SUSTAINABLE URBAN DESIGN AN ENVIRONMENTAL APPROACH

SUSTAINABLE URBAN DESIGN AN ENVIRONMENTAL APPROACH

2ND EDITION

Edited by Adam Ritchie & Randall Thomas

Taylor & Francis
Taylor & Francis Group

LONDON AND NEW YORK

First published 2009 by Taylor & Francis
2 Park Square, Milton Park, Abingdon, Oxon, OX14 4RN

Simultaneously published in the USA and Canada by Taylor & Francis
270 Madison Avenue, New York, NY10016

Taylor & Francis is an imprint of the Taylor & Francis Group,
an informa business

First edition © 2003 Max Fordham LLP selection and editorial matter;
individual chapters, the contributors

This second edition © 2009 Max Fordham LLP selection and editorial matter;
individual chapters, the contributors

Designed and typeset in ITC Officina Sans and Avenir
by Sutchinda Rangsi Thompson / Crown4to

Printed and bound in India by Replika Press Pvt. Ltd, Sonepat, Haryana

British Library Cataloguing in Publication Data
A catalogue record for this book is available from the British Library

Library of Congress Cataloging- in-Publication Data
A catalog record for this book has been requested

ISBN10 0-415-44781-X (hbk)
ISBN10 0-415-44782-8 (pbk)

ISBN13 978-0-415-44781-2 (hbk)
ISBN13 978-0-415-44782-9 (pbk)

CONTENTS

NOTES ON CONTRIBUTORS

Anthony Alexander is Director for Studies and Research at Alan Baxter & Associates where he leads an extensive research and communications programme, with a particular focus on sustainability. He has been an advisor on strategic sustainability work for London and Hong Kong, as well as for the UK Government's Carbon Challenge programme.

Patrick Clarke (MSc PhD) is a Director of Llewelyn Davies Yeang where he leads much of the practice's planning policy and research on sustainability, design and urban quality. His recent work has focused on exploring how urban areas can accommodate new development in ways that foster more sustainable patterns of urban living.

Eva Dalman (MSA) is an architect and planner working for the City of Malmö planning department. She is project manager of the Western Harbour project, and is currently engaged in a major consultation exercise for the Western Harbour, involving developers, city officers and the general public.

Bill Dunster is a graduate of Edinburgh University, and worked with Michael Hopkins and Partners before forming Bill Dunster Architects. He has been involved in research projects working towards zero energy urban buildings. This includes BedZED, the urban village at Beddington in Surrey, where his practice is situated.

William Filmer-Sankey is a Director at Alan Baxter & Associates where he works in the urban design and conservation team.

Graham Haworth studied architecture at the universities of Nottingham and Cambridge and founded Haworth Tompkins with Steve Tompkins in 1991. The creative philosophy of the practice focuses on the potential of new architecture to bring about positive change and support a strong social and cultural agenda. The practice was recently short-listed for the 2007 Stirling Prize for the Young Vic Theatre in London.

Adrian Hornsby is a writer and researcher in the field of urban design. He has lectured in Europe and China on the role of creative communities, and is co-author of *The Chinese Dream* (010 Publishers, 2008), a major study on the societal and environmental implications of China's high-speed urbanisation.

Rachel Moscovich is a sustainability analyst at Merrick Architecture Borowski Lintott Sakumoto Fligg Limited in Vancouver. She holds a BA from Barnard College in New York and a Master in Environmental Studies from York University in Toronto. She is a LEED Accredited Professional.

Richard Partington is principal of Richards Partington Architects, established in 1998. He is currently working on regeneration and urban design projects in Belfast, Newcastle, Woolwich and York.

Adam Ritchie joined Max Fordham LLP in 1998 as a building services engineer. He now leads the practice's sustainable urban design group, which is currently involved in a number of regeneration projects with particular emphasis on renewable energy sources.

Sarah Royse (BSc MCIBSE) studied physics and maths at Durham University before joining Max Fordham LLP in 2002. She is on the steering committee of the CIBSE's energy performance group and on the management team of the Association of Consulting Engineers Progress Network. She won the ACE/NCE young consultant of the year award, and is currently a principal sustainability consultant at Inbuilt Ltd.

Alan Short trained at Cambridge and Harvard universities. He is principal of Short & Associates, Professor of Architecture at the University of Cambridge and Fellow of Clare Hall, Cambridge.

Randall Thomas (Eur lng PhD (Arch) CEng FCIBSE MASHRAE) is a consultant to Max Fordham LLP and has over 25 years experience in an environmental approach to buildings and cities. He is currently Professor of Sustainable Environmental Design at Kingston University, London, and Course Organiser for Sustainable Urban Design at the Architectural Association. He is also a Royal Academy of Engineering Visiting Professor at the University of Cambridge.

Robert Thorne is a Director at Alan Baxter & Associates, where he helps lead the urban design and conservation team. He was principal author of *Places, Streets and Movement* (DETR, 1998) and *Achieving Quality Streetscapes* (CABE/DETR, 2002), and contributed to the *Urban Design Compendium* (English Partnerships, 2002).

Katie Tonkinson is an Associate at Hawkins\Brown Architects. Since joining the office in 2002, she has worked on large-scale transport schemes, such as Tottenham Court Road station, and is currently involved in several large regeneration projects, such as the refurbishment of a Grade II listed building at Metropolitan Wharf in London.

David Turrent trained at Manchester University and worked in private practice and local government before setting up ECD Architects in 1980. He has been responsible for numerous award-winning low energy buildings and is a member of the RIBA Sustainable Futures Committee. He is also a member of the CABE Enabling Panel and editor of *Sustainable Architecture* (RIBA, 2007).

Christina von Borcke is a freelance urban designer and landscape architect. She holds a Bachelor in Landscape Architecture from the University of British Columbia, Canada, and a Masters in Urban Design (Dist.) from Oxford Brookes University. Her professional work focuses on setting the scene for sustainable development through master planning and urban design.

Cecilia von Schéele is studying political science at Lund University, Sweden. She is currently working on the Flaghussen development in the City of Malmö Planning Department.

Chris Watson studied architecture at Cambridge University, and has worked for several practices, including Tim Ronalds Architects, where he was project architect on the award-winning refurbishment of the Hackney Empire Theatre. Since founding Witherford Watson Mann Architects in 2001, Chris has been co-director for Amnesty International UK's new headquarters, and the extension to the Whitechapel Art Gallery.

FOREWORD

2ND EDITION

The Royal Commission's 2007 report, *The Urban Environment*, took evidence from the team behind the first edition of this book. We found that best practice in urban design is often very good, but it is also frustratingly rare. We need to embed it as the norm, especially when we consider that more than half the world's population now lives in urban areas.

Books like this play a key role in delivering best practice and are crucial to inspiring and realising sustainable communities. We know what we have to do; this book provides us with insightful examples from home and abroad demonstrating how it can be achieved, so that best practice becomes the norm.

There is huge scope to reduce carbon emissions from the UK's existing housing stock, as well as supporting the building of new homes and business premises that are low-energy consumers. But it isn't just about buildings. We need to engender low-energy lifestyles by reducing the need for private car use. Planned shake-ups in the planning system offer a real opportunity to better integrate the economic, social and environmental objectives for sustainable development of our urban areas.

Also, outside buildings, the natural and semi-natural environment of our urban areas, including green spaces and rivers, provide important aesthetic and community benefits. In addition, restoration and management of these sites can provide flood mitigation through the creation of wetland sites and enhanced habitats for biodiversity. As climate change is likely to lead to more unpredictable weather patterns, the importance of such areas should not be underestimated.

In the spirit of the Vancouver 2010 Olympic and Paralympic Winter Games mentioned here in Chapter 19, the UK Government is planning for the London 2012 Olympics to be the first 'sustainable' games, setting new standards for major events, and perhaps new standards for the sustainable design and use of our urban areas. This book provides the inspiration and practical 'know-how' to demonstrate what is achievable, not just for the UK Olympics but for urban areas all over the world.

SIR JOHN LAWTON
Chairman
Royal Commission on Environmental Pollution

PREFACE

2ND EDITION

When the first edition of this book was written in 2002, we felt like pioneers. However, the need for an update shows how sustainable urban design has entered common parlance in the intervening years. The level of public perception and acceptance of environmental sustainability, or 'green' issues, are unrecognisable now compared to then, and the subject is dominated by our changing climate, caused by man-made emissions of greenhouse gases, particularly carbon dioxide.

In 2005, mayors from 18 of the world's largest cities, including New York, Melbourne, Paris and Beijing, met in London to agree how they should work together to show global leadership by achieving major cuts in carbon emissions from cities. By 2007, this group had grown to include government representatives from 40 cities, but the challenge remains: how can they turn good intentions into firm action?

This book should help illuminate their path towards that vision. It is informed both by years of study undertaken by a range of experts, and, importantly, by years of practice delivering their ideas, and will be of interest to mayors, planners, practitioners as well as students. The book is divided into two parts. Part I introduces the main concepts and issues in sustainable urban design, and Part II consists of a collection of case studies showing real-life application of the concepts. Appendices and a glossary of useful terms are found at the end of the book.

Figure 0.1 is an aerial view of one of our case studies (Chapter 17). It shows the key elements involved in sustainable urban design that are discussed in Part I. Those who are involved in urban design must consider a range of new solutions in order to be truly sustainable. This and the other case studies draw on some of the best experience of sustainable urban design from the UK and around the world.

0.1   The environmental agenda for sustainable urban design.

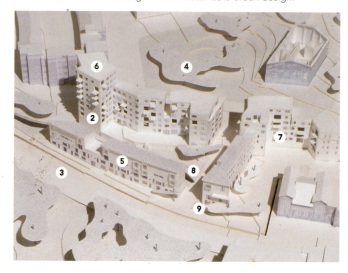

2	Urban planning and design	**6**	Energy and information
3	Transportation	**7**	Materials
4	Landscape and nature in the city	**8**	Water
5	Building design	**9**	Waste and resource

Albert Einstein once said: 'We can't solve problems by using the same kind of thinking we used when we created them.' We hope that this book will stimulate you to take up the challenge of leading an urban renaissance, and then guide you on the journey. Sustainable cities are few in number and many more are needed.

NOTE ON THE TEXT

The aim of this publication is to provide an overview for those involved, professionally, as students, or in any other way, with cities. It is not intended to be exhaustive or definitive and it will be necessary for users of the information provided to exercise their own professional judgement when deciding whether or not to use it.

Readers are advised to consult all current Building Regulations, British Standards or other applicable guidelines, Health and Safety codes and so forth, as well as up-to-date information on all materials and products.

PART ONE SUSTAINABLE URBAN DESIGN CONCEPTS

1 INTRODUCTION

ADAM RITCHIE

Sustainability

Sustainability is about poetry, optimism and delight. Energy, CO_2, water and wastes are secondary. The unquantifiable is at least as important as the quantifiable; according to Louis Kahn, 'the measurable is only a servant of the unmeasurable'[1] and ideally the two would be developed together. Using a term coined by the eighteenth-century author Jonathan Swift, this is a modest proposal.

This book identifies the major issues in making cities environmentally sustainable. By the time you are reading this sentence, we will, for the first time in history, have reached a milestone when more than half the world's population, 3.3 billion people, are living in urban areas.[2] Cities offer tremendous opportunities for community, employment, excitement and interest, which attract many of us. They can also create problems of congestion, noise and pollution which repel many others, or at least those who have the choice. These problems can be addressed, in part, through design, but success depends on recognising trade-offs and getting the balance right.

It is vital that we evolve towards sustainability in urban form, transport, landscape, buildings, energy supply, and all the other aspects of vibrant city living. Part of this will involve making cities more suitable for people, and therefore moving away from the previous policy of cities being for cars. Creating streets for pedestrians, cyclists and public transport is a key aspect of sustainable development.

Cities must also become greener for the sake of the diversity of many species (as well as humans) who inhabit them. Nature's ecosystem, with its robust and stable systems, is one model for future cities. However, in addition to an ecosystem's variety, diversity, redundancy and richness, we need poetry, whimsicalness, playfulness and excitement. Aristotle's view was that a city should be designed to make its people secure and happy.[3]

This book is meant to inspire rather than be prescriptive. Ideas of planning, space and form are a backdrop to many of the points made, but our built environment suffers enough at present from people who were too sure of their solutions and those who thought in 'silo'-based terms and over-planned and, thus, over-constrained development. Our contributors, however, believe that an integrated approach is needed. Density and the means of moving about the city are related. Landscape affects buildings. Noise influences the ventilation system selected and thus energy use. In turn, the energy use currently results in increased atmospheric pollution and CO_2 emissions at power stations, which affect our health. Similarly, the built form affects access to sunlight and this influences both the energy use and our well-being. Cities are the very definition of a complex system and the preceding examples are only small strands of a tangled web of inter-connected causes and effects.

Some general themes run through the book. One is that appropriate solutions often depend on an understanding of the context: environmental, historical, social, etc. A second is that the appropriate scale for solutions is something larger than the individual building – it could be the block, the neighbourhood, the city, the region. Another is that solutions that require fewer resources are more likely to be robust. And so, for energy, the first step is to reduce demand and then examine how to meet it. In terms of movement in cities and towns, the robust solution is the dense walkable community, which does not have a high demand for either public or private transport. There is also a view that passive solutions are best. Things that move in the urban world tend to be less robust and require more maintenance. This is true whether one looks at cars, London Underground's escalators, or pumps for heating systems.

The book is divided into two distinct parts. Part I provides an overview of the main issues affecting sustainable urban design, and discusses the tools and resources needed to tackle the subject. Part II features case study projects that demonstrate how these issues have been successfully negotiated by a range of expert practitioners. Our subject has essentially been cities in temperate climates that are neither bitterly cold in winter nor desperately hot and humid in summer. Our emphasis has been on new build, in part because that is where most of the contributors have had the best opportunity to develop new approaches. Improving the existing building stock is an even greater challenge, so, fortunately, a number of the ideas discussed in the book apply equally to upgrading existing buildings (see, for example, Chapter 18). Our case studies draw on some of the best experience from the UK, Europe and beyond, for example, Southwark in London (Chapter 11), Malmö in Sweden (Chapter 16) and Vancouver in Canada (Chapter 19). Many of these projects are brownfield sites where new buildings have often led to the regeneration of neighbourhoods. The increased densities that are likely to help us reduce CO_2 emissions will depend in part on our ability to creatively recycle land, buildings and methods.

Reference is often made to the three interdependent aspects of sustainability: social, economic and environmental. This book will concentrate on the environmental. The emphasis on this aspect arises naturally – it is the field in which most of the contributors are working. A (readable) book is, of course, also necessarily limited in length and one needs to choose one's focus. Sustainability is dependent on communities for its success, and developing the social dimension is often an arduous process. It could be said that the environment is the easiest aspect (in spite of the resistance to environmental improvement by some companies and governments), because it is much simpler to assess if, for example, CO_2 emissions have been reduced rather than whether a scheme will successfully lead to economic regeneration. We also try to avoid the misconception that these three aspects can be equated simply to a 'triple bottom line' which is to trivialise sustainability somewhat by reducing it to a matter of simple economics. While there certainly is a price to pay for the transition to a sustainable future, see, for example, the review by Sir Nicholas Stern[4] which evaluates the cost of action to reduce greenhouse gases, it misses less tangible but equally important aspects of sustainability, such as individuality.

Individuality creates space for the unexpected and the extraordinary as well as centring itself, in the best humanist tradition, on the person. If the social dominates the individual, everyone suffers from the deadening mediocrity that one finds outside the historic centres

1.1   De Montfort University, Queens Building, Leicester.

of cities as diverse as St Petersburg, Paris and London. This theme of uniqueness surfaces in urban design, landscaping and in individual buildings and will recur throughout the book. The exceptional towers of De Montfort University's Queens Building (see Figure 1.1) are an example. The structures are symbolic of urban regeneration and yet also functional, serving as an integral part of the ventilation system.

Cities must have a rich set of interconnections or they will not be sustainable. For example, a city for walkers and cyclists needs more visual variety, more diversity, more 'accidentals' (in the musical sense) in its street patterns and its buildings, because the pace is slower and the mind both desires more and can take in more. We need to develop a rhythm in the city that will include places we can enjoy; this rhythm will be about moving – and stopping. This will help us return to cities designed for people, rather than for cars.

A city's 'accidents' include such extraordinary views as this one down a narrow mews in London (see Figure 1.2), which combines dramatic changes of scale, buildings from different centuries, backs and fronts. One small image indicates the diversity and vitality of real cities. 'Accidents' are part of the normal pattern of our historical cities and appear to be anathema to many modern planners obsessed by regular patterns from an impossible aerial view. They are part of our past, our memory and thus a part of our poetry. They tell us that nothing was

1.4a–f Urban space.

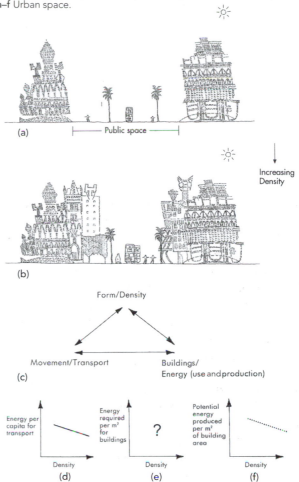

(a) — Public space —

Increasing Density

(b)

Form/Density

Movement/Transport

Buildings/ Energy (use and production)

(c)

Energy per capita for transport — Density

Energy required per m² for buildings — Density

? Potential energy produced per m² of building area — Density

(d)   (e)   (f)

1.2   View down a narrow street in central London.

1.3   Figure ground plan showing Malmö's Western Harbour street pattern.

designed in an instant and so reinforce our sense of time. A delightful modern exception to conventional planning is the irregular streets of Malmö's new Western Harbour, its grid described by principal architect Klas Tham as 'distorted by the wind like a fishnet hung out to dry'[5] (see Figure 1.3 and Chapter 16).

In many urban areas, public space, including parks and streets, constitutes more than half the total area of land. Buildings provide us with homes and workplaces and with commerce, industry and leisure. The space in between the buildings (see Figures 1.4a–1.4b) provides vitality, light, amenity, room to travel and room to rest. Landscape is essential – plants soothe us and improve the microclimate. Our open space is home to wildlife, thus promoting biodiversity. It may incorporate vegetable gardens, and reed beds for waste treatment.

The interrelationship of three of the key factors in environmental sustainability can be viewed simplistically as a triangle (Figure 1.4c). One apex is form/density, a second is movement/transport and the third is buildings/energy (use and production). We are only beginning to start to think about how these factors (and others such as landscape and social conceptions of privacy) can work together. This approach is in its infancy and in this book we describe some of the first steps being taken.

Urban form will affect energy use for transport and buildings. There is some agreement that the energy per capita for transportation decreases as density increases (see Figure 1.4d), but what happens to the energy required for buildings (see Figure 1.4e) and the energy that the buildings can produce (see Figure 1.4f)? These are important issues for environmental sustainability – and ones to which we return.

The Background

There is considerable scientific evidence that the Earth's temperature is rising and will continue to do so as a result of human activities. These, particularly the burning of fossil fuels – coal, oil and gas – for our buildings and our transport, manufacturing and agricultural systems, result in increased CO_2 in the atmosphere, which contributes to global warming. The likely negative impacts of global warming (which will probably outweigh the positive effects) include increased storms, flooding, droughts and the probable destruction of some ecosystems. Climate change affects us all – we must act quickly to reduce its impact by changing from fossil fuel-based systems to renewable energy-based ones. Much of what is written about climate change concerns its mitigation, that is, what can one do to reduce the scale of its impact in the future? On the basis that the climate will warm as a result of CO_2 already emitted, equal consideration must be given to how cities and their occupants can adapt to its likely effects. Although many of the ideas for adaptation in this book are described in terms of new construction, they are often applicable for retro-fitting to existing buildings as well.

In urban areas, there is a 'heat-island' effect resulting from the production and accumulation of heat in the urban mass.[6] Cities can be several degrees warmer than their surroundings. Figure 1.5 shows London's temperature relative to a rural reference temperature at 2am on a calm day in August 2000. The difference is in excess of 6°C and was measured at 9°C in the summer of 2003.[7]

The heat-island effect will lead to temperature rises being more marked; local air pollution may increase; drainage systems may need to be altered to cope with periods of higher rainfall, and night-cooling ventilation strategies will be less effective at times. Global warming will probably lead to social, political and economic disruption, so it seems wise to abide by what is known as the 'precautionary principle', which maintains that we should take action now to avoid possible serious environmental damage even when the scientific evidence for action is

1.5   Urban heat-island effect in London on a clear night (figures in degrees centigrade).

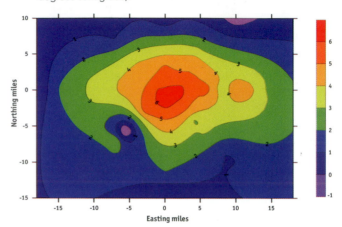

inconclusive.[8] We should therefore put considerable effort into designing our cities to reduce the emission of CO_2 and other greenhouse gases. The technology and know-how to reduce climate change are largely available, we just need more resolve, more government support and more individual initiative.

In 2006, 21 per cent of the UK's final energy consumption was used in industry, 29 per cent in the domestic sector, 38 per cent in the transport sector, and 12 per cent in the service sector (including agriculture).[9] Of course, in all these sectors much of the energy use is in buildings – in the European Union, buildings account for about 40 per cent of consumption.[10] Table 1.1 shows the current source of primary energy supplies in the UK in 2006.[11]

TABLE 1.1

Primary Energy Consumption 2006	
	Percentage of consumption (a)
Coal	18.7
Gas	38.4
Oil	33.2
Primary electricity (mainly nuclear)	7.9
Renewables and waste	1.8
Total	100

(a) Total annual energy consumption is approximately 9,700 million GJ

1.6 A small urban system at Coopers Road (Phases 1 and 2), London.

Anticipated occupancy: 664
Site area: 16,900m² (1.69 ha; gross floor area: 12,500m²)
Dwellings: 154 (91 dwellings/ha; 367 habitable rooms/ha)

Energy in food (a):   761,700 kWh/y
Energy to produce and
transport the food (b):   3,322,700 kWh/y

Rainfall 600 mm/y (c): 10,140m³/y   Water use: 24,236 m³/y (d)

Energy in goods (l)

Vegetation
CO_2 uptake (e):
1083 kg/y

Household waste (j)
a. 347,936 kg/y
b. 727,196 kWh/y (k)

Energy used in
transport (f):
3,762,224 kWh/y

Human waste:
30,196 kWh/y (i)

CO_2 produced
by occupants:
247,672 kg/y (m)

Wind energy
crossing at boundary

Heating energy (primary) (g):   1,225,927 kWh/y
CO_2 due to heating: 220,667 kg/y

Electrical energy (primary) (h):   1,166,210 kWh/y
CO_2 due to electricity: 164,435 kg/y

NOTES

(a) This is an approximate figure for the energy content of the food based on Mellanby (1974).[14]

(b) Energy to transport the food based on Peace (1997).[15]

(c) The rainfall figure is an approximate average.

(d) With water-saving measures (see Chapter 8), it should be possible to reduce household water consumption to 100 litres/person per day or 24,236m³/y for the site.

(e) A very rough estimate is that the grass and small trees of Coopers Road might assimilate 50 per cent of the CO_2 of cultivated fields and forests thus giving a figure of about 0.55kg CO_2/m²/y of planted area. The uptake is based on planted areas of 1490m² and lawn areas of 479m² or a total of 1969m², roughly 11 per cent of the site area.[16]

(f) An average person in the UK has a transport energy consumption of about 5666 kWh/y; approximately 82 per cent of this is for car travel, 5 per cent for rail and 7 per cent for bus.[17] This average figure may very well be significantly lower in urban situations such as Coopers Road.

(g) Gas delivered energy: 1,103,334 kWh/y; therefore primary 1,225,927 kWh/y.[18]

(h) Electricity delivered energy: 349,863 kWh/y; therefore primary 1,166,210 kWh/y.[19] (Note that delivered energy is assumed to be equal to useful energy.)

(i) This is calorific value and is estimated as 4 per cent of the calorific value of the food.[20]

(j) Household waste: average person 524kg/y (see Chapter 9).

(k) Waste energy content.[21]

(l) Not quantified here. This term will include the energy in goods (papers, tins, packaging, etc.). A thorough analysis will need to take into account such subtleties as the non-consumed part of food, e.g. vegetable parings, bones, etc.

(m) Estimated from an energy intake of 10,000kcal per day per person; 373kg CO_2 per person per year.

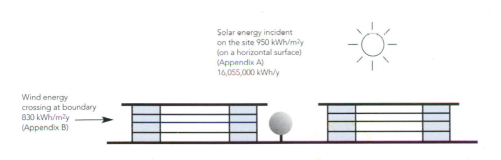

Solar energy incident
on the site 950 kWh/m²y
(on a horizontal surface)
(Appendix A)
16,055,000 kWh/y

Wind energy
crossing at boundary
830 kWh/m²y
(Appendix B)

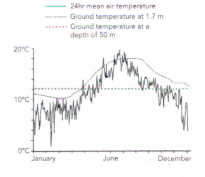

— 24hr mean air temperature
···· Ground temperature at 1.7 m
---- Ground temperature at a
     depth of 50 m

There is an urgent need to increase the contribution from renewables, and governments are (slowly) beginning to respond; the UK, for example, has a target of renewable energy providing 10 per cent of electricity supplies by 2010, which is the UK share of the EU's target of 22.1 per cent overall. In 2003, the London Borough of Merton became the first local authority in the UK to include a planning policy that requires new non-residential developments to generate at least 10 per cent of their energy needs from renewable energy and many other authorities have since followed suit.[12] The Mayor of London also now places a similar requirement on all new major development in London. How the renewable contribution could be increased in the urban context is discussed below, and particularly in Chapter 6.

The city as a complex system

In beginning to consider cities, it is useful to think of systems, as ecologists do when looking at energy flows in natural communities. A system can be defined as 'regularly interacting and interdependent components forming a unified whole'.[13] Figure 1.6 shows how the new housing at Coopers Road in Southwark, London (see Chapter 11), might be viewed as a small urban system, and gives very approximate energy and material flows. A simple, but useful approach to sustainability is to look at each flow and ask: where does it come from?; how does it get there?; who looks after it?; what does it do?; and where does it go? Clearly, it will be more productive to work with a somewhat larger system since, in energy and environmental terms, urban areas operate within the context of the city as a whole, the city works with the region, and the regions function at a national or international level. This, however, gives us a way of thinking about some of the issues. The city and its region have historically relied on one another for markets and resources but this relationship must be carefully managed to maintain its delicate balance.

At Coopers Road, approximately 25 per cent of the primary energy is for the buildings, 40 per cent for transport and 35 per cent for food (see also BedZED in Chapter 15). The resources, which are discussed in more detail in Chapter 6 and Appendix A, are a set of opportunities. Thus, the incident solar radiation is 16,000,000 kWh/y, but our systems won't be 100 per cent efficient. If we assume that they are 10 per cent efficient, we would have 1,600,000 kWh/y from solar energy or roughly 1.5 times our primary energy demand for heating very energy-efficient housing. This is encouraging, but a closer look at the figures suggests that a high level of sustainability in cities will not come easily. For example, CO_2 production is high and uptake is low; rainfall is low and water use is high. At a worldwide level, the total annual solar radiation falling on the Earth is more than 7,500 times the total annual primary energy consumption.[22]

One can look at the demands as the 'environmental footprint' (see Glossary) of the site, and the challenge is to reduce it over time and increase our 'footprint' of the use of ambient energy sources concurrently, as shown in Figure 1.7.

It will also be helpful to develop a way of thinking about how the city will change with time and to set out a clear and coherent strategy for improvement. We, of course, need to agree on a time-scale for our activities. Optimists are aiming for environmentally friendly cities by 2020. Realists sometimes cite 2050. We would rather not tell you what the pessimists say! Throughout the book there is pragmatic advice on how to reduce our impact and exploit our opportunities.

Integral to this is an appreciation of how to 'look' at an urban site. This is best viewed as a complete analysis of assets, including the social aspects of the neighbourhood (its meeting places, communication routes, safe areas), circulation routes (both for pedestrians and for vehicles), previous uses, historical monuments, important places, good architecture, interesting geology, trees, and so forth. This has been described succinctly as to 'know thyself'[23] and is equally important at

1.7   Evolving environment 'footprint'.

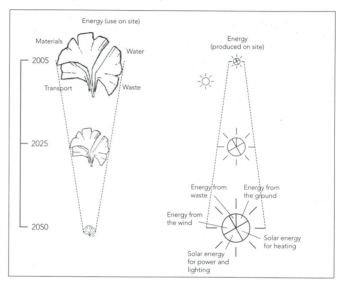

the city level as at the site level. The principal environmental concerns are touched on below.

Site Analysis

Solar energy is our starting point, and there is a long history of philosophers and architects attempting to find an 'optimum' form that would give residents a healthy environment with daylight, air and space. In the twentieth century, Le Corbusier, Frank Lloyd Wright and Lubetkin were three of many influenced by such concerns. A key element is to maximise the solar potential of the site. To do this, some knowledge of solar geometry will be useful.

Figure 1.8 shows the shadow cast by Barry Flanagan's delightful horse in a Cambridge College garden; the solar elevation angle at noon on 22 September is about 38°. Figure 1.9 shows the intriguingly named Devil's Passage in Paris. Buildings in London of similar height (about 14m) and separation (about 9m), orientated with the long axis east–west, will have most of the south façade in sun at noon in September. (Of course, earlier and later during the day in September and later in the year the façade will be more shaded.)

Urban designers need to take into account the sun's path for many reasons, ranging from the poetic effects of light and shadows, to the

1.8   Horse and shadow.

1.9   Devil's Passage, Paris.

bringing in of sunlight to ground-floor living rooms, to ensuring that roof-mounted solar panels are not overshadowed. Fortunately, tremendous progress is being made in modelling the urban environment. Figure 1.10 shows an analysis of yearly solar irradiation on part of the San Francisco financial district.[24]

A more detailed discussion of solar geometry is found in Appendix A. Solar considerations in planning and design are discussed particularly in Chapters 5 and 6 and also in the Stonebridge case study (see Chapter 17). The other principal items to consider are wind, air quality, noise, temperature, rain and biodiversity.

The wind crossing a site is potentially beneficial. It can assist in the natural ventilation of buildings (see Chapter 5), remove pollutants and heat, and be a potential source of energy (see Chapter 6). Urban environments may also exacerbate the adverse effects of the wind.[25] One of the reasons for the irregular street pattern in Malmö (see Figure 1.3) was to reduce the effect of the sea wind coming off the Öresund. Wind-tunnel testing, as shown in Chapter 14 where the Contact Theatre in Manchester and its immediate urban setting were being studied, allows us to create a more amenable environment both for buildings and for people (as pedestrians and idlers).

Air quality affects our comfort, our health and our ability to use natural ventilation. As the inhabitants of a number of Californian and other cities throughout the world know only too well, high levels of pollution can also shield the sun and reduce daylight levels.

With regard to temperature, as we have seen, the urban climate is warmer. Microclimates exist throughout the city and, through design, there is enormous potential for creating sunnier, warmer spaces in winter and cooler, shaded ones in summer. The use of temperature differences between ground and air (see Figure 1.6) is also a potential source of low CO_2 cooling and heating. Chapter 6 and Appendix A provide more detail.

The rain falling in an area is a precious resource but, as parts of England have seen recently, if it is not managed well it carries a risk of flooding. Chapters 4, 8 and 9 provide more information, and in Chapter 18 the Deptford Wharves project describes a design solution to limit the danger should the deluge come.

Sound and noise are almost a defining feature of urban life. Chapter 5 and Appendix D discuss these further.

Designers and specifiers need better information when choosing the materials with which to construct cities of the future. Chapter 7

1.10   Yearly solar irradiation on surfaces in the San Francisco financial district.

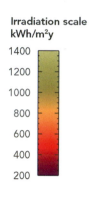

Irradiation scale
kWh/m²y

1400
1200
1000
800
600
400
200

describes some of the important factors, and the techniques to reduce material waste as well.

Clearly, the impact on the environment is not simply one of energy and material flows. There may be a reduction of biodiversity. This is because the number of species tends to increase with the availability of area, thus a loss of space through building is likely to be deleterious. We need to mitigate these effects, and maintaining (or, we hope, increasing) biodiversity is considered in more detail in Chapter 4.

Cities for People

Urban design is, of course, only part of the story. We also need to reconcile our modern living standards and expectations with the aspirations we have for a sustainable future. The association between environmentalism and sandals and hair-shirts is now firmly consigned to the past.

How sustainability is introduced into people's daily routine will be the key to the success of our cities. Many of the solutions outlined in this book require some changes to the way we go about our everyday lives, both personally and professionally.

The shift to a 'greener' lifestyle can be encouraged by a number of catalysts that get people talking and bring about new social norms.

Legislation, fashion, economy, and even the simple desire to 'keep up with the Joneses' can all play a part. Take, for example, the impact on public attitudes to energy when UK home improvement stores began stocking micro-generation technologies like solar water-heating and wind turbines. Surveys suggest that home energy generation rarely leaves families unchanged in their outlook and behaviour. 'It seems that microgeneration provides a tangible hook to engage householders emotionally with the issue of energy use. Householders described the sheer pleasure of creation and of self-sufficiency: "It's like growing your own vegetables."'[26]

Conclusion

Sustainable urban design is vital for this century – it is not too much to say that our health, welfare and future depend on it. Achieving a transition to a sustainable, solar society will involve us all – everyone should share in the environmental, social and economic benefits (solar is used here in the broad sense of renewable energy sources, including wind and biomass, which are effectively derived from solar energy).

We will need to develop flexible ways to 'shape' and design our future cities. Land-use planning can contribute to reducing travel demand and, thus, CO_2 emissions and, similarly, it can increase our use of the solar potential of the site.

Sustainable urban design is, in part, about balance. There are many good reasons for cities that are dense, have mixed uses and are varied. But such cities will need to manage potential conflicts between varying conceptions of urban form and living, between public transport and individual cars, between public distribution of energy supplies and private control, between man-made environments and more natural ones, and many others. This challenge is about our future – it is demanding and exciting. Its outcome will not be one single solution, but many. There will be some clarity but it is more likely that, if we are successful, our cities will be 'magnificently equivocal'.[27]

Further reading

Boardman B, *et al.* (2005) '40% House', ECI Research Report 31,
    Environmental Change Institute, University of Oxford. Available:
    http://www.eci.ox.ac.uk/lowercf/40house.html

Girardet, H. (1999) *Creating Sustainable Cities*. Dartington: Green.

IPCC (2007) *Intergovernmental Panel on Climate Change, Fourth Assessment
    Report: Climate Change 2007*. Geneva: IPCC. Available:
    http://www.ipcc.ch/ipccreports/assessments-reports.htm

Jenks, M. (2005) *Future Forms and Design for Sustainable Cities*. Oxford:
    Elsevier.

Lawton, J. (Chair) (2007) Royal Commission on Environmental Pollution,
    Twenty-Sixth Report, *The Urban Environment*. London. Available:
    http://www.rcep.org.uk/urbanenvironment.htm

Low, N. (2005) *The Green City Sustainable Homes, Sustainable Suburbs*.
    London: Routledge.

New London Architecture (2006) *Sustainable London, Addressing Climate
    Change in the Capital*. Exhibition pamphlet.

Rogers, R. (1997) *Cities for a Small Planet*. London: Faber & Faber.

Urban Design Group (2007) *Urban Design: Topic: Adapting to Climate Change*.
    Issue 102. London: UDG.

Urban Task Force (1999) *Towards an Urban Renaissance*. London: E&FN Spon.

(All websites accessed 2 February 2008.)

2 URBAN PLANNING AND DESIGN

PATRICK CLARKE

Introduction

This chapter seeks to draw out some of the planning and design principles that underpin attractive, successful and sustainable urban environments. The aim is to encourage a wider understanding of how basic layout and design principles can help create a robust urban form in which innovative design and the application of emerging construction and service technologies can flourish.

The key starting point is the recognition that, in large measure, the way in which people and goods move around urban areas determines their structure and how they function. When the means of movement changes, so too do patterns of human activity with direct consequences for the planning and design principles that guide the development and renewal of urban areas.

Most recently, the car has turned the established structure of urban areas inside out by drawing jobs, leisure and shopping away from traditional centres to locations that are easily accessed by car. Roads have been designed according to vehicle flows and speeds, and buildings have been pushed back from the pavement to make space for parking, and, perhaps for the first time in history, children are no longer able to play safely in the streets around their homes.

Now, in seeking to reduce our reliance on the car and to re-establish walking, cycling and public transport as the preferred means of moving around urban areas, we are again engaged in a process of change (see Figure 2.1). This has profound implications for planning and design thinking at all levels; from how we think about the structure of towns and cities and where we locate new development right through to how we lay out individual street blocks and design the buildings within them.

Central to much of the discussion in this chapter is the belief that, while designing for the car took us into uncharted territory (often with

2.1 A historic approach to urban transport in a contemporary form: Le Tram, Strasbourg.

disastrous consequences), there are clear historical precedents that can guide us when attempting to create places that work, based on the movement of pedestrians, cycles and public transport rather than the ubiquitous automobile. Indeed, it is ironic that while much energy is expended debating approaches to higher density, mixed-use environments, we are almost unconsciously surrounded by places that exhibit many of these same attributes and that have succeeded in meeting the needs and aspirations of successive generations.

This introduces the second main thrust of this chapter: that people's requirements and technology change faster than places. Bespoke places or buildings that are designed to fulfil a specific function are in danger of becoming obsolete as requirements or technology change.

2.2   A robust and enduring Victorian suburb. Jesmond, Newcastle.

2.3   A polycentric urban structure of walkable communities.

▦ Metropolitan Centre

▥ Urban and suburban areas

◉ Walkable communities 800m
   around town centres

▬ Higher density along road links

- - - Rail links

○ Transport interchange

The key point in creating places is to remember that while a street may have a life of 1,000 years or more, and a building perhaps 200 years, utility and building services may have a life of just 25 years. It is crucial that these can be upgraded during the buildings' lives as technology develops.

Many Victorian neighbourhoods, such as that illustrated in Figure 2.2, have seen the coming and going of different approaches to space heating, and have responded to changing household size through subdivision. These areas have adapted to mass car ownership better than many areas designed for the car, and today, given many have the essential attributes of density and street layout to support buses and trams, are ready to welcome the return of these means of transport.

Sustainable Urban Structure

Thinking about sustainable urban structure begins with the urban region: the town or city and its rural and/or coastal hinterland. The town or city depends on its hinterland for food and water, clean air and open space and, looking to the future, perhaps on biomass or wind for energy. The hinterland is dependent on the town or city as a market for its produce and for employment and services but is also affected by urban waste and pollution. Sustainable planning demands a more holistic and integrated approach to the urban region, which recognises the interdependence and potential of both town and country.

At the level of the town or city, the walkable community or urban village provides a fundamental building-block in creating a sustainable urban form. The concept is of a polycentric urban structure in which a town or city comprises a network of distinct but overlapping communities, each focused (depending on the scale of the urban area) on a town, district or local centre, and within which people can access on foot most of the facilities and services needed for daily living.[1] Each of these communities is defined by the walking catchment or 'ped-shed' around the centre. This is generally taken to be c.800m, equating to a 10-minute walk.

Figure 2.3 illustrates this concept in relation to a large metropolitan area in which the polycentric structure developed typically as the city spread outward, engulfing surrounding villages and towns and with new centres being created along new railway corridors. It shows what could be described as 'a centres and routes' model, which can be observed in London, Birmingham or Manchester, for example. In this model, town centres are the principal community focus but there are also linear communities developing along the main movement routes between centres and especially along the principal routes to the city centre. In other places, different structures can be seen reflecting differences of geography, landform and economy. In Belfast, for example, the structure is of linear communities that have developed along the principal arterial routes leading from surrounding towns to the city centre. This structure is described further and illustrated in Chapter 12 (see Figure 12.2).

In neither case is all the urban area within the walking catchment of a centre. In general, the proportion of remote areas (that is, those lying beyond walking distance of a centre) increases with distance from the city centre, reflecting both diminishing densities of population and more widely spread movement routes.

The Walkable Community

Figure 2.4 looks in more detail at the characteristics of a typical neighbourhood. A number of planning and urban design principles can be drawn out:

- Shops and services tend to be focused along a main street running through the heart of the neighbourhood, at the convergence of movement routes and around key facilities such as a railway station. The degree to which shops and services spread outwards into surrounding streets is a function of the scale and role of a centre, the density of population (and spending power) within its catchment and the degree of competition from neighbouring centres.

- Community facilities such as schools, health centres and open spaces are distributed around the neighbourhood, reflecting more localised catchments and their greater requirements for space.

- The neighbourhood provides a wide range of different housing opportunities not just in terms of dwelling size but also in terms of affordability and tenure. This provides the basis for a mixed community representative of society at large rather than having a narrow social focus.

- Housing densities are highest around the edges of the town or district centre, along the principal transport routes leading to neighbouring centres and overlooking parks, waterfront areas and other amenities. Densities reduce towards the edge of the walking catchment.

- Movement routes are shared by cars, buses (or trams), cyclists and pedestrians and go through the centre rather than around it as well as through residential neighbourhoods.

Figure 2.4 also highlights a number of issues concerning existing neighbourhoods and their ability to accommodate new development and change:

2.4   Attributes of a walkable community.[2]

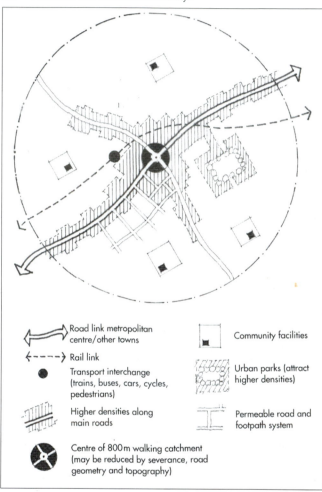

Road link metropolitan centre/other towns

Rail link

Transport interchange (trains, buses, cars, cycles, pedestrians)

Higher densities along main roads

Centre of 800m walking catchment (may be reduced by severance, road geometry and topography)

Community facilities

Urban parks (attract higher densities)

Permeable road and footpath system

- The potential for new infill development is often greatest in the 'shatter zone' or 'interface area' between the established retail, commercial and administrative centre and the consolidated residential hinterland. Here, land is often in marginal or short-term use, reflecting uncertainty or speculation over the optimum future use, outdated development-plan zonings or uncertainty over proposals such as for new roads. Such areas therefore often offer rich potential for new housing and mixed-use development.

- The opportunities for new mixed-use development are likely to be greatest within and on the fringes of the town/district centre

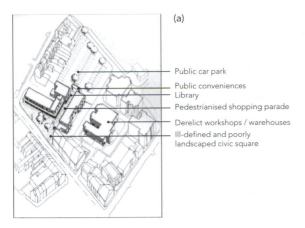

(a)

Public car park
Public conveniences
Library
Pedestrianised shopping parade
Derelict workshops / warehouses
Ill-defined and poorly
landscaped civic square

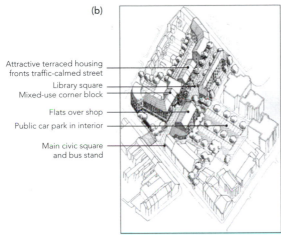

(b)

Attractive terraced housing
fronts traffic-calmed street
Library square
Mixed-use corner block
Flats over shop
Public car park in interior
Main civic square
and bus stand

2.5a–b Regeneration of an existing district centre.[3]

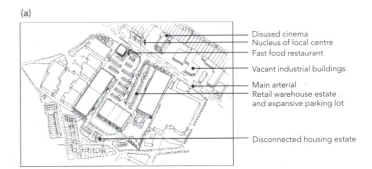

(a)

Disused cinema
Nucleus of local centre
Fast food restaurant
Vacant industrial buildings
Main arterial
Retail warehouse estate
and expansive parking lot
Disconnected housing estate

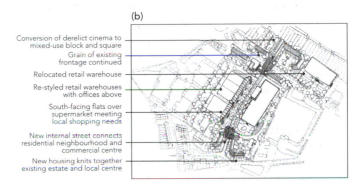

(b)

Conversion of derelict cinema to
mixed-use block and square
Grain of existing
frontage continued
Relocated retail warehouse
Re-styled retail warehouses
with offices above
South-facing flats over
supermarket meeting
local shopping needs
New internal street connects
residential neighbourhood and
commercial centre
New housing knits together
existing estate and local centre

2.6a–b Replanning a stand-alone retail park to create a new
district centre.[4]

and along the main movement routes to other centres. These areas often have a mixed-use character and can offer the greatest potential to support a range of uses, including shops, offices, leisure and housing.

Planning and Design Implications and Opportunities

This idealised concept of walkable communities provides the basis for planning and design thinking at a variety of levels and in particular about how new development and urban management approaches can reinforce and strengthen a sustainable urban structure. This includes:

- directing new shopping, leisure and commercial development towards existing centres and ensuring that off-centre development does not undermine the viability of existing town and district centres;

- enhancing the attractiveness of existing town and district centres by extending the range of facilities and services they offer and improving the quality of their physical environment. Figures 2.5a–b illustrate the potential to improve the quality of an important district centre along one of Southampton's linear communities. This thinking can also be broadened out to address the

surrounding catchment area in terms, for example, of improving the quality and attractiveness of walking and cycle routes, open spaces and play areas as well as reinforcing community identity through well-designed signage and street furniture;

- making the most of the opportunities for new housing and other uses in the catchments around existing centres by developing at appropriate urban densities;

- seizing the opportunities to create new local centres in areas that are currently remote from local facilities and services. Figures 2.6a and b show how the nucleus of a local centre could be developed through the replanning of an adjacent but free-standing retail park to become an integrated piece of the urban fabric. Similar possibilities may arise through the planning of urban extensions that could be designed so as to serve both a new and an existing community.[5]

Streets and Street Blocks

The development structure within the neighbourhood takes the form of street blocks defined by movement routes. These blocks are arranged in such a way as to enable direct pedestrian movement to and from

2.7   Removing the requirement for off-street parking increases this site's capacity from 10 houses to 32 apartments.[6]

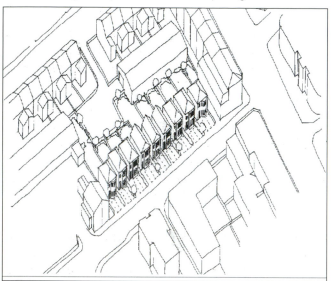 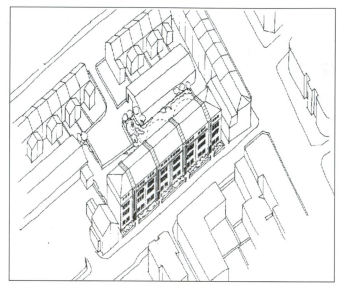

important facilities and amenities including the centre and public transport routes and stops. The pattern of routes is open-ended, providing a choice of paths to and from any given point. In general, the street blocks become smaller closer to the centre to optimise pedestrian permeability.

Individual street blocks take the form of perimeter development with buildings facing outwards towards the edge of the block and the street. This provides the basis for active street frontage with windows and doors overlooking and opening out onto the street to provide good surveillance of the street and the activity within it. In residential areas, rear gardens (whether private or shared) are enclosed by building frontage and walling.

There are no hard and fast rules to street and block dimensions. What is important is that both are designed in relation to their context and role. This implies a variety of street widths from wide avenues to intimate mews courts. However, a number of important guidelines can be identified:

● Corners need careful design both to recognise their prominence at the junction of two routes and to ensure that they are turned with active frontage and continuity of passive surveillance of the public realm. Often this is more easily achieved with apartments, which can give greater scale and which do not require

individual rear gardens which are difficult to accommodate within the corner.

● The orientation of blocks needs to be considered with solar potential in mind. A balance is needed here between seeking the optimum east–west alignment of streets to maximise solar potential and other design objectives, such as providing direct movement routes to local facilities and creating a robust perimeter block structure with continuity to the relationships between the fronts and backs of buildings. Variation in building heights and breaks in the building line can reduce shadowing and increase solar access within the block.

● Solar orientation will also influence thinking about the internal layout of the dwelling. For example, locating principal living rooms to maximise solar access could imply having kitchens and bathrooms to the front on one side of a street and to the rear on the other.

● Care needs to be taken over the design of the threshold between the street and the dwelling. Services, bins, cycles, space for home deliveries all need to be thought about here, together with the need to balance surveillance of the street with privacy for the home.

● Streets should fulfil a variety of roles – a place to live, shop, park, drive, walk, cycle and catch the bus, and even, in quieter side streets, for children to play.

2.8   Analysis of the facilities and services within walking distances of the site informs decisions on density car parking and layout.[7]

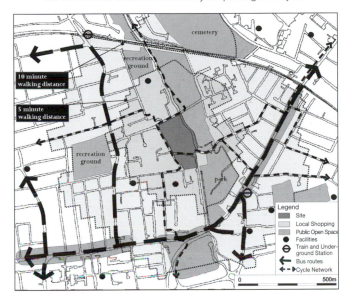

Optimising Development Density

Making efficient use of land and supporting local services by developing at appropriate urban and suburban densities is an important thrust of the new design approach. The term 'appropriate' is deliberately used because development density will vary according to the location and accessibility of different sites, their context and setting, and the different types of housing being provided. Indeed, an important principle is that development density should be the outcome of a design approach that responds to these and other issues creatively rather than to a fixed design requirement.

Against this background, a number of planning and design principles can be identified when seeking to create attractive and sustainable environments that make more efficient use of land and energy:

- Requirements for car parking can have a major impact on both the density of development and its quality. This is especially true of small sites of up to 1 ha where cars are parked on the surface. In some cases, reducing the off-street requirement from two to one space per dwelling can increase site capacity by 50 per cent. Figure 2.7 illustrates the differences in both townscape character and site capacity associated with different approaches to car-parking provision.

- The efficiency of the street network and the arrangements for parking are critical factors on larger sites. For example, a traditional

street grid with cars parked on-street can reduce the percentage site area required for roads and parking from 35–40 per cent to around 20 per cent, assuming a terraced housing form and around one parking space per dwelling.

- Thinking about requirements for new community facilities in relation to existing provision in the area is important. For example, instead of seeking further open space in an area that is already well served by open space, it may be more beneficial to seek a financial contribution towards improving an existing space or play area or making better streets.

The logic of the walkable community again provides a useful starting point when thinking about appropriate levels of density and car parking. The starting point is to build up an understanding of how the site fits in with its surrounding context. For example, where are the local shops, schools and open spaces? Where are the bus, tram and train stops, and what destinations do they serve? Where can you walk to in 5 minutes? What can be reached in 10 minutes?

Figure 2.8 shows how this approach can be used to build up a picture of the walkable neighbourhood around a 3 ha-site in outer London. In this case, the analysis pointed to a level of accessibility to both facilities and public transport that was significantly better than that which would have been assumed from a cursory analysis.

This then provided the basis for proposing reduced levels of parking provision and no on-site provision of public open space. The analysis also helped in identifying pedestrian desire lines (see Figure 2.9) from surrounding residential streets that had effectively been blocked by the site's former industrial use. These desire lines provided an important starting point in defining the structure for the site's redevelopment. The resulting development concept is shown in Figure 2.10.

Some Density Rules of Thumb

Development density will vary across an urban area, reflecting different levels of proximity to the city, town and local centres, the public transport network and other facilities and amenities, such as open spaces and waterside areas. The matrix set out in Figure 2.11 provides some guideline housing density ranges derived from case study design analysis of densities achieved on 70 sites across London that were designed with different mixes of houses and apartments and different levels of

2.9   Redevelopment provides the opportunity to reconnect the surrounding community to local shops and open spaces.[8]

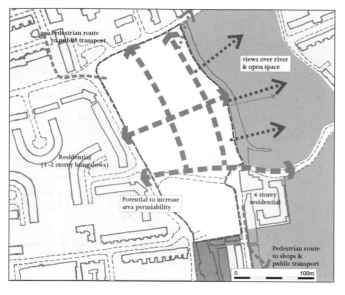

2.10   A mix of town houses and apartments achieves a density of 110 dwellings per hectare with 0.6 parking spaces per dwelling.[9]

car parking. It indicates a very wide range of densities from 35 dwellings per hectare (dph) in areas away from facilities and public transport right through to over 400dph in the very accessible city centre.

The foregoing discussion has been concerned with what planners term 'net housing density', that is, the ratio of dwellings (or habitable rooms or floorspace) to an area of land developed primarily for housing. But, clearly, towns and cities need to provide a range of other uses, such as shopping, employment and leisure, which need to be either within walking distance of home or accessible by public transport. A 'town' or 'district' density includes allowance for these non-housing uses and should be much lower than the net housing density. The important principle is that moderate to high net housing densities are supported by good quality local facilities, including parks and open spaces. This produces lower 'town or district' densities but maximises the proportion of the population which can access local facilities and amenities on foot.[10]

Some Broader Issues and Key Points

The discussion in this chapter has largely been concerned with the structure of the urban environment. This is a fundamentally important component in planning for a more sustainable future, but in itself will not deliver sustainability. That depends also on more detailed design

considerations, explored in subsequent chapters of this book, but it also turns on a number of broader issues. These include the following:

● *The creation of socially mixed and inclusive communities*. One of the lessons of much post-war housing is that the split between market and social provision has helped to polarise society into ghettos of rich and poor, imposing incalculable economic and social costs on future generations. The lesson must be about recreating a wider mix of housing opportunity and choice, and avoiding concentrations of particular housing types and tenures.

● *The provision of services and facilities that meet a range of needs*. Pristine out-of-town shopping centres may be efficient places to shop for those with access to a car, but they lack the character, serendipity and community focus of a town centre or high street with its mix of high-fashion, second-hand, ethnic and convenience stores, pubs and access for all.

● *Engaging local communities in discussion* about how they see their neighbourhood and their priorities and aspirations for the future. The dialogue should be honest, open, ongoing and with a real commitment to changing plans and designs to reflect people's views.

● *The provision of quality public transport services*. This is a funda-mental prerequisite in reducing reliance on the car. Chapter 3 sets

2.11 A matrix giving guideline density ranges for sites with different levels of accessibility to local facilities and public transport.[11]

Setting	Public transport Accessibility Level (PTAL)		
	0 to 1	2 to 3	4 to 6
Suburban	150 – 200 hr/ha	150 – 250 hr/ha	200 – 350 hr/ha
3.8 – 4.6 hr/d	35 – 55 dph	35 – 65 dph	45 – 90 dph
3.1 – 3.7 hr/d	40 – 65 dph	40 – 80 dph	55 – 115 dph
2.7 – 3.0 hr/d	50 – 75 dph	50 – 95 dph	70 – 130 dph
Urban	150 – 250 hr/ha	200 – 450 hr/ha	200 – 700 hr/ha
3.8 – 4.6 hr/d	35 – 65 dph	45 – 120 dph	45 – 185 dph
3.1 – 3.7 hr/d	40 – 80 dph	55 – 145 dph	55 – 225 dph
2.7 – 3.0 hr/d	50 – 95 dph	70 – 170 dph	70 – 260 dph
Central	150 – 300 hr/ha	300 – 650 hr/ha	650 – 1100 hr/ha
3.8 – 4.6 hr/d	35 – 80 dph	65 – 170 dph	140 – 290 dph
3.1 – 3.7 hr/d	40 – 100 dph	80 – 210 dph	175 – 355 dph
2.7 – 3.0 hr/d	50 – 110 dph	100 – 240 dph	215 – 405 dph

KEY

Abbreviations

hr	=	habitable rooms
d	=	dwelling
ha	=	hectare
dph	=	dwellings per hectare
hr/ha	=	habitable rooms per hectare

Definition of site setting

Central = areas with very dense development, a mix of different uses, large building footprints and typically buildings of four to six storeys, located within 800 metres walking distance of an International, Metropolitan or Major town centre

Urban = areas with predominantly dense development such as terraced houses, mansion blocks, a mix of different uses, medium building footprints and typically buildings of two to four storeys, located within 800 metres walking distance of a District centre or along main arterial routes

Suburban = areas with predominantly lower density development such as detached and semi-detached houses, predominantly residential, small building footprints and typically buildings of two to three storeys

Definition of Accessibility

The PTAL is a measure of the time taken to walk to an existing public transport node

Note:
3.8 – 4.6 hr/d is typically detached and linked houses
3.1 – 3.7 hr/d is typically terraced houses and flats
2.7 – 3.0 hr/d is typically flats

out the key challenges and potential in seeking to turn around decades of under-investment in public transport.

- The delivery of excellent local facilities and services. If people are to walk to local amenities, then these must meet their needs, as well as any to which people can drive. This applies to schools, open spaces and play areas, local shopping facilities, as well as the walking routes to and between these facilities.

- The recognition that long-term management and maintenance are as important as the initial design. New development must be designed with management and maintenance in mind, not just in terms of the choice of materials and landscape but also with a clear definition of who will be responsible for what and a commitment to pay for maintenance over the long term.

- The vision of new development as a catalyst for the improvement of existing areas. This demands excellent design, but it could also include a local 'community chest' to pool contributions from a range of development schemes to be spent on local community projects. This could help encourage a more positive public attitude to development and change, which becomes increasingly important the more development moves from a few large sites to a multitude of improvements to the physical environment and community facilities. Such approaches also increase in importance as more emphasis is placed on the re-use of very small sites.

It is clear from this wide range of issues that sustainable planning and design do not belong to one discipline. Success requires a holistic and integrated design approach that draws on skills in planning, urban design, architecture, landscape design, building and services engineering, community consultation and development, and much more besides.

Further reading

CABE (2001) *Better Places to Live: By Design*. London: Thomas Telford
    Publishing. Available: http://www.cabe.org.uk/publications.aspx

Department for Transport (2007) *Manual for Streets*. London: Thomas Telford
    Publishing. (Note, this document supersedes Design Bulletin 32 and
    its companion guide *Places, Streets and Movement*.) Available:
    http://www.dft.gov.uk/pgr/sustainable/manforstreets/pdfman-
    forstreets.pdf

Department of Transport, Local Government and the Regions/Commission for
    Architecture and the Built Environment (2000) *By Design: Urban Design
    in the Planning System – Towards Better Practice*. London: Thomas Telford
    Publishing. Available: http://www.communities.gov.uk/documents/
    planningandbuilding/pdf/158490

English Partnerships and the Housing Corporation (2002) *Urban Design
    Principles, Urban Design Compendium*. London: English Partnerships.
    Available: http://www.urbandesigncompendium.co.uk

English Partnerships and the Housing Corporation (2007) *Delivering Quality
    Places, Urban Design Compendium 2*. London: English Partnerships.
    Available: http://www.urbandesigncompendium.co.uk

Greater London Authority (2004) *The London Plan: Spatial Development
    Strategy for Greater London*. Available: http://www.london.gov.uk
    /mayor/strategies/sds/london plan/lon plan all.pdf

Rudlin, D. and Falk, N. (1999) *Building the 21st Century Home: The Sustainable
    Urban Neighbourhood*. Oxford: Butterworth-Heinemann.

Urban Villages Group (1992) *Urban Villages*. London: Urban Villages Group.

(All websites accessed 2 February 2008.)

3 TRANSPORTATION

ROBERT THORNE, WILLIAM FILMER-SANKEY AND ANTHONY ALEXANDER

Introduction

Travel is a natural human urge; it broadens our experience, brings new contacts and can help keep us fit. It is also essential for moving food and supplies to maintain the fabric of urban life. Travel, furthermore, is not just a means but an end in its own right; the act of travelling is in many cases as important as reaching the destination.

In short, travel is both a sustainable and a sustaining activity and all urban settlements, from villages to cities, rely on it. The problem of recent years is that the means of travel – motorised transport – has come to dominate our lives and our cities. The distances travelled by people and goods have been increasing exponentially, prompted by expanding levels of trade (especially international trade), business travel and tourism.[1] Since the 1980s, when a model of urban development was encouraged in the UK that promoted private car use over public transport, the distance of essential journeys to work, school and shops has increased by up to 40 per cent. The unrestrained growth in car use has made traffic congestion inevitable, and attempts to provide ever greater amounts of road infrastructure only bring temporary relief as the slowest parts of any network always create bottlenecks. In 2000, the average speed of cars in many cities was slower than the horse-drawn carriages of 100 years before, around 10 mph/16 kmph.[2]

The enormous social change that began with the Industrial Revolution of the nineteenth century was based on the stationary machinery that ran factories and the new mechanised transport of railways, steamships, trams and eventually cars, trucks and ultimately planes. These transported the fuel and raw materials in and the goods out. The population also became more mobile than ever before and in the twenty-first century this has reached a level of hyper-mobility of people and products. The liberation, progress and economic growth that this has brought are spoiled by the then unforeseen potential consequences of climate change. Fundamental to industrial civilisation has been the ability to exploit and consume fossil fuels (coal, oil and gas) for energy and materials, but the resulting emissions of the greenhouse gas, carbon dioxide, have had a significant impact on global warming. In London, in 2006, ground-based transport emitted 9.68 Mt (megatonnes) of carbon dioxide into the atmosphere and aviation transport emitted 22.78 Mt.[3] Although the carbon dioxide emitted by transport is not currently as great as that emitted by power stations, reducing the overall carbon intensity of transport is a vital part of the challenge of mitigating dangerous climate change.

This merely adds a new, sharper dimension to a long-recognised series of social, economic and environmental problems related to the excessive use of transport. As journeys become longer, slower and more wasteful of energy, they cease to fulfil their enriching role. Travel by car (70 per cent of people in the UK commute to work by car[4]) gives virtually no physical exercise when compared with walking or cycling, which also extend life expectancy (see Table 3.1). Although car driving creates a sense of personal empowerment through mobility,

TABLE 3.1

Nature and scale of some impacts of transport on health in London [5]	
Impact	Scale
Road accidents, fatalities (2000)	286
Road accidents, total casualties (2000)	46,003
Percentage considering noise from road traffic a nuisance (GB figure, 1991)	63
Calories consumed for 70kg person (kcal/h), driving a car	80
Calories consumed for 70kg person (kcal/h), walking at 5km/h	260
Calories consumed for 70kg person (kcal/h), walking at 7km/h (brisk walk)	420
Estimated net life extension, compared to whole population, of those who walk or cycle to work	2 years

Source: *Informing Transport Health Impact Assessment in London,* AEA Technology/NHS Executive London, 2000, and TFL, 2001.

3.8   Velib' bicycle hire station near Gare du Nord, Paris.

(see Figure 3.7), thus encouraging cycling or walking and giving new opportunities for social contact and interaction. Locating major centres of work and retail near public transport interchanges and connecting them to the local cycle or footpath network will help to persuade people to leave their cars at home for at least some of the time. An integrated approach to transport whereby suburban trains and buses are designed to also take bicycles, or where bicycle hire or parking facilities are available next to major transport nodes, helps reduce total car dependency (see Figure 3.8).

Detailed Design

When designing places, built-in flexibility is essential. A problem with previous trends in land use or zone-based planning is that the underlying ideas are proving to be more short-lived than the urban designs they produced, which continue. An important element of designing for sustainability is that it is not bound by dogma, but can be adapted to meet future demands. This is particularly true of streets and services. Houses scattered around a cul-de-sac can easily be demolished but the infrastructure that feeds them and the low density, block size or street pattern is far harder to replace. However, sustainable transport solutions cannot be limited to the design of new settlements but must also be applied to the existing urban form. Sometimes this may require a concerted effort on many different levels, ranging from major interventions such as removing over-sized transport infrastructure

to counter physical isolation, to merely informing local residents of sustainable transport alternatives such as bus routes or cycle paths via a local travel awareness campaign. The example of Malmö (Chapter 16) shows how a local mobility office can help facilitate sustainable transport patterns. The challenge also exists of how to continue to accommodate the private motor vehicle since we must recognise the empowerment private vehicles give elderly or disabled people, and that they are essential for many commercial and public services. Inclusive design ensures that the rights of all members of the community are considered.

Total segregation of different modes of travel can create problems where retail suffers from lack of visibility from nearby transport corridors. Walkable neighbourhoods are fine but we need to beware of creating areas that turn their backs on their surroundings, as UK housing built to the Radburn Principles[16] has done. Levels of natural surveillance offered by passing traffic improve security, and since some of the earliest towns were founded on transport connections such as ports, river crossings or crossroads in order to maximise the potential to capture passing trade, traffic has been fundamental to urban economic life.

Design has a vital role to play in making places feel good for pedestrians and cyclists within a hierarchy of movement that still includes motorised transport. Block sizes can be designed to give a balance between ease of access, mix of uses and privacy, while the careful layout of connections between places ensures that routes for pedestrians and cyclists are as direct as possible. Street widths, the treatment of different types of street, and frontages contribute to the variety of experience which those on foot or cycle can notice and appreciate, but those in cars cannot. The current classifications and definitions of roads and streets reflect their subservience to the needs of cars. Changing those descriptions is more than a symbolic gesture. It reflects a changed perception of what streets are for and for whom (see Table 3.3).

Pedestrians and cyclists have very practical needs that must be addressed by good urban design. As well as routes that are easy to use and well located, adequate cycle parking is also clearly important. The UK Government's Code for Sustainable Homes requires dedicated cycle parking to be provided for new homes, recognising that security and convenience are major barriers to increased cycle use. Where this is not

TABLE 3.3

Redefined street types[17]	
Conventional capacity-based terminology	Street types that combine capacity and character
Primary ditributor	**Main road** Routes providing connections across the city
District ditributor	**Avenue or Boulevard** Formal, generous landscaping
Local ditributor	**High street** Mixed uses, active frontages
Access road	**Street or Square** Mainly residential, building lines encouraging traffic calming
Cul-de-sac	**Mews/Courtyard** Shared space for parking and other uses

3.10   High quality cycle rack in Melbourne, Australia.

3.9   Residents in this high-rise block resort to storing their cycles on balconies in the absence of better alternatives.

provided, residents often make do with inappropriate solutions (see Figure 3.9).

One important issue lies in the belief that public transport is of a lower status than private transport and this is preventing a modal shift from cars to public transport. High quality design of buses, trams and trains, as well as their stops, stations and interchanges, is widespread in many continental European countries, counteracting the prevailing impression that public transport is only for those who cannot afford a car. At the level of designing street layout, the relationship between the urban grid and architecture can emphasise the central role of public transport. High quality bus stops, cycle racks and traffic-free routes all help to make sustainable transport attractive (see Figure 3.10).

Future Technologies

The key point to note is that we will be living differently in the future. Technology, whether mode of transport, vehicle design or information technology services, inevitably evolves, but predicting winners in advance can be extremely difficult. At an intercity level, trains like France's TGV or Japan's bullet train are competing with aeroplanes for travel time, and massively outperform them in terms of their environmental impact. For LEVs, electric, hybrid or hydrogen fuel cell engines represent new frontiers for the motor industry and are becoming

All outdoor spaces form the basis of our landscape, whether natural or man-made, and contribute to the general quality of our immediate environment. The following discussion will highlight how landscape can contribute to the creation of more sustainable urban areas in strategic terms as well as in detail.

The Wide-ranging Benefits of Landscape in the City

When thinking about landscape in the city, one should not forget the primary role of urban areas – they provide the main locations for human habitation, commerce, trade and interaction. They are places where people live, work and conduct their daily lives. The sustainability debate recognises this and pushes the point even further by suggesting that compact cities can lead to a more sustainable society. Living at higher densities will limit travelling distances and hence use less energy and fewer resources for transport. The reality, however, is that many people *choose* to live outside of cities even when otherwise dependent on them for work and facilities. Research has shown that there are two main reasons for this trend: the lure of living in a physically attractive environment, and the search for a different type of community and lifestyle.[1] These are environments that offer more space in the home as well as in the public domain, such as parks, fields and open spaces. The straightforward solution to the 'urban exodus' then seems to be more spacious dwellings, together with more public and private green space in cities in the form of urban parks, communal gardens, gardens, roof terraces, balconies, and so forth. These can and should be of different characters and sizes, providing pleasant green views and contrast, and helping to make cities more desirable places to live for a wider range of people. This solution can change the perception of the city and improve the quality of life that cities offer.

This idea is easily translated into the overall sustainability of the city (see Figure 4.3). The traditional function of the city focused on the economic and social aspects with the environmental dimension taking a back seat. However, with rising affluence and mobility, environmental options have increased tremendously, highlighting the fact that, given the choice, the means and the opportunity, more contact with our natural environment is very desirable. By improving all natural and landscape elements in the city, it becomes a better place to live as well as work. Ironically, this in turn strengthens the economic and social sustainability of the city as a whole.

4.3   The need to improve the sustainability balance in the city.

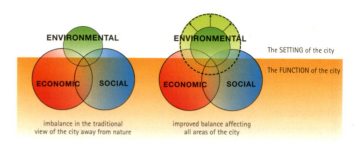

imbalance in the traditional view of the city away from nature

improved balance affecting all areas of the city

The role and benefits of more nature and landscape in the city are multiple and often interlinked. They affect and improve:

- the micro-climate of the city, making it a more pleasant place to live;

- people's health and quality of life in the city, creating more green spaces of varied nature with more trees and greener views;

- property values, through better access to open space;

- the biodiversity, as more species live in the city, creating a real and diverse ecosystem with a range of habitats for wildlife.

Micro-climate

It has long been understood that vegetation in any form influences the micro-climate around it. Vegetation has been shown to do the following:

- extract CO_2 from the air through the process of photosynthesis and produce O_2 in turn (for example, over 100 years, six trees take up as much CO_2 as is produced by driving one family car for one year);[2]

- bind airborne particles, thereby reducing dust (foliage acts as an impingement filter, trapping airborne particles until they are washed away by rain);[3]

- bind numerous urban pollutants;

- absorb noise;

- raise local humidity by evapotranspiration;

4.4   Avenue planting creates a more pleasant environment on the
street and deflects attention from parked cars. Fulham, London.

- retain rainwater and/or delay it entering the drainage system;

- make the ambient temperature more temperate (lowering it in summer, raising it in winter) and hence counteracting the urban heat-island effect;

- act as a windbreak, reducing wind speeds by up to 50 per cent and hence reducing the associated wind-chill factor – this in turn can lower the heating requirements for buildings.[4]

Elaborating on all these processes and their benefits is not possible in the space available here but it is important to understand that vegetation positively influences climatic conditions (Appendix F provides more detail). It should therefore be better integrated into the design and layout of new urban and suburban areas.

People's health and quality of life
Vegetation has a positive effect on our physical and mental health through cleaner air, fewer airborne particles, a better micro-climate and by providing visual respite. However, there is a further dimension.

The factors that have attracted people out of urban areas to live in the suburbs can give us clues as to what is missing in the city – namely greener environments that contrast with the hard lines and rigidity of buildings.

The influence of landscape goes further than improving the aesthetic value and ecology of cities. Landscape in the city can influence the human psyche and mental well-being. Clinical trials have shown that hospital patients looking out over trees have a faster recovery rate, lower blood pressure and need less medication than patients who look out over paved areas.[5] If something this simple can help the sick recuperate, there surely must be lessons we can learn to improve our daily environment.

The presence of trees and mature landscape can to some degree also influence human behaviour. There is anecdotal evidence that people living in tree-lined streets are less prone to show violent behaviour, be depressed or abuse drugs.[6] Trees along streets can influence driving behaviour. People drive more calmly and are more alert. This is not to suggest that our physical environment can solve all our problems, but it can help stimulate more positive responses. Even if further research is needed to substantiate these claims, everybody agrees that avenue planting visually improves the quality of streets by deflecting attention from cars and should therefore be taken more seriously in the design process (see Figure 4.4).

But why does the existence of planting, or the view over landscaped areas, affect our well-being? Could it simply be colour? According to colour therapy, green is the neutral colour in the middle of the visible light spectrum (between red/orange and blue/violet). The lens of our eyes focuses green light exactly onto the retina so minimal muscular adjustment is needed.[7] Green is therefore the easiest colour for the eye to see and functions like a 'tonic' when we are exhausted. It also soothes and comforts the mind of those who are tired and weary. Craftsmen in ancient Greece used this knowledge by using a green byrol (transparent material) to rest their eyes, while today many sunglasses have a green tint to achieve the same effect. It is not without reason that the colour green represents peace and balance – attributes not currently associated with cities.

Incorporating such landscape as parks, trees and general planting into the city can therefore help to visually counteract the stress created and experienced in cities as a result of traffic, noise and pollution. These landscapes do not have to be large parks but can also be integrated as small greens and 'pocket' parks within the urban fabric. Green vistas can calm our senses and reduce tension. Even a small balcony overflowing with plants and flowers has an effect, not only on the owner tending it, but on everybody who sees it. The urban environment becomes more pleasant and some of the reasons why people move out of cities begin to be addressed.

Property values

In the past, it was difficult to quantify the benefits of the natural environment and the quality of the natural setting in the city. Research in the past few years has highlighted a clear link between proximity to parks and property values. Because people want easy access to open spaces, properties overlooking them or close to them are more desirable than properties further away. This is reflected in house prices with an 8 per cent increase for properties with views over a park and 6 per cent increase for properties in the vicinity of a park.[8] Furthermore, higher density development is generally more acceptable around open spaces as this offsets the reduction in private open space in the properties.[9] Providing good visual and physical access to open space ensures that more people are able to benefit.

Unfortunately no research has yet been conducted to quantify the value of private outdoor space in the UK. While most people agree that even a balcony or terrace would make any property more desirable, the development industry perceives this as cost, without being able to evaluate its return. This is different in other countries. In Germany, for example, outdoor space is considered in the purchase or rental value of any property at 25–50 per cent of the internal price per square metre.[10] Consequently more urban developments in Germany provide dwellings with private outdoor space of usable dimensions and size.

Biodiversity

Plants are a source of food and shelter for insects, birds, and small mammals. These in turn are the food sources for other animals. Plants need soil, water and light to grow and sustain this simplified food chain. But not any planting will do. A diversity of plant species is needed to attract different insects and birds. Native species are generally more attractive to local wildlife than exotic species, as their fruits and flowers are more palatable,[11] but this does not exclude the use of exotic species *per se*. Often they are very useful for their striking shape and/or ability to grow in stressed and polluted environments, but choosing to plant them must be justified as part of the overall aim.

While vegetation is the key to creating and sustaining biodiversity, one plant or tree species by itself will not attract wildlife; it is the combination and, especially, diversity of species that form the attraction. The combination of plants used is dependent on the type of soil, the availability of water and the existing climate. Together these form the local habitat that is attractive to different birds, insects and small animals. Creating a large number of different but interlinked habitats (such as forests, open tree planting, hedgerows, meadows, grassland, ponds, riverbanks and streams) offers the best chance of attracting wildlife and improving the biodiversity of the city. It also creates a variety of environments for people to experience, creating diversity in contrast to the occasional monotony of the city.

Not all plants, however, will grow in all situations or locations. Some are better in dry soils or wet locations, sunny or shady, exposed or protected. Care needs to be taken when selecting plants for specific

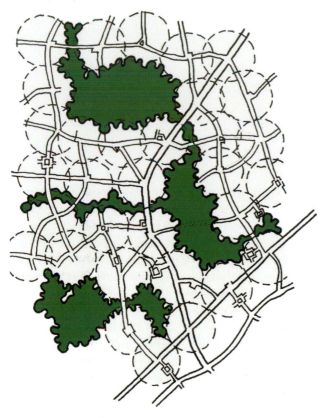

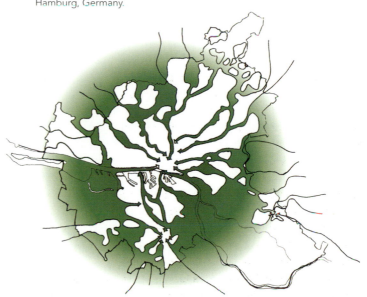

extreme situations. Table F.1 in Appendix F lists a large variety of plants with their suitability for different purposes and situations. In general, one can assume that local species are better adapted to local climatic conditions and therefore need less care and water. Pollution-resistant plants are well suited as street trees, while plants attracting insects and birds are best suited for open spaces and gardens.

From Landscape Strategy to Detailed Implementation

In the context of making places more sustainable, one needs to address the issues at different scales. Some fundamental principles need to be put in place at a strategic level so that detailed solutions can be effective. Detailed solutions strengthen the effects of the strategic principles. This general statement is also true for making landscapes more sustainable and, through its role, leads to more sustainable urban design. The slogan 'think globally – act locally' neatly expresses the relationship between strategy and detail.

Relating strategy and detail to sustainable landscape design is fairly straightforward. There needs to be enough space for nature and land-scape elements to grow in the first place, before we can select the most appropriate and beneficial plants for the desired effect. This can, to some extent, be enforced through detailed planning regulations. The 'Bebauungsplan' in Germany is a site-specific planning tool that clearly sets the minimum and maximum height, scale and site coverage (among other guidance) of any development. Thus it is ensured that enough land remains permeable to water on each site. The city of

Berlin, for instance, 'adopts a 50 per cent rule, whereby every square metre of built footprint has to have the equivalent amount of biodi-verse rich landscape (soft surfaces and water)'.[12]

To increase biodiversity in the city, open-space networks are advanta-geous in that they can form wildlife corridors that help a variety of animals to pass through or move deep within our urban areas (see Figure 4.5).[13] With these corridors in place, the potential increase in biodiversity is far higher than with isolated pockets of open space. The type of soil, access to water and selection of plants further influence the biodiversity of these places in detail. On the city scale, these corri-dors and networks are made up of parks, back gardens, allotments, trees and hedges, but more importantly of leftover land, riverbanks, lakes, railway cuttings, green roofs, climbers and buffer planting.

A landscape strategy outlining landscape corridors and important linkages on a city scale can safeguard land from future development and hence retain its ecological function as well as providing improved access to open spaces. The city of Hamburg has embedded such a land-scape strategy in its planning system. Landscape corridors stretch from all directions deep into the city centre (see Figure 4.6).[14]

The principle of having a landscape strategy relates to sites of all sizes. Any large development site should have its own landscape network, while smaller ones should relate and create linkages within the wider strategy. When setting out a new development site, some strategic landscape principles should be considered at the outset to create a more sustainable development. These include:

- *Conduct a landscape assessment* of the site, including a tree survey and a habitat survey. Identify sensitive areas and landscape elements that deserve retention, such as mature trees, natural watercourses, low-lying land (potentially good areas for natural drainage), unique habitats and ecosystems.

- *Consider the local landform of the site*. Avoid grading the site to a uniform slope for ease of construction and development but instead use it to create a site-specific response. This will preserve the natural ecology and hydrology of the site. When major grading occurs, the drainage pattern of the land is altered significantly and its downstream effects may be unclear.

- *Reserve steep land that is otherwise unbuildable as escarpment and linear open spaces*. These are unique landscape features that are part of the history of the site and are impossible to recreate at a later stage. They provide immediate amenity value to new residents and retain an existing feature within a newly emerging open-space network.

- *Understand the local microclimatic conditions*. What aspects can be exploited through design (i.e. south-facing slopes have a higher solar-gain potential) and what aspects need careful attention in order to mitigate possible harsh conditions (i.e. buffer planting on the side of prevailing winds can minimise the reduction of the ambient temperature and heating requirements)?

Using these as a starting point for site layout will create a natural network of intrinsic landscape elements that give the site its own special character, and they can become a focus in layout and design. Furthermore, they not only help create a development that responds to its setting and functions environmentally, but also create a unique, site-specific solution that feels natural in its location and contributes to the 'sense of place'. One can then consider their detailed articulation to fulfil the strategic thinking behind them.

Drainage in the City and Landscape
A well thought-out natural drainage strategy can have a profound effect on the strategic and local level. We know that buildings, tarmac (see Glossary), paving and parking seal vast areas of our cities. Statistics show that a startling 97 per cent of an inner city block is

sealed and impermeable (see Table 4.1). Little room is left for plants to take root and little if any water can trickle through to help replenish the groundwater. Instead, water is channelled into gullies and fed into the municipal sewers or straight out into our rivers, lakes and oceans. This is not however an argument against increasing density since the amount of impermeable area per dwelling/km² can be lower in urban areas when compared with suburbia. Reducing the amount of rainwater entering municipal sewers is advantageous as it means less wastewater needing treatment in sewage plants and hence less wasted energy.[15] The extreme storm conditions in South-east England in August 2004 illustrate this further. Since some stormwater run-off combines with sewage during extreme conditions, the system simply overflows and the waters have to be discharged without treatment into the rivers. More than 1.5 million tonnes of sewage were discharged into the Thames in London to deal with the water quantities. This had a disastrous effect on water quality and wildlife, killing some 100,000 fish.[16] In July 2007, the flooding of the River Severn in Gloucester caused by consecutive storms disabled power supplies to drinking-water pumps, leaving thousands of people up to their knees in water but with none to drink.

TABLE 4.1

Degree of impermeability of different uses[17]	
Inner urban areas	0.97
Dense residential areas	0.75–0.80
Mixed-use areas	0.80
Terraced housing	0.52
Semi-detached with small gardens	0.50
Semi-detached with medium gardens	0.42
Detached houses with large gardens	0.20

Collecting surface-water run-off in gullies and flushing it away has become common practice in past decades. It is therefore not surprising that floods are more severe, have a shorter 'lead time' and are more likely to occur more frequently since the time between rainfall and run-off into the sewer is greatly reduced. This again costs more energy and money in man-made prevention through flood defences.

To illustrate how the effect is compounded, consider this example: within the watershed (see Glossary) of a small river, the developed/

impermeable land has increased threefold from 7 per cent to 20 per cent over 20 years (so it is still a suburban/rural form of development). The effect of the additional run-off has been a fivefold increase in volume of water in the river and has caused freak flood levels.[18] Rather than allowing free drainage, water is collected in gullies and feeds into the municipal drainage system. More water reaches the rivers in less time and this is the main cause of flooding.

Rainwater is a relatively clean form of grey water. There is some contamination from the atmosphere and surfaces, but much of this can be dealt with by fairly simple filtration systems and in many cases treatment will not need to be extensive. The collection and use of rainwater are discussed in more detail in Chapters 8 and 9. Even when taking all possible rainwater harvesting options into account, the slowed release of water into the ground and/or sewage system will still aid the natural water cycle and replenish the aquifers. On-site natural drainage systems can also help improve water quality, and reduce the risk of flooding.

Many factors influence natural drainage, including:

- the amount of permeable and impermeable ground to be drained;
- the type of soil with its rate of percolation;
- the intensity and duration of typical rainfalls and severe storms.

Water retention systems

In the early stages of design it is important to allow enough land to be able to implement a natural drainage system that can absorb all the rainwater falling on all permeable and impermeable ground on the site. This can occur on a small scale on individual building plots, or on larger development sites where a sophisticated interconnected water system can provide an important amenity function as well. At Stonebridge (see Chapter 17) and at Deptford Wharves (see Chapter 18), both sites benefit from the amenity of the surface water system.

The possible retention systems are:

- low area drain;
- ditches and swales;
- permanent retention ponds;

- underground collection cisterns;
- planted roofs.

Depending on the specific aims to be achieved in the development, different systems offer various advantages. The land-take necessary (the site area required for natural drainage systems) depends on the depth of the drain, which in turn depends on the local soil. The approximate land-take given in Table 4.2 is a percentage of the total site area to be drained and forms a rough guide. This enables the planning of natural drainage systems during the early stages of development. The exact land-take for a natural drainage system relates to the actual quantity of sealed land on site and the degree of impermeability of materials used (see Table 4.3). Figures 4.7a–e illustrate the different systems, and further information on drainage is given in Chapter 9.

The dramatic difference between the three roof types listed in Table 4.3 is most interesting, especially for inner urban settings where flat and low pitch roof construction is most common and where less open ground is available for free drainage. Creating planted roofs should therefore be considered part of a more sustainable design solution.

Planted roofs

Planted roofs are all types of green roofs and brown roofs that support some form of vegetation. While green roofs have only recently become more popular in the UK, Germany is the centre of expertise in modern green-roof installations. An estimated 10 per cent of all flat roofs have been greened[19] and in 2000 and 2001 alone a staggering 25 million square metres of green roofs were installed on new or existing flat roofs.[20]

The water retention ability and slowed release of storm water are not the only advantages of green roofs. They can also help reduce costs by increasing the life of the roofing materials, reducing wear and tear, and can reduce the urban heat-island effect (see Table 4.4).

There are different types of planted roofs, and each has its own advantages and design considerations. Roughly speaking, one can differentiate between intensive and extensive green roofs, with brown roofs as a sub-category of extensive green roofs. Intensive green roofs are actually roof gardens intended for occupation and with the (see Glossary) sites and mimic the early ecosystem of plant invasion. Recolonisation is therefore relatively quick and the variation in materials used creates a better habitat for native flora and fauna to take hold than the often monocultural nature of sedum-based extensive roofs (see Table 4.5).

Conclusion

As this chapter has demonstrated, landscape and vegetation have a profound role to play in our lives and our physical environment. It is therefore difficult to understand why these have been neglected in the development process over the past 50 years. New technologies and standardisation have driven the development process, and speed and cost considerations have required sites to be uniform and free of any obstructions. The effects of these practices have only become clear years after being adopted as 'modern standards'.

Only now are we noticing that many of the places we have created are too artificial, and seem to show little regard to their setting and context. Many people who have the choice to move are leaving these places for more pleasant environments. We need to learn from the past and create developments with their very own sense of place, and which are influenced by their natural sites. The resulting development promises to be more humane and satisfying than modern standards have been. Considering the land, landform and landscape at the outset when laying out a design will create the conditions for urban developments that fit in with their settings. This major strategic decision will make numerous detailed options possible and lead to a more sustainable development overall.

GUIDELINES

1. Landscape and landform influence the appropriate form of development.
2. Landscape and vegetation affect the immediate microclimate by binding airborne particles, absorbing noise, raising humidity and reducing temperature fluctuations, as well as lowering wind speeds.
3. Trees and plants form a contrast to urban development and provide a calmer environment for urban life, while views over green areas soothe the eye and comfort the mind when tired. Parks, trees and planting can help to visually counteract the stress experienced in cities as a result of traffic, noise and pollution.
4. Creating wildlife corridors with interlinked habitats offers the best chance of attracting wildlife and improving the biodiversity of the city. A citywide landscape strategy can set the parameters for wildlife corridors to be developed and can make site-specific open spaces more meaningful.
5. The planning of any site needs to start with a landscape assessment, including topography and microclimatic conditions of the site. This will inform a unique development response with intrinsic landscape elements embedded within the 'place'.
6. Reserve 5 per cent of a site to allow for free drainage or on-site water retention. Sustainable drainage best occurs on the lowest-lying land of the site.
7. Consider green and brown roofs to provide additional landscape elements in urban development.

Further reading

CABE Space (2005) *Start with the Park: Creating Sustainable Urban Green Spaces in Areas of Housing Growth and Renewal*. London: CABE. Available: http://www.cabe.org.uk/AssetLibrary/1715.pdf

CABE Space (2006) *Paying for Parks: Eight Models for Funding Urban Green Spaces*. London: CABE. Available: http://www.cabe.org.uk/AssetLibrary/8899.pdf

Grant, G. (2006) *Green Roofs and Facades*. Berkshire: HIS BRE Press.

Hough, M. (1995) *Cities and Natural Process*. London: Routledge.

Town and Country Planning Association (2004) *Biodiversity by Design*. London: TCPA. Available: http://www.tcpa.org.uk/downloads/TCPA_biodiversity_guide_lowres.pdf

Wheater. P.C. (1999) *Urban Habitats*. London: Routledge.

(All websites accessed 12 January 2008.)

7. The services with their controls should be energy-efficient and 'intelligent' (but not necessarily more so than the people who will use and run them). Occupants should have some control over their environment.

8. Boilers should produce extremely low levels of pollutants and all materials selected should not contribute to indoor air pollution.

5.2   Thermal mass in the sinusoidal concrete ceiling at the BRE Environmental Building, Garston.

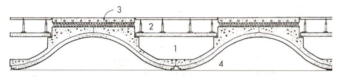

KEY

1   Ventilation paths through slab serving floor below
2   Raised floor zone for cables and pipes for floor above
3   Screed with heating/cooling pipes and insulation beneath
4   Pre-cast concrete (75mm) ceiling with in situ concrete topping
5   High-level windows
6   Side-hung casement windows
7   Bottom-hung translucent windows

5.3   A London terrace.

Meet the demand in sustainable ways

Maximise the opportunities for capturing energy and water. In terms of energy, this is principally directed towards maximising solar potential, and has four main aspects:

1. *Daylighting.* Daylighting and attractive views enhance the urban experience. Daylight needs to be appreciated as the precious commodity that it is. To paraphrase Blake, 'Light is eternal delight.' The provision of natural light in buildings has been an ongoing concern of architecture. Lack of light and air, unsanitary and overcrowded conditions (excessively high densities in today's terms) and congested streets influenced urban planning from nineteenth-century Paris to the Garden City movement.[1] The benefits of daylight have traditionally included better health and a sense of well-being, as well as enlivening the architectural character of spaces. A varied, poetic mixture of daylight and artificial lighting is desirable. Describing the interior atmosphere of an English nineteenth-century home (Melsetter House by Lethaby), one critic praised it saying that it seemed 'friendly not only to its occupants but to the very air'.[2] Providing more natural light in many spaces can reduce the CO_2 emissions associated with artificial lighting powered by conventional fossil-fuel power sources. The ongoing improvement of glazing has also meant that it has been possible to provide more natural light with lower heat losses in winter. Triple glazing with a mid-pane U-value of $0.8W/m^2K$ (compared with single glazing at $5.6W/m^2K$) is commercially available.

Successful spaces are those with good daylight – daylight from two sides, or a wall and roof, can be magical. The eighteenth-century Georgian home with its elegant proportions and tall windows facilitated gracious spaces. It served as a model for the London homes (built in the 1840s) shown in Figure 5.3 and is also of relevance to us today. Note too that the windows normally had wooden internal shutters, which were used at night to insulate, to maintain comfort and to ensure privacy.

Victorian schools used high ceilings and tall windows to bring light deep into classrooms, and the principle still holds. In Germany, where there is an active effort to ensure that office workers have access to daylight, office floor-to-ceiling height is generally about 3.5m compared with 3m (or less) in the UK. (The greater space can also be useful in providing flexibility for additional services, in deeper floor voids, for example, if required during the life of the building.) Narrow floor plans will tend to ensure that sedentary workers are close to windows.

An intriguing modern approach to using a technical requirement (the need for larger glazed areas on lower floors to maintain the same daylight level because of obstructions from neighbouring build-ings in urban contexts) as a generator for an aesthetic is shown in Figure 5.4.[3]

2. *Passive solar gain*. Passive solar gain takes advantage of the solar radiation falling on roofs, walls and, particularly, windows. Letting in the sun during the heating season will help to reduce the demand for fuel. Conversely, in the summer the potential solar gain that could lead to overheating needs to be controlled at the façade while also still ensuring a ventilation path.

5.4   The Crystallography Building, Cambridge.

What percentage of a façade should be glazed? There is no easy answer to this (architects will be relieved to hear). It will depend on the design intent, type of building, orientation, proportions of the interior spaces, U-value of the glazing and wall element, and the risk of overheating, to name just a few considerations. At the BRE Environmental Building, a careful analysis that included the value of daylight in reducing CO_2 emissions and seasonal heat loss through the wall and glazing led to a south façade with about 50 per cent window (see Figure 5.2). For modern housing, in part for reasons of privacy, a smaller percentage is common.

3. *Solar thermal panels*. These actively collect solar energy and transfer it to a fluid, usually a water and anti-freeze mixture (for more on solar thermal panels, see Chapter 6).

4. *Solar electric 'photovoltaic' panels (PVs)*. Developed in practical form especially by the US space programme, these devices convert solar energy directly into electricity (for more on photovoltaics, see Chapter 6).

Maximising the solar potential and dealing with ventilation in low-energy ways have important effects on building form and we can

5.6   Energy and density considerations

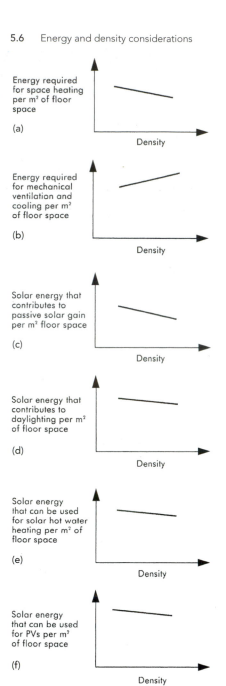

5.5   Energy and density considerations

expect to see more and more buildings that illustrate Mies van der Rohe's remark that 'form is not the aim of our work, but only the result'.4 This will also apply to urban form because solar potential depends so much on density of development, orientation, obstruction heights and other such considerations. Similarly, energy use will depend on some of these factors. Figure 5.5 (based on the simple, indeed, naïve schematic of Figure 1.4) sets out some very simple relationships between the main concerns as density increases.

If we first look at the factors that affect energy consumption (Figure 5.6), more compact developments will tend to have reduced heat losses (Figure 5.6a); this is, for example, because there will be less surface area for the volume enclosed, there will be more shared wall space and because higher densities will tend to encourage the heat-island effect. As density increases, it will become more difficult to use natural ventilation solutions and for reasons similar to those given for heating, the likely need for cooling is increased (Figure 5.6b). More compact developments will be less able to use passive solar gain (Figure 5.6c) and daylight (Figure 5.6d) (in the summer, though, this will reduce the cooling load). We can see that generally, and it should be stated

that the slopes of the lines in the figure are very notional, increasing density has a number of disadvantages.

In terms of suitability for solar thermal (Figure 5.6e) and PVs (Figure 5.6f), more compact forms will tend to mean that PVs can only be used on the roofs – less compact forms will allow PVs to be used on façades. Solar thermal panels, in part because of plumbing and maintenance considerations, tend to be used only on roofs, but wall-mounted installations can be designed to work, such as in the example in Figure 6.5 (page 59). Roof heights are an important factor, and where these heights vary (and they usually do), putting taller

5.7   Density, form and solar optimisation.

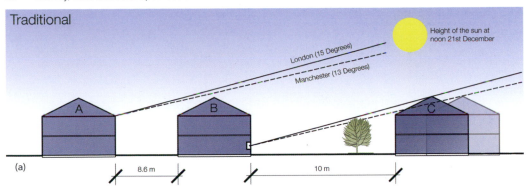

Traditional

London (15 Degrees)

Manchester (13 Degrees)

Height of the sun at
noon 21st December

A

B

C

(a)

8.6 m

10 m

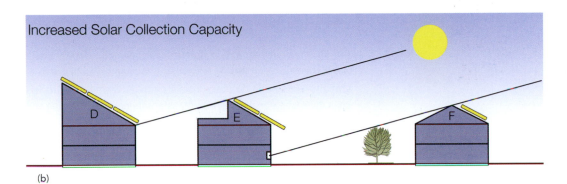

Increased Solar Collection Capacity

D

E

F

(b)

buildings to the north is a way of preserving the solar potential. In the future we should expect to see a sculpting of urban form, as was achieved, for example, at Parkmount in Belfast (see Chapter 12) and Stonebridge in London (see Chapter 17).

Many of these issues have been studied quantitatively.[5, 6] Very broadly, in a mixed grouping of homes and offices, all designed to a very high standard of energy efficiency and planned so that wherever possible the use of air conditioning is avoided, more compact forms will tend to mean that more energy per unit of floor space is required. It will also be more difficult to supply this energy from the sun (as an extreme example, it is easy to imagine that an isolated primitive hut, well-insulated and covered with solar thermal and PV panels, could easily meet the occupants' energy demands from the sun).

These are generalisations and need to be tested when looking at any particular development. It may be that providing all or most of the energy from the site itself is not actually that important if there are other sources of renewable energy available from outside the area. If it would seem that the situation is clear-cut and that higher densities result in a somewhat greater energy consumption in buildings, one should return to the overview provided by our systems approach of Chapter 1. It may also be that increased densities have advantages that outweigh their disadvantages. For example, it could be easier to use community heating and CHP (combined heat and power) schemes. Higher densities mean shorter distances, hence lower distribution losses; such schemes may also be able to take advantage of economies

of scale to extract energy from wastes (see Chapters 6 and 9). It is also likely to be easier to take advantage of large inter-seasonal energy storage. So that, even if energy consumption appears to increase with density, it might still be worthwhile having a higher density because it would mean that energy could be supplied in a different, more efficient way from alternative sources, thereby lowering the energy consumption and its associated CO_2 emissions.

And energy is only part of this complex web. Privacy, the need for light, fresh air for health, land values, ease of rainwater recycling and waste collection, increased noise and many other factors will influence the density and layout of developments. In practice, what is very encouraging is that the complexity will generate a variety of solutions which will contribute to the richness of the urban environment.

One should 'think south', or keep the sun's path in mind, when designing urban form and building orientation. This structuring need not be too rigid and should certainly be balanced against other factors, such as the grain of existing streets and the effect on building appearance. But there will be a tendency to favour street patterns that run broadly east–west so that buildings might face, say, anywhere up to 30 or 40 degrees of due south and still have good solar potential (see Chapter 6 and Appendix A).

What is the relationship between density, form and solar optimisation for housing? Traditional 'two-up, two-down' nineteenth-century English workers' housing as shown in Figures 5.7a–b was built to a

5.8a   Urban forms.

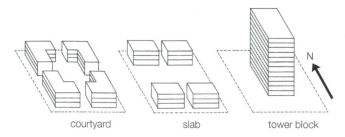

courtyard   slab   tower block

density of about 80–100 dwellings per hectare. It has been suggested that densities up to 200 dwellings per hectare – corresponding to an 'average obstruction angle' of about 30 – are possible before negative energy impact is significant.[7]

In Figure 5.7a, if the streets run east–west, passive solar gain and day-lighting are good on the rear floors of B. If solar thermal and PVs are used on the roofs, the roof of A will be partly overshadowed by B during part of the winter. Figure 5.7b also shows how the total PV potential can be improved by varying the architecture slightly.

From modest considerations such as these, and by keeping in mind other factors such as the existing streets (see, for example, Chapter 11), one could develop new patterns for development.

Figure 5.8a shows three typical urban forms: courtyard housing, parallel slabs and a tower block, all built to the same nominal density of about 100 dwellings per hectare; the floor area per home has been taken as 100m². The courtyard housing can create a strong sense of place and community but will have some self-shading; interruptions in the form add variety and bring the sun in. The slab forms may feel rather soulless if not handled with care, architecturally, but can use the sun well. The tower block has a distinctive character with both advantages and disadvantages; its solar potential (includ-ing the negative aspect of possibly overshadowing other buildings) depends very much on context. Orientation is shown as due south but considerable flexibility is possible (see, for example, photovoltaics in Chapter 6).

Figure 5.8b is an interesting study of the various urban forms in the im-mediate vicinity of the 'Made in Stockwell' site (see Chapter 18 for the case study), and shows the relative scale of each type in comparison with the proposed site. Note also that these forms can be analysed in terms of the space the buildings occupy on the site; the residual space can be examined to give, for example, an index of landscape potential.

Overall, probably the most important development currently under way is thinking about form in terms of the total potential to use solar radiation – not only for passive solar gain and daylighting, as has been done traditionally, but also for solar thermal water heating and electricity production through PVs.

This is leading designers to give more attention to roofscapes, which have been, until recently, the forgotten 'fifth façade'; home to lift over-runs and air-conditioning heat-rejection plant, and occasionally even a terrace. Increasing the sustainability of development and liveability of cities has put enormous pressure on roofs to serve as solar collectors, rainwater harvesters, green space for biodiversity and rainwater attenuation as well as gardens in the sky.

Allow for future adaptability to accommodate changes in use and advances in technology

It is important that buildings should be capable of being altered within their lifetimes to allow for new technologies and social changes; indeed, a building's life will be extended if it can be adapted – so-called 'long life, loose-fit'. An example of incorporating technical develop-ments is to plan for replacement windows that will lose less heat, admit more light and even produce electricity using photovoltaics. But this approach can be extended to roofs, internal partitions and external walls. This trend may lead to fewer buildings being conceived of as a work of fine art; instead we may see buildings that strive less to draw attention to themselves and contribute more to streetscapes and the comfort of their occupants. As one designer has noted, 'One of the problems of modernism is that beautiful objects have been created that are not kind to people.'[8]

Thermal Comfort

Cities tend to experience higher temperatures in both winter and summer because of the heat-island effect (referred to in Chapter 1). This is advantageous in the winter but potentially disadvantageous in summer, especially in offices where the likelihood of cooling may be increased.

5.8b Urban grain.

15 Stockwell Green
Net site area = 12,150 sqm
Built footprint = 7,570 sqm (63%)
Gross floor area = 26,495 sqm
Land use: Commercial (archive storage)

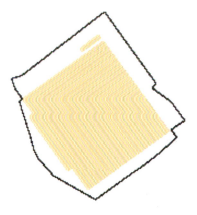

Slab block
Net site area = 12,150 sqm
Built footprint = 2,450 sqm (20%)
Gross floor area = 12,250 sqm
Land use: Residential (slab blocks)
Approximate units per hectare: 150

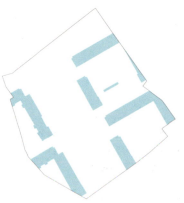

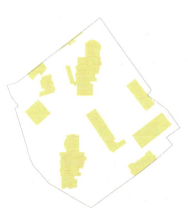

Point block and slab block
Net site area = 12,150 sqm
Built footprint = 3,090 sqm (25%)
Gross floor area = 27,810 sqm
Land use: Residential (point and slab blocks)
and education
Approximate units per hectare: 240

Terrace
Net site area = 12,150 sqm
Built footprint = 5,140 sqm (43%)
Gross floor area = 12,850 sqm
Land use: Residential (terraced homes)
Approximate units per hectare: 100

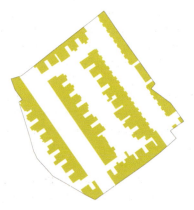

5.9   Selected urban ventilation strategies.

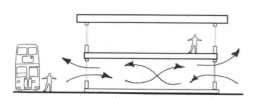

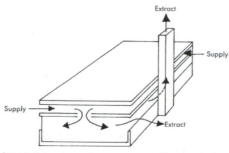

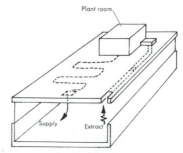

(a) Air in and out from perimeter

(b) High-level supply; extract at mid level or high level, e.g. stacks (see also Figure 7.3)

(c) Mechanical ventilation (i.e. supply air path incorporated in thermal-mass deck)

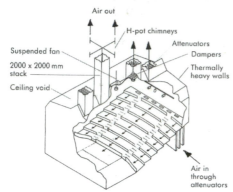

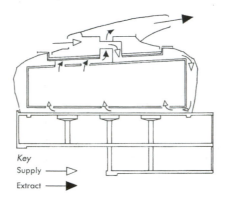

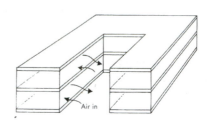

(d) Air in from perimeter, extracted via stacks (Contact Theatre)

(e) Wind-assisted high-level supply and extract

(f) Ventilation via a quiet courtyard

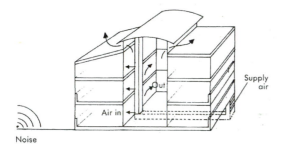

(g) Ventilation from a protected area

The occupants' ability to control their environment is known to be a key factor in the success of buildings. In homes, this is usually easy, but in offices it requires careful attention both to design and to the mechanical heating, cooling and ventilation systems. Allowing temperature levels to vary tends to be both a more robust solution and a less energy-intensive one. Being able to adjust one's clothing is important in winter and summer and a strong case can be made that human beings enjoy the variability and stimulation. In the winter, temperatures between 20°C and 23.5°C are felt to be comfortable by many; in the summer, a comparable range is between 23°C and 26°C. It should be noted that the entire field of comfort is complex, subjective and often controversial. Humidity, ventilation and even noise can affect temperature preferences. In developing the brief for the BRE Environmental Building, another approach was taken, which was to provide the occupants with control over their environment (openable windows, movable shades, overrides on the building management system) and design to pre-defined criteria that an internal temperature of 25°C should not be exceeded for more than 5 per cent of working hours, and 28°C not more than 1 per cent of the time.[9]

Acoustic Comfort

The exceptional variety of sound and noise in cities varies from the exciting to the deplorable, the attractive to the deafening, the poetic rustle of leaves to the screech of braking buses.

In many homes, background noise levels, without the sounds of, say, radios and televisions, will vary from about 25–35dBA (Appendix D gives some basic data and some definitions). In open-plan offices, with conversations, telephones, and photocopiers, noise levels are in the range of 45–55dBA. On busy city streets, with a mixture of cars, buses and the occasional motor bike, the noise level is likely to be 75–85dBA at the kerbside. Thus, attenuation of external noise is one of the most important issues for environmentally friendly buildings that rely on natural ventilation. Of course, noise problems in cities are nothing new. One of the reasons Gilby House in Camden Town, London, designed in 1937 by Chermayeff, had a mechanical ventilation system was the noise from the traffic over cobblestone roads, now long overed over by tarmac, and the noise and pollution of the adjacent mainline railway.

Another area of great importance is noise transmission – between buildings and, especially, between flats. Enjoyable urban living and acoustic privacy go together and are another part of the sustainability of our cities. Poor resistance to sound is so common that the Building Regulations in England and Wales control the allowable noise transmission between dwellings.[10] Performance in excess of this minimum standard is rewarded with credits by the Code for Sustainable Homes[11] scheme as promoting human health and well-being. Noise from internal sources has historically been an issue with mechanical ventilation systems but a well-designed system, with acoustic attenuators if necessary, should perform well.

Air and Ventilation

Urban air quality has been and remains notoriously poor. In 1393, King Richard II empowered the University of Cambridge to improve certain gutters, which were 'causing the air to be corrupted and many masters, scholars and others passing through the streets fell sick thereof'.[12] Some current key contaminants are listed in Appendix C – they too have pernicious effects on our health.

Designers need to consider how they will bring air into the building. Natural ventilation systems have the advantage of requiring very little energy but may need more space for a low-resistance air path. A guideline is that ventilation from one side is adequate for room depths up to 2.5 times the floor-to-ceiling height, and cross-ventilation is suitable for spaces 5 times the floor-to-ceiling dimension. In most housing, natural ventilation is the rule. Dual-aspect flats (that is, those laid out so that they have views to two sides) can be cross-ventilated and also have more access to the sun (see Chapter 17).

In offices and other buildings, though, the problems are often more complex. A number of solutions are being developed, ranging from assisted natural ventilation (or mixed-mode) approaches through to mechanical ventilation with assistance from the wind. A number of

5.10   Cartier Foundation, Paris.

5.11   Attenuators and student at the Contact Theatre, Manchester.

these methods incorporate heat recovery. It is also possible to add cooling to many of them, with the source being a natural one such as groundwater (see Chapter 6). The use of the Earth's cooling capacity is nothing new. Palladio describes the summer home in Costozza belonging to the Trentos, gentlemen of Vicenza. There, cool air from underground excavations from former quarries was led into the building by a system of underground passageways.[13]

Ventilation Strategies

Figures 5.9a–g show a variety of 'sustainable' ventilation strategies, but one needs to examine the comfort achieved, the energy required and the corresponding CO_2 emissions. Hybrid solutions combining natural and mechanical ventilation are one way of dealing with variable urban pollution rates; a mechanical boost might be provided when pollution was high and filtration, say, was needed. In a similar way, intelligent controls could shift the ventilation mode according to noise level, if required. These more sophisticated approaches could function on plan, reacting to local roads, say, or vertically in tall buildings.

Jean Nouvel's brilliant gambit at the Cartier Foundation in Paris (Figure 5.10) was to set a glass (unfortunately air-conditioned) building back behind a glass screen. The building is thus protected by its distance (probably more than by the rather perforated screen) from much of the noise and pollution of the busy Boulevard Raspail. Perhaps what is most important though is the integration and richness of the combination of architecture and nature because the screen allows one to see, in Nouvel's words, not only a tree but the reflection of the tree.[14]

A more common urban ventilation strategy is the traditional one of a building close to the road with air introduced at the perimeter – this is satisfactory provided that noise and pollution levels either are not excessive or are dealt with in some way (such as with attenuators for noise). Figures 5.9a–e show several options with air introduced and exhausted in a variety of ways. Figures 5.9f and 5.9g show other strategies, with air brought in from courtyards or quiet side areas.

The ventilation strategy at the Contact Theatre, Manchester[15, 16] (see Chapter 14), incorporated a low-pressure drop inlet with large acoustic attenuators to reduce the urban noise level to an acceptable level for stage productions. Figure 5.11 shows a visiting mature French student of environmental design experiencing the sound reduction at first hand when standing between the sound absorbing walls of one of the attenuators.

Dwellings

In order to overcome the problem of noise intrusion into flats, mechanical ventilation is sometimes adopted. The fresh air can be heated to offset the heat losses from the flat and avoid the need for radiators. By running the fresh and exhaust air past each other in a sealed heat exchanger, up to half the outgoing heat can be reclaimed.

A heat-recovery ventilation system is shown in Figure 5.12(a). A boiler provides hot water and heat to a water-to-air heat exchanger within the heat-recovery unit. A room thermostat in the living room starts the boiler when there is a demand for heat. A design ventilation rate of one-half an air change per hour is achieved by cycling the fans at normal speed: one-half an hour on, then one-half an hour off. With a demand for heat, the fans are run continuously at normal speed. When cooking or running a bath, a manual boost switch runs the fans at twice normal speed, automatically reverting to normal speed after two hours. Figure 5.12(b) shows a typical layout plan of the heat-recovery system within the flat (the airflows indicated are for the boost situation).

Façade and section

Note that the façade and section need to work together. Passive solar gain, overheating, ventilation, views, thermal mass, acoustics, aesthetics and many other factors meet here, not necessarily always happily.

A south-facing façade will need to have a way of controlling solar gain. This may be through external movable louvres, but for many buildings it is more likely to be through, say, retractable internal blinds or shades. Where the budget is more substantial and where life-cycle costing is encouraged, these blinds may be in between two layers of glazing. If air is to be brought in from the façade, solar control measures should not interfere with the air path, the classic example being roller blinds flapping against an open window. Blinds with guide rails at each side restrain the blind and can also be fixed to the opening pane. Alternatively, the ventilation path can be dissociated from the glazing by using separate openings, which avoids the problem in the first place.

Roofs

As discussed earlier, the roofs of buildings have many potential uses. One approach is to have a planted roof, which consists of vegetation such as sedums, herbs and grasses. The thermal performance of planted

5.12 A schematic and layout of a heat-recovery ventilation system.

BUILDING DESIGN

(a)

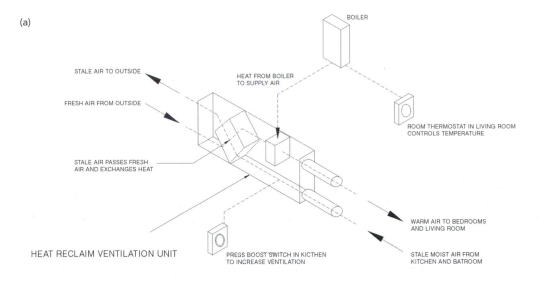

BOILER

STALE AIR TO OUTSIDE

HEAT FROM BOILER
TO SUPPLY AIR

FRESH AIR FROM OUTSIDE

ROOM THERMOSTAT IN LIVING ROOM
CONTROLS TEMPERATURE

STALE AIR PASSES FRESH
AIR AND EXCHANGES HEAT

WARM AIR TO BEDROOMS
AND LIVING ROOM

HEAT RECLAIM VENTILATION UNIT

PRESS BOOST SWITCH IN KICTHEN
TO INCREASE VENTILATION

STALE MOIST AIR FROM
KITCHEN AND BATROOM

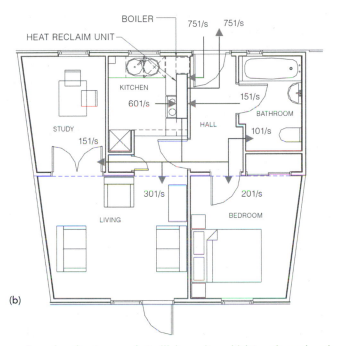

(b)

BOILER
HEAT RECLAIM UNIT
751/s 751/s
KITCHEN
601/s 151/s
BATHROOM
STUDY HALL 101/s
151/s
301/s 201/s
LIVING BEDROOM

roofs can be advantageous but will depend on which type is employed; more details are given in Chapter 4.

The advantages of soil and plants on a roof include the retention of rainfall during storms, thus reducing the risk of surcharging drains and flooding. Plants, as we have seen, will also take up CO_2, produce oxygen, release moisture into the atmosphere, remove dust particles, provide an environment for wildlife including birds and butterflies, gladden our lives and remind us of the changing seasons.

But a planted roof may compete for the same area as a solar collector; for daylighting or passive solar gain through roof lights; for solar thermal hot-water heaters, and for photovoltaic panels. Which strategy is appropriate will depend on the weighting given to each benefit.

High-rise Buildings

Le Corbusier drew high-rise buildings set in an urban park, but his vision of the city was a complex one and he said that 'family life would hardly be at home [in a city of towers] with their prodigious mechanism of lifts'.[17]

A key question when considering tall buildings is to ask whether they are being proposed out of desire or necessity. And if desire, whose desire? The images of strength and virility associated with tall buildings (and perhaps now challenged by the attacks on the World Trade Center) may suit both politicians and architects, but their role in a sustainable community requires careful analysis. A mixture of uses (homes, offices, shops, leisure) to create semi-autonomous communities may also make 'high rise' more sustainable. What is very clear as one studies London is that tower blocks only work both socially and environmentally if the space between them is successful and if they are well managed.

The Barbican, designed by architects Chamberlin Powell and Bon in the 1960s and still incorporating the tallest residential apartment buildings in London, now represents for many a desirable home. Its success is attributed in part to an arrangement of buildings around gardens and lakes, which makes use of all available space, underground car parking, and pedestrian walkways above ground level away from the busy street (see Figure 5.13).

Solar considerations

Light is an important issue. If a tower block deprives the adjacent buildings of light and thus of the opportunity to use photovoltaics and active solar thermal systems, problems might ensue. In energy terms, the PVs that might be mounted on the south façade of the tower, however, could possibly more than compensate for the energy loss of any buildings overshadowed by the tower. This would, of course, require some analysis.

5.13   The Barbican Estate, London.

Solar considerations may lead to us putting higher buildings at the north of a site unless they fulfil another function such as marking particular sites in a broader urban context.

As the use of solar energy becomes increasingly viable (and necessary), we can expect to see legislation to control urban forms to enhance solar access in a similar way that daylight access has influenced cities in the past. For example, much of Paris consists of areas of great beauty, planned and built in the nineteenth century with light as an important generator of form.

Wind considerations

Tall buildings may experience high wind speeds at both the top and the bottom. At the top this is a potential source of energy (see Chapter 6 and Chapter 18). If, however, winds hit the building and cascade down, this is likely to annoy pedestrians. The Lawson Comfort Criteria[18] define a scale of annoyance by the wind for particular pedestrian activities. Wind conditions around buildings may be tolerable to people depending on their activity. For example, wind conditions in an area designated for sitting need to be more benign than in a location where people merely walk past. Testing in wind tunnels, or Computational Fluid Dynamics (CFD) modelling can provide additional details of problem areas. Design and planning can help to mitigate negative effects; some towers are set on a plinth to protect pedestrians from wind at street level. Appendix B has further information on wind.

Energy consumption

Tall buildings will tend to have a greater surface-to-volume ratio and hence an increased heat loss. Exposure at higher levels is also likely to increase the space-heating energy use. Passenger lifts will, of course, require energy. A detailed study of the various options for both energy use and energy supply will need to be carried out for any particular site. We need also to keep in mind that if we increase density with high-rise buildings, this is likely to reduce the energy associated with transportation.

Plants in Buildings

Plants in buildings will require water and nutrients but have similar advantages to those outside: CO_2 uptake, oxygen production, a humidifying effect and the psychological effects of their presence and colour (see Chapter 4). In addition, plants can remove a number of indoor air pollutants. For example, bamboo palms will remove formaldehyde; lady palms, ammonia; areca palms and toluene. Other plants will remove nitrogen dioxide, carbon monoxide and benzene.

GUIDELINES

1. Always do the things that cost 'nothing' first, such as getting the orientation, form and massing correct.
2. The form of the building will be the result of considering many factors, from street pattern through to energy consumption and the potential for energy production.
3. Buildings should be well insulated and tightly sealed. The demand for energy should be reduced.
4. Design for daylight.
5. Occupant satisfaction is an important element of success. Buildings and cities are for people.
6. The use of low-energy ventilation (and, in some cases, cooling) systems is vital.
7. The building's main components, including façades and roof, should be conceived and constructed so that they can be altered over time to suit new uses and new technologies.
8. There are many ways to design sustainable urban communities. Success will come with the right balance (or something entirely opposite and extraordinary).
9. Design buildings so that they possess 'the lightness and joyousness of springtime which never lets anyone suspect the labours it cost' (Matisse).

Further reading

Edwards, B. and Turrent, D. (2000) *Sustainable Housing: Principles and Practice*. London: E&FN Spon.

Garnham, T. and Thomas, R. (2007) *The Environments of Architecture*. Abingdon: Taylor & Francis.

Latham, I. and Swenarton, M. (2007) *Fielden Clegg Bradley: The Environmental Handbook*. London: Rightangle Publishing.

Littlefair, P.J. et al. (2000) *Environmental Site Layout Planning: Solar Access, Microclimate and Passive Cooling in Urban Areas*. Garston: BRE.

Lloyd Jones, D. (1998) *Architecture and the Environment: Bioclimatic Building Design*. London: Laurence King Publishing.

Santamouris, M. (2006) *Environmental Design of Urban Buildings: An Integrated Approach*. London: Earthscan Publications Ltd.

Sassi, P. (2005) *Strategies for Sustainable Architecture*. London: Routledge.

Steemers, K. (2001) 'Urban Form and Building Energy', in M. Echenique and A. Saint (eds) *Cities for the New Millennium*. London: E&FN Spon.

Thomas, R. (2005) *Environmental Design*. Abingdon: Taylor & Francis.

Yeang, K. (1999) *The Green Skyscraper*. London: Prestel.

6 ENERGY AND INFORMATION

RANDALL THOMAS AND ADAM RITCHIE

Introduction

Energy and sustainability are inextricably linked. Energy-related emissions as a direct result of the combustion of fossil fuels – a finite resource – account for over 80 per cent of worldwide CO_2 emissions.[1] Energy also accounts for around one-third of the global emissions of methane, the second most important greenhouse gas. An alternative to fossil fuel-derived energy is renewable energy. Put into context, renewable sources, excluding wastes and passive uses of solar energy, provided 1.8 per cent of the UK's total primary energy requirements in 2006. This was only 0.1 per cent higher than in 2005.[2] The intention is to increase this and, as an example, the government is aiming to supply 10 per cent of electricity from renewables by 2010 and 20 per cent by 2020, mainly through an increase in large-scale wind power.

If one doesn't believe that nuclear energy is a reasonable alternative, one is essentially left with the transition to a solar society (solar is used here in the broad sense of renewable energy sources, including wind and biomass, which are effectively derived from solar energy). What form might a solar society take and what might be the time-scale? The principal options for forms are shown in Figures 6.1a–d.

In Figure 6.1a, solar generating stations using renewable energy sources such as photovoltaics (PVs) or wind turbines generate electricity which is then distributed via a national electricity 'grid' network to users. Figure 6.1b shows a similar arrangement, but here the electricity is used to split water into hydrogen and oxygen. The hydrogen is then distributed via a pipe network, as natural gas is now. This approach is sometimes referred to as 'the hydrogen economy', more on which, later.

Figure 6.1c shows solar energy being produced within the urban area itself. This has the advantage of producing energy near the point of use, thus reducing transmission losses. Another advantage (or disadvantage, depending on your point of view) is its visibility, which has been shown to influence people's attitudes and increase their awareness of energy use.[3] However, it has a number of difficulties which will be discussed below.

Figure 6.1d shows a mixture of 'on-site' generation, with the remaining demand being supplied from 'off-site' by a grid system. This has a number of advantages, including being the most pragmatic and the most adaptable, and so is the one we are most likely to see developed in the short term, unless legislation conspires against it.[4] In the longer term, we are likely to have a hydrogen economy in which electricity and hydrogen both play a role.

One of the encouraging aspects of sustainable design is the diversity that will result naturally, and so in England a supplementary source of energy will be from chicken litter, while in Thailand there are plans to produce biogas from agricultural waste water and elephant dung.

How much energy is available? In the London area, approximately 950kWh of solar energy are incident on every square metre of horizontal surface each year. The energy in the wind (available to a typical wind turbine) is very similar, at approximately 830kWh per annum per square metre (of vertical 'surface'). (Appendix A gives incident solar radiation data for the British Isles and Europe and Appendix B gives wind data for the British Isles.)

How much energy is needed? This, of course, is a much more difficult question to answer. Many buildings in urban areas are used for either offices or housing. Figures 6.2a–b show the energy demand and CO_2 production, respectively, of the low-energy housing at Coopers Road in the London Borough of Southwark (see Chapter 11). (These figures are for a 'base case' model; an 'improved' version having an estimated energy demand of 93kWh/m²y.) Figure 6.2c shows the energy demands of the low-energy BRE Environmental Office Building,

6.1 Solar options.

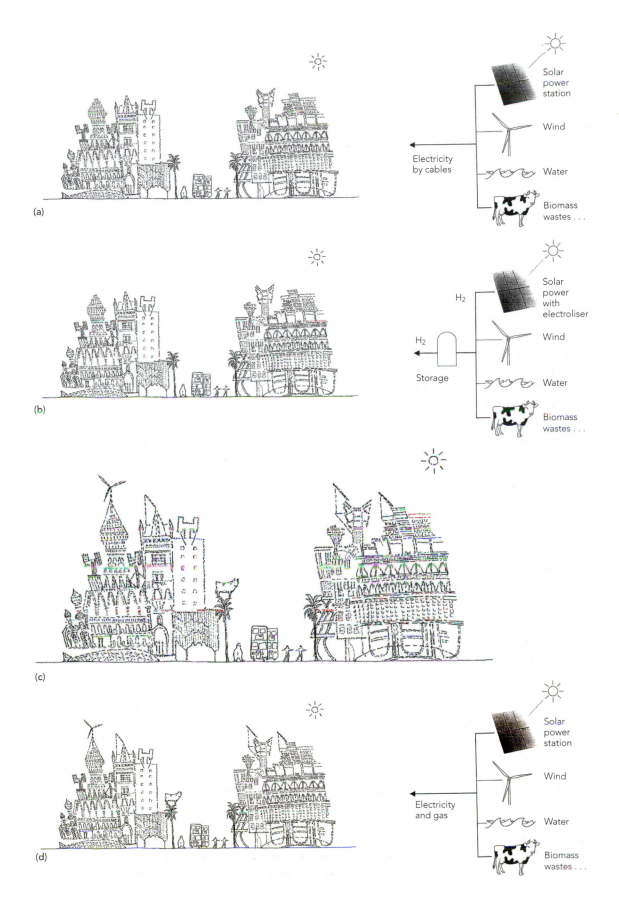

6.2 Delivered energy use and CO_2 production at Coopers Road.

(a) Coopers Road delivered energy use (i–ii) 100% = 116kWh/m²y
(b) Coopers Road CO_2 production 100% = 31kg CO_2/m²y
(c) BRE Environmental Building delivered energy use 100% = 83kWh/m²y (iii)
(d) BRE 'Improved Version' Delivered energy use 100% = 42kWh/m²y (iv)

6.3 Butterflies and elephants (not to scale).

(a)

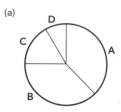

Key:
A. Heating 37% (43kWh/m²y)
 • Fabric heat loss (25kWh/m²y)
 • Ventilation heat loss (18kWh/m²y)
B. Domestic hot water (39%) (45kWh/m²y)
C. Power (16%) (19kWh/m²y)
D. Lighting (8%) (9kWh/m²y)

(b)

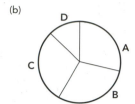

Key:
A. Heating 29% (9kgCO2/m²y)
 • Fabric heat loss (5kgCO2/m²y)
 • Ventilation heat loss (4kgCO2/m²y)
B. Domestic hot water (29%) (9kgCO2/m²y)
C. Power (29%) (9kgCO2/m²y)
D. Lighting (13%) (4kgCO2/m²y)

(c)

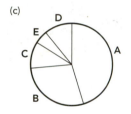

Key:
A. Heating 45% (38kWh/m²y)
 • Fabric heat loss (25kWh/m²y)
 • Ventilation heat loss (13kWh/m²y)
B. Small power (28%) (23kWh/m²y)
C. Lighting (11%) (9kWh/m²y)
D. Service power (5%) (4kWh/m²y)
E. Hot water 11% (9kWh/m²y)

(d)

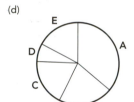

Key:
A. Heating 36% (15kWh/m²y)
 • Fabric heat loss (8kWh/m²y)
 • Ventilation heat loss (7kWh/m²y)
B. Small power (22%) (9kWh/m²y)
C. Power (19%) (8kWh/m²y)
D. Service power 7% (3kWh/m²y)
E. Hot water 16% (7kWh/m²y)

which, although outside London, is easily adapted to an urban environment; Figure 6.2d is a hypothetical 'improved' version.

To put this in perspective, each home at Coopers Road produces about 2,500kg of CO_2 a year. A pair of homes will annually be close to the weight of an elephant (about 5,000kg). We really want to be more like butterflies (Figure 6.3) and a strategy is discussed in Chapter 11 for achieving this.

For housing, it should be possible to reduce the space heating demand to, say, 10–15kWh/m²y but there will always be a need for some energy. There will be some fabric heat loss and a ventilation heat loss that cannot be eliminated since even if heat is recovered, the process will be somewhat inefficient. Hot water requirements might be reduced to 300–400kWh/y per person but there will be a demand and one has the same issue with heat recovery. With regard to electricity, we should be able to reduce the need to, say, 10kWh/m²y by using low-energy appliances and by greater use of daylight.

It is interesting to note also the sensitivity of demand to urban density, and some indication of this is given in Table 6.1. Thus, very approximately, two-thirds of the energy demand in housing (see Figure 6.2a) is independent of density and only one-third will be affected.

We can now examine in more detail an energy strategy for an urban site. In the background, as always, is the concept of reducing demand

Notes for 6.2:

i. Largely based on data kindly provided by ECD Architects.

ii. Note that the distinction between Figure 1.6 and this figure is one of primary energy and delivered energy. For converting delivered energy to useful energy (see, for example, Figure 6.20) we assume all of the delivered electrical energy is useful and that boiler efficiencies are 85 per cent. Power includes some cooking.

iii. Based essentially on a performance specification for the Energy Office of the Future Report 30, BRECSU, Garston, Watford. Note that for comparison CO_2 production figures have been updated to be consistent with figures of 0.47kg CO_2/kWh of electricity and 0.20kg CO_2/kWh of gas.

iv. Estimates by Max Fordham LLP of feasible reductions. Ventilation heat loss assumes heat recovery on extract air.

TABLE 6.1

Energy demand for housing as related to density	
Item	**Comments**
Space-heating load/person	
a. Fabric heat loss	Decreases with density
b. Ventilation heat loss	Weak connection but will be reduced slightly by urban heat-island effect
Domestic hot-water load/person	Independent of density
Electricity for lighting	Will increase somewhat with increasing density
Electricity for small power (appliances, computers, etc.)	Independent of density
Electricity for lifts	Will increase with density

6.4 (a) View from a distance.

(b) Positioning sketch.

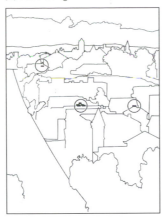

6.5 Evacuated-tube solar thermal array.

(c) Detail.

and then meeting that demand in a suitable way. Our first appropriate solution will be the use of solar energy.

Solar Energy

In Chapter 5, we looked at maximising the solar potential. Here we will examine in more detail the technology needed to harness solar energy, active solar thermal and photovoltaics.

Solar thermal

With solar thermal, the sun's energy is actively collected by either water or air and the heat is then used inside the building. Solar water heating has been with us for well over a century. Early photographs of the urban roofscape in Los Angeles, California, in 1900 show solar collectors fitted on roofs (see Figures 6.4a–c).[5] Figure 6.5 shows a more recent, evacuated-tube solar thermal array on the south-facing wall of an organic-food restaurant in Malmö (see Chapter 16). Figure 6.6 shows the Zero Energy House in Amersfoort, in the Netherlands, and is indicative of how many of our future roofs will be used for solar thermal, PVs and daylighting.

As with all forms of solar collector, one should try to avoid overshadowing by other buildings (and parts of the building itself) and obstructions, including trees. Figure 6.7 shows solar thermal panels on a roof in Seville being overshadowed by the adjacent Cathedral's Giralda Tower.

6.6 Roof of the Zero Energy House, Amersfoort.

Solar Thermal   PV   Rooflight

Small-scale solar thermal systems in the South of England can be expected to provide about 400kWh/m²y. Thus, if 4m² of panel were installed on the roof of an average home at Coopers Road (with four occupants, on average), it would make a significant contribution (47 per cent) to the annual hot-water demand. Solar thermal is suited to the demands of residential development for hot water but, as with many other renewable energy sources, the supply is intermittent, and therefore a technique for storing energy is needed. One advantage of solar

6.7   Shadow cast by the Giralda Tower, Seville.

6.8   District heating with thermal storage at Friedrichshafen, Germany.

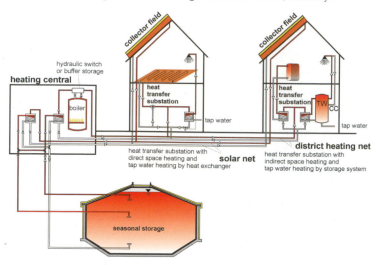

Solar Thermal Panels

6.9   A 1,000m³, 18m x 18m thermal store under construction.

thermal is that heat can be stored easily and cheaply as hot water (remembering that the specific heat capacity of water is 4.2 kJ/kgK), and most installations will employ a thermal store or 'buffer tank' to store heat collected during the day until it is needed, in the evening, say. Solar energy is also more abundant in the summer, and as output reduces in the winter, a back-up would be provided by the main heating system. Some large projects have investigated the storage of heat for longer periods, later in the year, say, when there is also a space-heating demand. Figure 6.8 shows a simplified schematic arrangement for a so-called 'seasonal' thermal store connected to solar thermal panels mounted on individual dwellings, and Figure 6.9 is a seasonal thermal store at the UK's first zero-carbon office building, near London.[6]

In urban areas, economies of scale are possible and a number of large-scale residential developments are underway in London (see 'Made in Stockwell', for instance, in Chapter 18) with solar-thermal arrays of 500m² or more. The potential for solar thermal is significant and its use in the UK has increased by 175 per cent in the period 2001–6.[7] One reason for this rapid rise is the recent introduction of planning policies requiring on-site renewable energy generation (see Chapter 1) as well as government grant-funding schemes.[8] Solar thermal is ranked second only to passive design in order of preference

by the Greater London Authority[9] and it will undoubtedly be one of a number of ways of moving towards more sustainable cities.

Photovoltaics

Photovoltaics (PVs) are materials that produce electricity directly from solar radiation. The PV phenomenon was discovered in 1839 by Antoine Becquerel, but it is only in the past 50 years or so that extraordinary progress has been made, driven by research and development in the space and computer industries. PVs are a very low-polluting, established and reliable technology, and are found everywhere from marine buoys to solar planes (see Figure 6.10). Appendix A provides a more technical introduction.

In buildings, PVs are in use on roofs and walls (see Figures 6.11 a–f) and can also be parts of sunspaces (see Chapter 15) and sunshades. The optimum orientation and tilt in the UK are due south and at an angle from the horizontal of about the latitude minus 20 degrees. So, in the London area, the optimum tilt to maximise the year-round

6.10   Solar plane.

6.11   PVs on buildings.

(a) The Netherlands National Environmental Education Centre.

production of electricity is about 30 degrees. There is, however, considerable scope for flexibility and orientations within about 30 degrees east or west of due south, and tilts of 10 to 45 degrees will give approximately 95 per cent of optimum performance (see Appendix A). This can be important in the layout of urban streets and in optimising the solar potential of the site. PV output can be significantly reduced by slight overshadowing, and this will argue for putting PVs on roofs unless the southerly facing walls are relatively unobscured, on tall buildings for instance. The Parkmount development in Belfast (see Chapter 12) is an example of how to model the urban space to use solar energy for photovoltaics. It is also an example of how one can quantify the extent to which the PV potential of the site has been realised.

PV systems can be connected to the electricity grid to 'export' electricity to other users rather than store it in, say, batteries when supply exceeds demand. In Germany, central government legislation requires utility companies to purchase electricity from PV installations at a fixed so-called 'feed-in' tariff, which for PV equates to approximately 0.5 Euro per kWh[10] (37p/kWh) compared with an average purchase price (in 2008) of 0.17 Euro per kWh (12p/kWh). A wide range of products is available in varying module sizes (from roof-tile dimensions to, say, 2 x 4m panels) and varying colours, for use on façades and roofs. It is also likely that windows incorporating PVs that transmit visible radiation but capture the infra-red will be available.

Certain forms such as railway stations may also be particularly suited to PVs because of their large roof expanses in often relatively open urban space. The new train station in Naples, Italy proposed by architect Zaha Hadid is one example (see Figure 6.12).

One area that will become extremely important is the solar potential equivalent of rights-of-light. Clearly, one will not want to invest in PVs and solar thermal only to see the output reduced by future developments if they overshadow the solar installations.

There are a number of different types of PVs but high-quality monocrystalline with an efficiency of 12–15 per cent in a grid-connected system will provide very roughly 100kWh/m²y when installed facing due south and at a tilt of 30 degrees.

Atrium

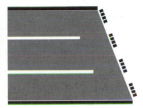

(b) Doxford Solar Office.

Inclined wall with windows

(c) The BRE Environmental Education Building.

Vertical

Costs

It is generally accepted that PVs will become less expensive and that they will become economic – the only matter for debate is when. PV manufacturing capacity is rapidly expanding and this should help reduce costs. A recently completed three-year field trial of 25 large-scale building integrated photovoltaics (BIPV) installations concluded that, based on a system lifetime of 25 years, costs varied from 20.9p/kWh to £1.85/kWh. Removing the two most expensive sites, which were under-performing, gave an average cost of 39.1p/kWh.[11]

6.12   A 450kWp solar array on Naples TAV railway station.

6.13   Wind speeds over varying terrains.[13]

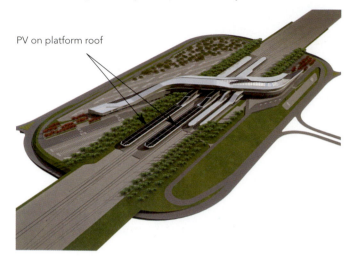

PV on platform roof

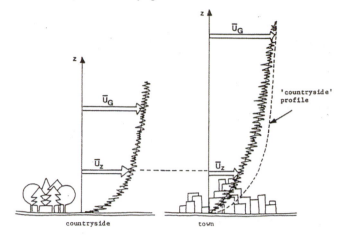

6.14   Horizontal-axis wind turbines at Castle House, London.

Despite the potential economy of the PV material displacing a roof material, new-build frame-mounted systems were the cheapest overall, costing £5.11/Wp, and new-build tile-integrated systems were the most costly at £8.28/Wp.

Wind Energy

At a time when large wind turbines are being constructed around Europe and the USA, and the price of energy from them is becoming more and more competitive, one may ask why we should bother considering smaller urban versions.

One reason is that although wind farms can be things of beauty, some consider that they spoil the countryside visually and acoustically and that Wales, for example, would be better off without them. For off-shore wind farms there are the inevitable issues of construction and maintenance costs, as well as the need to transmit the energy produced to users who are likely to be hundreds of (if not more) kilometres away. However, successful businesses are proving that wind generation is now commercially viable in many parts of the world, including numerous areas in the UK.

Of course, in urban environments there are noise and safety issues that need to be considered. There is, nevertheless, wind in the city. How much is there? And how much energy is available?

In Appendix B, there is a map of the availability of wind energy in the UK. In the London area, the mean annual wind speed is approximately 4m/s at a height of 10m. The effect of the urban environment on this is complex. Generally, there will be a reduction of wind speed due to the uneven urban terrain (an effect called wind shear), and Figure 6.13 shows a simplified diagram of wind speeds over varying terrains.[12] However, this may be compensated for by an increased wind turbulence in some parts of cities (other parts, such as urban courtyards, will be sheltered – and deliberately so). Buildings also may serve as masts for wind turbines where height and turbulence may be advantages. Figure 6.14 shows one form of urban wind turbines integrated into a tall building being built in London.[14] Another is described for Deptford Wharves (see Chapter 18).

Small-scale wind turbines have overall efficiencies of approximately 15–30 per cent and, allowing for losses in the system, in the London area (in relatively open ground), the output very roughly might be about 150–300kWh/m²y; the area used is the swept area (see Appendix B).

6.15
(a)   Vertical-axis devices.

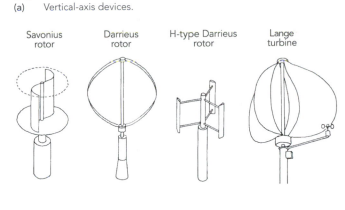

Savonius rotor   Darrieus rotor   H-type Darrieus rotor   Lange turbine

(b)   Chinese windmill.

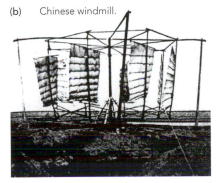

6.16   Building types for urban turbines.

Building types

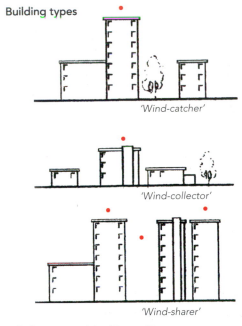

'Wind-catcher'

'Wind-collector'

'Wind-sharer'

● Indicates potential turbine positions

Figure 6.15a shows some less common vertical-axis turbines and Figure 6.15b is a delightful vertical-axis Chinese windmill. Keen observers of vans and buses will know that vertical-axis Savonius rotors are used on roofs for ventilation.

In Appendix B, Table B.1, there is a comparison drawn from a Dutch study of the advantages and disadvantages of axis position for 'urban' turbines. The same study examined urban building types and charac-terised three as suitable for small-scale wind power; these are:

1.   the 'wind-catcher' – good height plus relatively free flow;

2.   the 'wind-collector' – a somewhat lower building in an area with more surface roughness and more turbulence;

3.   the 'wind-sharer' – experiences high wind speeds and high tur-bulence.

Figure 6.16 compares the characteristics of these types. Obviously, the descriptions are somewhat subjective, but this research work is a valuable step in assessing the resources available at a site.

The first generation of low-cost wind turbines that can easily be connected to the grid is now being marketed by home improvement stores for homeowners. While their sales have been encouraging, there

has been considerable discussion on the subject of the appropriate-ness of small-scale wind turbines for the retro-fit, urban market, given turbulence caused by adjacent buildings, the significant 'stand-by' losses of the inverter and public safety concerns as a result of poor maintenance.

In the future we are likely to see combined systems of wind turbines and PV modules fully integrated with the roof design (including easy access for maintenance). Wind turbines, with or without PVs, may also be located in open spaces such as car parks. Key questions will be those of appearance, noise and output.

The Ground

The ground temperature is much steadier than the air temperature (see Figure A.3a–b), therefore it is possible to use the ground directly as a source of cooling or indirectly as a source of heating.

Where water is trapped in an aquifer, it is possible to extract it at, say, 12°C, use its cooling capacity (usually via a heat exchanger to avoid contamination) and then return it to the aquifer at a slightly higher temperature. This has been done at numerous buildings throughout the country, such as the BRE Environmental Building in Garston and the Royal Festival Hall in London (see Chapter 8), and provides an environmentally friendly way of cooling. Aquifers are common in the

6.17   Groundwater levels beneath London.

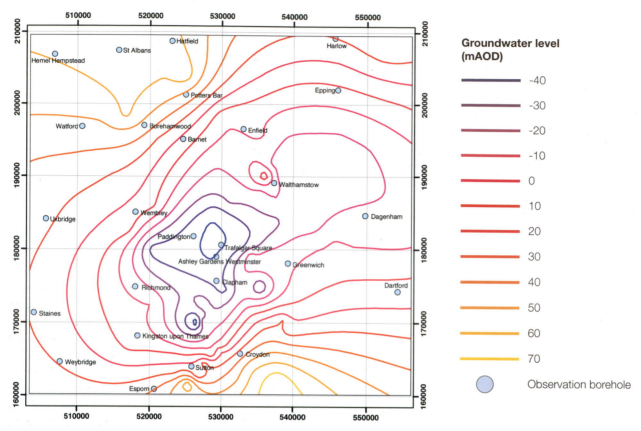

UK (see Appendix B) and we can expect to see this resource used more frequently in the future. Chapter 18 describes how boreholes drilled into the aquifer beneath London in the 1930s to supply a brewery could be re-used for cooling offices.

The energy available in groundwater from aquifers, surface water in ponds and reservoirs, waste water in sewers (see Chapter 19) or even from the ground itself, can also be upgraded using heat pumps to provide a source of heat. However, most heat pumps currently available use refrigerants which, if released, deplete the ozone layer and are potent greenhouse gases, and so a brighter, long-term future for them awaits new materials (or the reuse of old ones, such as ammonia).

In some cities, groundwater is, curiously, a growing problem. This is because we are extracting less water from the aquifers for manufacturing and processing industries than we did in the past, so the water level is rising. In the case of London, it had been rising at a rate of 2m per year until 2000 when the level began to drop again as a result of increasing abstraction rates due to water shortages and pumping (up to 30 million litres per day) to reduce the risk of flooding of underground tunnels. An innovative pilot scheme is currently under way to use some of this water to cool the London Underground. Figure 6.17 shows how groundwater levels vary across central London.[15]

Geothermal[16] energy may also be available, depending on the geology of the area. For example, in a number of areas in the Paris region, geothermal energy is exploited by extracting water at 73°C from an aquifer at a depth of 1,500–2,000m and using it for the hot-water service.

Community Heating (CH) and Combined Heat and Power (CHP)

In urban situations, with higher population densities and thus higher energy demands, it is possible to provide heat from a central boiler plant and then to distribute it via a pipework system to adjacent buildings. In the past, this was often known as district heating and is now more commonly known as community heating (CH). It was especially popular in modernist housing schemes in England after the Second World War. Figures 6.18a–b show housing by Lubetkin (the architect of the delightful Penguin Pool at London Zoo in Figure 6.18c and the circular building with its tall chimney that served as boiler house and laundry (now a community meeting room).

In cities, there will also be a high demand for electrical energy and so it is common to consider a CHP plant that produces electricity and recovers the waste heat from this process to supply part of the heating load. Often this can have a significant environmental benefit

6.18 Priory Green and the Penguin Pool by Lubetkin.

(a) View of the Priory Green estate, London.

(b) Boiler house and laundry at Priory Green.

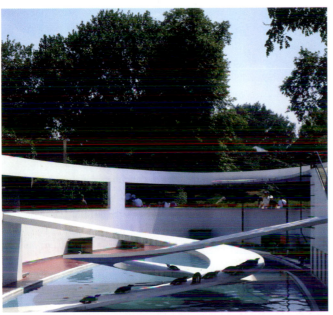

(c) Penguin Pool, London Zoo.

in that less CO_2 is produced than with conventional separate heat and electricity supplies.

CH/CHP is being used at the Greenwich Millennium Village and at the Peabody BedZED development (see Chapter 15). Other important initiatives include Woking's development of a community-energy system in the town centre, including CHP, thermal storage and absorption cooling.[17] Mixed-use developments, with their variety of load patterns and a constant base load, will tend to favour CHP.

The case for CHP is a complex one that is continually varying with changes in technologies available; the cost of fuels, particularly gas

and electricity; and the CO_2 produced. Normally, a comparison is made between the efficiency of a CHP unit and the efficiency of the separate supply of heat and electricity. Figure 6.19 shows a typical comparison, and it appears to be quite clear that CHP is more efficient and so the 'better' choice. However, in reality, for many CH/CHP schemes the CHP unit is part of a system in which back-up is provided by both gas and electricity from national distribution systems. The reasons for this are technical and economic. For simplicity, if we consider a group of, say, 200 new energy-efficient homes, for much of the year no space heating at all will be required. However, there will be a year-round demand for hot-water heating for showers, washing-up, and so forth. It thus makes sense to size the CHP unit on the hot-water demand so that one can maximise the number of hours it runs (a common rule of thumb is that the unit should run at least 4,000 hours annually to be viable) rather than size it on the combined space heating and hot-water load and then have costly, unused spare capacity. The back-up then comes from the national gas distribution system. Similarly, the unit is not based on peak electrical demand but rather uses the grid as a back-up (and indeed exports electricity to the grid when it is not needed on site). Thus, for a 'real' system, in which perhaps 40 per cent of the heating demand, and the equivalent of about 57 per cent of the electricity load are met by the CHP unit, the more appropriate comparison is between separate supplies and CH/CHP with back-up from gas and electricity. The analysis of such a system is shown in Figure 6.20; the primary energy efficiency corresponds to about 65 per cent.

A detailed analysis of the feasibility of CH/CHP was carried out for phases 1 and 2 of the Coopers Road housing development (Chapter 11). The four courtyards are fairly compact and the plant rooms were all located on the closest corners of the blocks in order to reduce the pipework linking the buildings to the main plant room with its boilers and CHP unit. The pipework connecting homes within each courtyard is extensive.

6.19   CHP comparison with separate generation of heat and power.

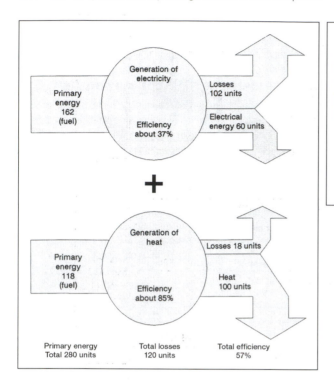

The (delivered) energy demand of the total of 154 homes amounts to approximately 1,103,334kWh/y for space and hot-water heating and 349,863kWh/y for electricity (see notes to Figure 1.6 on page 7). The options considered were:

1.   individual gas boilers for space and hot-water heating to each home, and grid electricity;

2.   CH/CHP with gas-fired boiler back-up to provide space and hot-water heating. Electricity from the CHP unit to be used for the 'landlord's' supply (e.g. corridor and external lighting, and central heating pumps), and the rest sold to the grid. Each home to have grid electricity.

The CHP (70kWth, 35kWe) unit was sized on the basis of supplying the hot-water load. A traditional reciprocating engine unit was selected, using availability, size and cost as the criteria.

The unit (as suggested above) will supply approximately 40 per cent of the annual total heat demand and will produce the equivalent of 57 per cent of the annual electrical demand. Compared with the option of individual boilers in each home and standard grid connections, the annual CO_2 saving is 18,000kg. The figures assumed that individual heat metres were not included because of the high additional cost – this could be considered to be optimistic because energy use might be higher than allowed for in such a case.

The estimated additional capital cost of CH/CHP is £200,000 and so the cost per kg CO_2/y saved is £11.10. This is compared with a number of other measures in Figure 6.23 on p.70. The overall economic calculations are based on electricity being sold to the local electricity supplier at a none-too-optimistic tariff. If instead the electricity (provided there was sufficient surplus) were sold directly to occupants by the system administrator, the return on capital would improve;[18] such an arrangement is sometimes referred to as a 'private wire'. Nevertheless, the straight payback period was encouragingly estimated to be 6–7 years; this would of course be lower if a grant were received.

This discussion raises quite a few issues. There is clearly an environmental advantage in lower CO_2 production, but it is less than was anticipated. One reason for this is that heat losses in the pipework distribution system can be significant, another is that energy is needed for pumping. In catering there is a saying among chefs that the closer the kitchen is to the dining room, the better the food. Something similar is true here where the debate is, in essence, at what point to convert the energy of fuel into heat. Piping gas to individual homes and only then turning it into hot water has its merits.

What we see is that CHP can be useful, but as buildings are better designed and require less and less heat energy, maintaining the hours of use required to make CHP efficient and cost-effective becomes more difficult. Similarly there are potential conflicts with other sources of energy. If solar thermal water heating is used, it will compete directly with CHP for demand. Supplies chasing a demand tend to make for bad economics.

The central plant associated with CH/CHP has the advantage (over many smaller plant dispersed across a site) of being able to change to alternative fuels such as biomass or wastes (see below) in the future. There may be a saving of plant space and there is perhaps less maintenance; or at least this is in the hands of centralised organisations, which is a great advantage to landlords, and, as it would seem from feedback (see Chapter 11), to tenants as well.

6.20 Energy balance for Coopers Road Estate (154 homes).

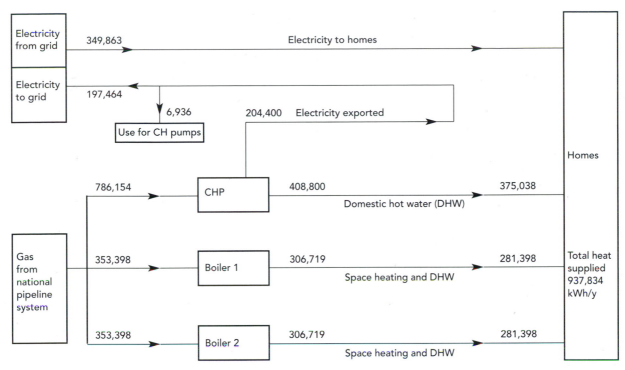

6.21 A (simplified) PEM fuel cell.

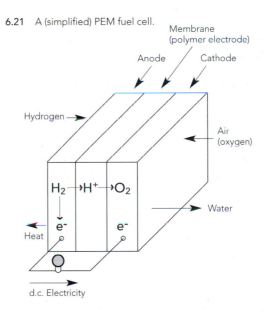

What is clear is that each site needs to be carefully evaluated. Also, as energy demands fall through better design, more efficient equipment and other such factors, the argument for supplying energy as close as possible to the demand is strengthened. Of course CH/CHP did this for electricity in comparison with the national grid but it was saddled, in a sense, with the problem of efficiently distributing the waste heat. Dense urban situations can present advantages, such as being able to route distribution pipework through corridors or basements. This will reduce the cost of the pipework, and reduce the potential heat-loss (or at least those heat losses may make a useful contribution to heating the space through which they pass).

There are opportunities for new technologies and this will create competition among all options. The most common CHP units are gas-fired reciprocating engines but technological advances have meant that new forms of CHP are either commercially available now or soon will be. They are sometimes referred to as micro or mini technologies and include fuel cells, micro-turbines (with gas as the fuel) and Stirling engines (see below and Appendix E).

Fuel Cells

There are many types of fuel cell using a variety of 'fuels' (described in more detail in Appendix E), but most interest is centred on cells using hydrogen, which when combined with oxygen produces electricity

(d.c.) (see Glossary) and water, giving off heat in the process, thus making these cells candidates for CHP plants. Figure 6.21 shows a schematic of a common type – the proton exchange membrane (PEM) cell. The fuel, hydrogen, enters at the anode and the oxidant at the cathode. Both anode and cathode are coated with a platinum catalyst. Between anode and cathode there is an electrolyte, which is a polymer

6.22 Schematic for a 'hydrogen' economy.

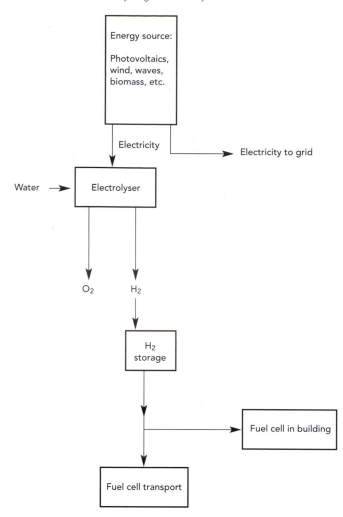

membrane similar to Teflon. At the anode, hydrogen yields protons (H+) and electrons (e−). At the cathode, oxygen, protons and electrons form water.

Fuel cells were described as long ago as 1839 but the only long-term programme of research on them has been carried out by NASA, which has used them, and continues to do so, in space missions. NASA's reasons for developing fuel cells included an assessment that they were safer than nuclear power and were able to produce potable water. Generally, their advantages are an absence of moving parts and thus very low noise levels, high efficiencies and the fact that they produce almost no pollution. Disadvantages to date have principally been cost and issues relating to the use of hydrogen as a fuel (see below).

Part of the reason for the current optimism about fuel cells is that they could be an integral part of an all-encompassing hydrogen economy (with its appropriate sources, infrastructure and users) that would link buildings and transport, solar and wind energy, urban and agricultural waste in an efficient, low-polluting, cost-efficient way. This may sound utopian but numerous initiatives are under way to form the first building-blocks of this enormous, exciting enterprise. Figure 6.22 shows the basic elements of a scheme. What we are likely to see is a mixture of energy sources (PVs, wind and biomass) being used concurrently.

Hydrogen, like other fuels, has its risks – it burns and is capable of forming explosive mixtures. It is not a common fuel (although, during the Second World War in England, buses ran on town gas, which was largely hydrogen), and its properties, particularly in use, will require further study to ensure that it can be introduced safely. This applies particularly to its use in transportation systems, where mobility creates more complex conditions for fuel cells than in stationary building applications. Refuelling, for example, is the subject of intensive study, but fuel cells themselves are very safe.

Hydrogen can be stored as a compressed gas; in special hydrogen storage alloys; or carbon-based materials that offer advantages of lower weights, especially important for use in transport.

Regenerative fuel cells, that is fuel cells that convert electrical energy to chemical energy and back again, are also likely to be part of the storage element of the infrastructure. The hydrogen economy with storage can help deal with the variability of the energy available from ambient energy sources such as solar and wind power. Energy from PVs during day-time, for example, could be stored to meet night-time lighting loads.

Fuel cells are beginning to make their way into our terrestrial world. A 200kW cell supplies electricity and heat to a New York Central Park police station and a similar-size unit has been installed in a recreational centre with a pool in Woking, south-west of London.[19] Back-up heat is from a boiler, and electricity can either be topped up from the grid, or sent to the grid if there is a surplus. This idea of using energy (both electricity and heat) in the building so that there are no transmission losses is one of the great attractions of building-based CHP. What is less clear, though, is whether fuel-cell costs will be competitive with other environmentally friendly technologies, and as Table 6.3 shows, experts are reluctant to make estimates.

Fuel cells used as CHP plants for groups of buildings will tend to favour higher densities and more compact forms so that distribution losses are low. In other respects they are likely to be discrete, and if they replace traditional boilers it will be a quiet revolution. But, as always, it is a question of balance: in this case there needs to be a demand for both the electricity and the heat, and well-designed buildings and cities will require less of both.

Waste

Future sustainable waste policies are likely to include recycling (see Chapter 9), composting and recovery of energy from waste.

Waste is currently used as a source of energy in a number of large-scale incineration plants, and during the post-war period in England, when large housing estates were being built, engineers regularly considered incinerators as sources of heat for community heating schemes. Looking at Figure 1.6 on page 7, we can see that the energy in domestic waste is significant. Of course, as more waste is recycled, this use of the resource would reduce.

The incineration of waste is criticised particularly on grounds of poor design and management of the facilities, which can lead to the release of dioxins into the environment, as well as being a sheer loss of material resource. Somewhat more acceptable alternatives to incineration are available, including pyrolysis (see Glossary) and gasification.[20]

In the UK, much of our waste still goes to landfill sites, and in some cases the methane produced by its anaerobic degradation is captured and used as an energy source. Sewage sludge can also be treated in digesters to produce methane gas. This can then be burned in an engine to produce 'green' electricity.

At the Vauban Passive House in Freiburg, Germany, organic kitchen and garden wastes, as well as human wastes, are treated in a digester and the methane produced used as cooking gas.[21] A similar arrangement has been installed at Bo01 in Malmö, Sweden (see Chapter 16).

When considering the extraction of energy from waste, it is important to keep the waste hierarchy in mind: the embodied energy as well as the raw material itself can be more valuable than the energy extracted. See Chapter 9 for more discussion of the waste hierarchy.

Biomass

Biomass is a term used to describe plant material used as an energy source for either buildings or transportation. The astonishing thing about biomass is that we can produce it relatively quickly. If one considers that 1,000kg of dry biomass has about the same energy content as 400kg of crude oil,[22] one can appreciate the potential.

Biomass is considered to be CO_2 neutral because its combustion does not result in a net increase in atmospheric CO_2; this is because such crops absorb CO_2 during photosynthesis. It is accepted, however, that its production and transport currently require fossil fuel and therefore, strictly speaking, there will be some net CO_2 emission.

For space heating, biomass has included beech and willow coppicing and wood chips from farms or urban areas (see Chapter 15). Recently in the UK, interest has been growing in more exotic fuels such as refined vegetable oils derived from rape or sunflower seeds and tests are under way on a grass, Miscanthus. Research is also being carried out into the use of biomass for fuel cells.[23]

Table 6.2 shows the primary energy saved when biomass replaces fossil fuels, and for a projected cost comparison of biomass fuels (i.e. energy crops) with other alternatives, see Table 6.3.

TABLE 6.2

Energy characteristics of biomass fuels[24]		
Item	Primary energy saving of biomass compared to fossil fuel kWh/ha.y	Fossil fuel replaced
Rapeseed oil	10,300	Diesel fuel
Willow	19,500	Light oil
Miscanthas	41,700	Light oil

Is biomass an appropriate energy source for heating and powering our cities, one might ask? In dense urban areas, it is unlikely to be grown in the vicinity of the site (the 1.69ha Coopers Road site would need 9.4ha of Miscanthus field to meet its electricity needs alone[25]). It also requires space for storage and fuel handling, which is usually at a premium on urban sites, and there is the increased potential for particulate emissions from biomass combustion (PM_{10} in particular – see Appendix C) to have a 'revenge effect' of actually adding to urban air pollution. In short, biomass will not be the solution to the energy crisis. It has been suggested that within Europe's borders it has the potential to supply only 10–15 per cent of European energy needs without negatively impacting on our ability to be self-supporting in terms of food production.[26]

TABLE 6.3

Estimated future power costs			
Technology	2020 cost (pence/kWh)	Mean of range	Ranking based on mean
PV (solar)	10–16	13	7
Onshore wind	1.5–2.5	2.0	1
Offshore wind	2.0–4.0	3.0	3
Energy crops	3.0–4.0	3.5	4
Wave	3.0–6.0	4.5	6
Fuel cells	Unclear		
CHP	1.6–2.4	2.0	1
Micro CHP	2.0–3.0	2.5	2
Nuclear	3.0–4.5	3.8	5

Ranking Energy Measures

So where should one put one's money, given these options? Generally, one is trying to arrive at a reasonable economic balance of providing environmentally friendly energy to meet a low-energy demand. A very simple approach is to be guided by data like that in Figure 6.23.

These data come with numerous warnings: full life-cycle costs would be much more meaningful; economies of scale are possible; market costs vary constantly; and so on. None the less, it is a start; further refinements will be made with time and much more work is required. Energy-saving measures will also tend to reduce radiator and boiler sizes.

Data such as that above can be used in conjunction with an energy consumption and CO_2 production analysis to decide an appropriate environmental and economic strategy. What one needs to do is keep two cost curves in view, as shown in Figure 6.24. One starts at the left of the graph in Figure 6.24 and introduces energy-reduction methods. Then, as these start to become more expensive because of diminishing returns, at a cross-over point, one switches to supplying energy in

6.23   Approximate economic costs of CO_2 reduction measures.

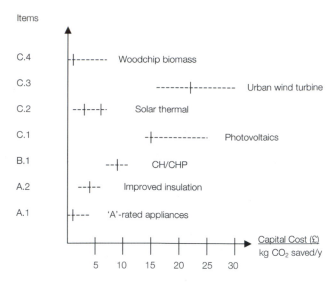

Key
A Items that reduce energy demands
B Items that change the way energy is supplied but still use fossil fuel
C Items that supply energy

Notes to Figure 6.23

The convention used is that if an item costs, say, £100,000 and it saves 10,000kg CO_2 each year, the capital cost per kg of CO_2 per year saved is £10. Emissions: 0.47kg CO_2/kWh (electricity); 0.19kg CO_2/kWh (gas). For comparison, 20-year lifetimes are assumed throughout

There is a wide range of items that are not necessarily strictly comparable and so caution should be employed. Thus, for PVs, there is a straight capital outlay but with CH/CHP, it is the differential between two capital costs. The horizontal dashed lines are very rough estimates of ranges. The intersections of the vertical lines with the horizontal lines form the points referred to below.

A.1   Based on a 6.4 cubic foot refrigerator with a base energy consumption of 230kWh/y and an improved consumption of 153kWh/y. Indicated point: 0.5.

A.2   Additional insulation, e.g. increase insulation from 100mm to 150mm and roof insulation from 150mm to 200mm to 300mm. Indicated points: 3 to 4.

B.1   Change from individual boilers and grid electricity to CH/CHP with boiler and grid back-up. Indicated point: 11.1; based on the Coopers Road site discussed in this chapter. Running costs and maintenance costs are likely to be lower with CH/CHP, but as these are highly variable, they have not been considered here.

C.1   Installed cost of a monocrystalline PV system: £715/m² based on Reference 13. Assumed annual output: 100kWh/m²y. Saving 47kg CO_2/m²y. Indicated point: 15.

C.2   The lower point of 2 is based on large solar roofs. The higher one of 6 is based on a family-size unit of approximately 4m² of collector area at a cost of about £2,000, including hot-water cylinder and controls.

C.3   Central London, small-scale, the range is probably quite wide, say, 15 to 30 or more. For a 2.5kW roof-mounted wind turbine in central London: Assumed cost: £1,300/m² of swept area. Assumed output: 120kWh/m² of swept area per year. Indicated point: 22.

C.4   Mixed-use site on city outskirts, with swimming pool and theatre. Change from a 1,250kW gas-fired boiler to 2 no. 500kW woodchip-fired boiler plus a 300kW gas-fired boiler at an additional cost of £150,000. Saving 326,000 kg of CO_2 per year. Maintenance and fuel costs not considered. Indicated point: 0.5.

6.24   Generalised cost curves.

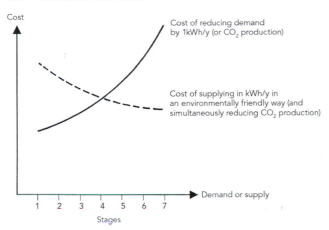

Cost

Cost of reducing demand
by 1kWh/y (or CO_2 production)

Cost of supplying in kWh/y in
an environmentally friendly way (and
simultaneously reducing CO_2 production)

Demand or supply

1   2   3   4   5   6   7

Stages

environmentally friendly ways and continues (until one's money
runs out).

The Future of Energy and its Design Implications

For much of the twentieth century, the energy supply industry was
concerned with developing massive power stations that used fossil fuels
or nuclear power to provide electricity via a centrally organised, highly
controlled grid. Environmental arguments (some of which have been
described above) now favour a transition to a solar society where
renewable sources of energy provide in a more decentralised way for
our needs, taking into consideration local conditions. It goes without
saying that this transition should take into account economic and social concerns as a new framework is put into place. The framework needs
to consider demand reduction and provision of supply simultaneously.

In this transition there are a number of unknowns. The first is whether
energy will be supplied locally or remotely and the answer is a combination of both, although the proportions of each are unknown. To generate electricity remotely involves transmission losses of, say, 7 or 8
per cent. This is significant but it may be reduced in the future with
technological advances such as super-conducting cables. Urban space
is, of course, limited and it is easier to collect energy (e.g. wind) or
process materials in order to extract it (for example, waste and biomass) outside the city limits.

These new sources, ranging from solar, wind, hydro (waves and tides),
landfill, sewage gas, small-scale CHP, biomass and so on, are known

loosely as 'embedded' generators because they are local and not
operated by the transnational corporations that own the grid.

Within the city we will see a multiplicity of energy sources all competing
with each other. Selection will be based on the local environment (in
the best Darwinian tradition) and on costs. In some cases we are likely
to see systems operating in parallel, for example, fuel cells with boiler
back-up to allow for varying seasonal and diurnal demands for heat and
power. There is likely to be a miniaturisation of components, including
boilers, to suit the much lower loads that will occur as demands are
reduced through thoughtful design.

But what should the poor urban designers, architects and engineers do
now? They should design for flexibility in this exciting but somewhat
unpredictable future. Buildings are likely to see three or four different
energy-supply systems in this century (as the authors' nineteenth-
century homes have seen over a period of about 120 years). Pragmati-
cally, this means shaping the urban form to allow for solar energy,
laying out the services distribution and allocating space (even if it is
not constructed) on the urban site to incorporate either a centralised
source or individual building sources. Also the allocation of riser space
so that services can be supplied from the ground up or the top down, for
example, PVs and solar thermal. Nothing could be easier.

Energy and Transport

In the next decade or so, we can expect to see continuing improvements
in current internal combustion engine technology, resulting in
improved fuel consumption and less pollution; we will also see more
trams in cities. The radical hope is that new solutions, including
electrically powered vehicles in the first instance and then fuel-
cell-powered ones, will become widely available to mass transportation, and should help reduce problems of congestion and pollution in
urban areas.

Low Emission Vehicles (LEVs) are available now but are constrained by
battery technology (see Chapter 3 for further discussion and Chapter
15 for an example of electric car use). Fuel-cell vehicles use essentially
the same technology discussed above for fuel cells in buildings, but
with the additional constraints imposed by the need to deal with
a moving fuel. Car manufacturers, in collaboration with some oil
companies, are putting their research efforts into hydrogen fuel cells
and storage in particular. Hopefully, fuel-cell innovation in buildings

will drive costs down through economies of scale, which then will lead to increased fuel-cell use in transport. There are the same potential advantages of being able to use renewable sources of energy and of significantly lower pollution levels.

As part of a European initiative called Clean Urban Transport for Europe (CUTE), nine cities, including London, took part in a fuel-cell bus trial.[27] So successful was this trial period that it was extended by one year and went on to include additional cities, such as Beijing and Perth.

The most popular fuel options are either to have an on-board reformer that takes another fuel, usually methanol, and produces hydrogen from it, or, to rely on hydrogen being available directly at filling stations. The latter requires an infrastructure to supply it and sufficient vehicles to make it economic. London is shortly to have 60 hydrogen-powered vehicles in a public service fleet including vans, cars, motorbikes, even a fork-lift truck.[28]

An embryonic hydrogen economy is currently under development in British Columbia where the 'Hydrogen Highway', stretching from the coast at Victoria to Whistler in the hills, offers a network of refuelling stations, including demonstrations of stationary and portable fuel cell applications, where one can see hydrogen fuel cell technology in action.

This is a field of enormous potential, which is likely to affect urban form in that PV-generated electricity could be used where required and, to a large extent, when required. Transport and building will be another link in our complex urban future. We should also be able to breathe more easily because of PVs.

Information Technology

Information Technology (IT) will make possible the sustainable city. Very broadly, we can expect to see it blossom in at least two major areas:

1. control of systems and components;
2. provision of information to users.

Control

IT is already being employed to control building engineering systems more closely. In a rather simplified way, this means providing energy only when it is needed, where it is needed, and in the required quantity.

In addition, predictive techniques for the weather will have a growing influence on urban buildings and transport systems.

IT will become more and more widespread and we are likely to see, for example, low-cost energy-collection devices that track the sun. We will also see common building materials such as concrete blocks and finishes incorporate IT, as well as components such as glazing, which will respond to changing environmental conditions.

In transport systems, IT will be used to give priority to public vehicles over private uses and facilitate safer trips by bicycle or foot. One recent suggestion is for a sophisticated localised weather-monitoring system to give cyclists and pedestrians improved priority at traffic signals when it is raining. The overall result of these developments should be a more efficient use and production of energy and lower CO_2 emissions.

Provision of information to users

At the design level, detailed databases using local information will enable better-informed choices to be made about urban forms (as we saw in Chapter 1), material selection, choice of ambient energy source, and so forth. It will be possible to predict and monitor performance.

IT will enable people to participate in the design process and will inform them, as users of the designs, of the status of systems both artificial and natural. This will include data on air quality (see Appendix C), energy stores, water reservoirs, the energy production of their PV panels, their electricity consumption, security at the front door and in the street, availability of seats in the next bus, the status of the shared cars, recycling results, the number of bird species in the city at any one time and much other information. This in turn will create a greater individual and communal awareness of our environment and how it can be improved. This role of education and stimulation will grow. IT will also allow occupants greater and more efficient control of their environment.

Finally, IT will change our social patterns with, for example, video-conferencing which can reduce the need to travel, and thus will lead to environments rich in information in both urban and rural areas.

GUIDELINES

1. Solar design affects both urban and building form.
2. Keep your options open. In designing the site and its buildings, allow for change. During the lifetime of the project, it will probably see at least three or four different sources of energy.
3. Analyse demand and supply simultaneously. Reducing the energy requirements can have environmental, economic and other benefits.
4. A mixture of renewable energy sources, from PVs to wind to biomass, is likely to be the way forward for most cities (and their surrounding regions).
5. Community heating with combined heat and power has an important role to play in carefully selected applications.
6. Fuel cells hold the promise of providing a pollution-free source of heat and electricity. They will be an essential part of the future hydrogen economy.
7. Our 'waste' is an important potential source of energy that should not be neglected. How it is treated has a number of impacts, including those on land use and health.
8. Energy and transport are related and should be considered together.
9. IT will touch every aspect of the sustainable city, from design through to the comfort and security of its citizens.

Further reading

Boyle, G. (2004) *Renewable Energy: Power for a Sustainable Future*, 2nd edn. Oxford: Oxford University Press.

Department for Communities and Local Government (2004) *Planning for Renewable Energy: A Companion Guide to PPS22*. London: TSO. Available: http://www.communities.gov.uk/documents/planningandbuilding/pdf/147447

Greater London Authority (2004) *Green Light to Clean Power: The Mayor's Energy Strategy*. London: GLA. Available: http://www.london.gov.uk/mayor/strategies/energy/docs/energy strategy04.pdf

London Energy Partnership (2006) *Towards Zero Carbon Developments*. London: LEP. Available: http://tinyurl.com/2tpr4k

Royal Commission on Environmental Pollution (2000) *Twenty-second Report: Energy – the Changing Climate*. London: RCEP. Available: http://www.rcep.org.uk/newenergy.htm

Royal Commission on Environmental Pollution (2004) *Biomass as a Renewable Energy*. London: RCEP. Available: http://www.rcep.org.uk/biomass/Biomass%20Report.pdf

Thomas, R. (2001) *Photovoltaics and Architecture*. London: Spon Press.

Town and Country Planning Association (2006) *Sustainable Energy by Design*. London: TCPA. Available: http://www.tcpa.org.uk/downloads/TCPA SustEnergy.pdf

(All websites accessed 2 February 2008.)

7 MATERIALS

SARAH ROYSE

Introduction

Cities cover only 2 per cent of the world's land surface yet they consume over 75 per cent of the planet's material resources.[1] The ongoing improvement and expansion of our urban environment are making increasing demands for the creation of new, and the upgrading of existing, buildings, roads, and landscape (some 40 per cent of worldwide raw material flow is attributed to construction[2]). In the UK, the production of construction materials contributes over 5 per cent of national CO_2 emissions,[3] and a further 5 per cent is incurred in their transport.[4]

By continuing to consume materials at this rate, we risk irreversible environmental damage. We must, therefore, change the way we manage material flows to and from our cities. The aim of this chapter is to look for ways in which we can design and construct more environmentally-friendly cities. Furthermore, the uncertainties over future weather patterns as a consequence of global warming will present challenges to our urban environment, and a careful choice of materials will help us adapt and future-proof our cities. Fortunately, designers, manufacturers and developers have already begun investigating material efficiency, alternative materials, and new production techniques. But where does one start, given so many (sometimes conflicting) factors? Some of the principal considerations are outlined below.

Selection of materials

Traditionally materials were chosen based on factors such as local availability and function, but a global market and cheap transport have given designers the possibility of making selections from a much larger palate of materials, based on fashion, appearance and cost. More recently, however, the environmental implications of some supply chains have become apparent, and have shown this approach to be unsustainable.

The principal selection criteria for sustainable materials should be:

1. Suitability, in terms of performance, appearance, ease of maintenance, lifetime and cost.

2. Economic cost, both capital and operational/maintenance.

3. Impact on the local environment by sourcing the material, e.g. felling, quarrying, etc.

4. Impact on the global environment, e.g. CO_2 emissions and the depletion of finite resources.

5. Health hazards associated with processing and using the material.

Closer to home, decisions based on material suitability are familiar to us all: in warm weather, we select light, breathable fabrics, such as linen, to help keep us cool; if it is cold or raining, a woollen jumper or waterproof jacket is likely to be the garment of choice.

It is often the case that a number of materials fit the selection criteria, and the decision is then based on capital cost. However, one should also consider how the material will be used, and its potential impact on operational cost. Whole life costing[5] (WLC) is one method of determining best overall economic value. For example, whether or not the investment in a more expensive, higher performance thermal insulation material may actually result in a saving over a 'normal' thermal insulation by reducing the energy consumed on heating.

It is also important to compare a building's embodied energy against its operational energy. The energy used by many buildings during their lifetime is much greater than their embodied energy content. However, in the future, as energy-efficiency measures become the norm, the embodied energy (which to date has received little attention) will constitute an increasingly significant part of the overall energy 'budget'.

7.1   Sheep's-wool insulation and a sheep.

Fired materials, such as engineering bricks and clay tiles, have a high embodied energy content due to the energy consumed by drying kilns, while imported materials have a higher embodied energy than their locally sourced equivalents due to the energy consumed in transport. The primary embodied energy content (measured in GJ per Tonne) of some materials is given in Table G.1 in Appendix G.

A fair comparison of two or more materials should consider the energy consumed in material extraction, processing, transport, use, maintenance, and eventual disposal. A life cycle assessment[6] (LCA) assesses the energy consumed over the lifetime of a material, analysing when and where the environmental impact occurs.

Key materials
Timber
Viewed by many as one of the most environmentally-friendly materials, timber is an organic renewable resource and can be produced using little energy, if the wood is locally sourced. However, there is often a geographical disparity between where wood is grown and where it is used; 55 per cent of softwood used in UK construction comes from UK sources, and 45 per cent from overseas, principally Scandinavia.[7] With the demand for timber-frame construction expected to increase in line with the forecasted growth in the UK housing market, sustainable timber sourcing will become increasingly important.

Deforestation and illegal logging are bigger problems. Research has shown that forest degradation and land-use change are responsible for 25 per cent of all man-made carbon emissions into the atmosphere every year,[8] and according to a report by the World Wildlife Fund, up to 26 per cent of the UK's imports of timber could be illegal.[9] Efforts are under way to stop illegal timber imports by requiring that timber products come from legal or sustainable sources. A number of certification schemes have been established to ensure that logging is properly managed, and will not result in the loss of biodiversity or habitat. The problem is to ensure that products are from well-managed sources, and there has been much controversy over so-called 'eco-labelling' of timber products with dubious provenance. Certification schemes include the Forest Stewardship Council (FSC) and the Programme for the Endorsement of Forest Certification (PEFC),[10] and others can be found in the Glossary.

Further environmental considerations become apparent during the life cycle of timber. For example, research has identified that about half of the total impact of a timber-framed window (over a 60-year life) is incurred during maintenance and disposal.[11] Concerns of durability, to which this research alludes, provide some explanation for the tendency towards over-specification of timber structures, and their preservation methods. If timber is to succeed as a long-term viable option, more research is needed on this aspect.

Other materials
Other organic materials include sheep's wool for insulation (see Figure 7.1). It is claimed to have a much lower environmental impact than mineral wool, yet achieves comparable specific thermal conductivities (0.04W/mK),[12] as well as being tolerant of moist conditions sometimes found within constructions. Drawbacks include the need to treat the wool with chemicals to prevent mite infestation, and to reduce the risk of fire spread.

The use of natural plant fibres, such as flax, hemp and cellulose, in buildings has also increased recently. The Adnams bottle bank in Southwold, Suffolk, is the UK's first commercial building to use lime hemp construction. The double-skin blockwork wall with fibrous hemp cavity fill (see Figure 7.2) was chosen for its high thermal mass and low embodied energy content. Straw, the waste product from wheat production, is attracting some interest, and straw bales have been used

7.3   Concrete construction at the Environmental Building,
       showing guiding arrows for the incoming air.

7.2   Wall with fibrous hemp cavity fill.

as 'building blocks' with good insulating properties. Susceptibility to rodent attack, however, remains an issue.

Concrete

Concrete is one of the most widely used construction materials, primarily due to its structural properties when combined with steel reinforcement, but also because it provides thermal mass and acoustic insulation. Figure 7.3 shows the concrete floor/ceiling construction at the BRE Environmental Building where the ventilation path has been combined with the thermal mass to take advantage of night cooling.[13]

Notwithstanding the impact on the physical environment of acquiring the constituent ingredients for concrete, the embodied energy content of cement is a particular concern. Since 1990, the concrete industry has achieved a 25 per cent improvement in energy efficiency, and yet a staggering 8 per cent of global CO_2 emissions are still currently attributed to cement production.[14] Alternatives exist, and so-called 'eco-concrete' can include pulverised fuel ash (PFA) and ground granulated blast furnace slag (GGBS) – both waste products from power generation[15] – as a substitute for up to 50 per cent of the cement in a concrete mix. Research has shown that these can achieve respectively a 15–25 per cent and 35–45 per cent reduction in CO_2 emissions attributed to the concrete.[16] However, the disadvantage is that the concrete takes longer to cure, and therefore buildings take longer to construct.

Light-transmitting concrete is a relatively new product being developed in Germany. Invented by Hungarian architect Aron Losonczi, Litracon[17] contains glass optical fibres that transmit light from one side of the material to the other (see Figure 7.4). By using a variety of diameters of optical fibres (from 2 microns wide up to 2 millimetres), different illumination effects can be achieved.[18] Use of this translucent material in partition walls could allow internal rooms, without access to the external façade, to benefit from daylight.

Self-cleaning concrete is another new and interesting product. Here photocatalysts added to concrete become highly reactive when exposed to ultraviolet light, and decompose organic material such as dirt, air-borne pollutants and nitrous oxides on the surface of the concrete. Research suggests that covering 10–15 per cent of the roads and building surfaces in a city such as Milan could reduce air pollution by 40–50 per cent.[19]

Metals

The use of metal in construction is widespread, ranging from structural frames and concrete reinforcement, to railway tracks and bridges, as well as lightning conductors and cables that conduct electricity, to name but a few.

The energy consumed in making one tonne of steel is about 5,500 kWh (roughly similar to a typical UK household's annual electricity consumption) and this is only for the smelting process; a full life cycle

7.4   Litracon™ construction; effectively bringing sunlight through a wall.

7.5   ETFE construction at the Eden Project, Cornwall.

assessment covering raw material extraction (iron ore, coke and lime-stone), transportation, and production would give a higher figure (Appendix G suggests a range of 8,500–16,500 kWh). The case for using steel may be strengthened by the fact that steel is 100 per cent recyclable, and although the re-smelting process does consume energy, the embodied energy content of the material falls with each re-use (the recycling rate for steel construction products in the UK is 94 per cent[20]). Of course, it is lower still if the material is used without heavy reprocessing, such as in BedZED (see Chapter 15).

Glass

Continuous technological development has led to a wide-range of multi-functional glazing systems such as single or multiple panes with evacuated or argon-filled cavities, selective light transmission, low-emissivity (low-E) coatings and self-cleaning. It is important to compare and contrast glazing using LCA and WLC to realise the environmental and economic benefits that each function has to offer. For example, solar reflecting glazing can help reduce internal solar gain to a space, and hence the requirement for cooling. However, the coating can also reduce the level of daylight penetration, which will increase the requirement for artificial lighting.

New, translucent materials such as Kalwall and ethylene tetrafluoroethylene (ETFE) can be advantageous in terms of weight, cost, solar transmission and thermal insulation, in comparison with traditional glass. Figure 7.5 shows the use of ETFE on the Eden Project in Cornwall. Here the lightweight cladding material was chosen for its high durability, good thermal insulation, and light-transmission properties.

Another interesting innovation is to combine glass with photovoltaic (PV) cells, which serve the dual function of generating electricity and providing dappled shade. Advantages are that the system can fit into standard window profiles, and has the ability to change the level of light transmission by spacing the cells differently (see Figure 6.11a p. 61).

Novel materials

Phase change materials (PCMs) can provide similar benefits to a thermally heavyweight material. They act as a thermal store by exploiting the latent heat effect of the material's change of physical state.

7.6   Separation of demolition waste at the 'Made in Stockwell' site.

For construction applications, a typical PCM compound has a melting point of, say, 22°C. During the melting phase it absorbs heat from the room and stores it. When the interior temperature drops, it re-solidifies and releases warmth back into the room (the benefits of thermal storage are discussed in Chapter 5). PCMs have a high energy storage density, which means that less material is needed to achieve the same effect as a thermally heavyweight material. Concrete, for example, has a specific heat capacity of approximately 1kJ/kgK, while research has shown some PCMs can store up to 200 times more heat than the equivalent volume of concrete.[21] However, there are some concerns regarding the flammability and toxicity of organic PCMs which are subject to ongoing investigation. A number of trial projects are under way and should be followed closely.

Material waste

The reduction of waste at all stages of construction is a key message of the study Rethinking Construction.[22] Over 90 per cent of non-energy minerals extracted in the UK are used to supply the construction industry with materials, yet every year some 70 million tonnes of construction and demolition materials and soil end up as waste, 13 million tonnes of which comprise material delivered to sites and thrown away unused.[23]

The UK Government, in conjunction with the construction industry, is now considering a target to reduce by half the amount of construction, demolition and excavation wastes going to landfill by 2012, through

waste reduction, re-use and recycling.[24] The success of such targets depends critically on the correct procedures being in place, as demonstrated by the 'Made in Stockwell' site (see Chapter 18), which achieved 98.7 per cent recycling of demolition waste (see Figure 7.6). Chapter 9 discusses how information on construction waste is being shared between contractors and recycling companies.

There still remain environmental consequences, such as CO_2 emissions attributed to the transportation and processing of recyclable material, and the greatest benefit can therefore be realised from innovative approaches towards reusing materials. The BedZED project (see Chapter 15) used 98 tonnes of reclaimed structural steel, which amounted to 95 per cent of that used on the scheme. It is estimated that this resulted in 2,580 GJ embodied energy savings, which equates to a 3.8 per cent reduction in the total carbon footprint.[25] To facilitate these initiatives, Design for deconstruction[26] (DfD) is a concept that encourages designers to consider how a building might be dismantled at the end of its lifetime, and the re-useable materials reclaimed.

The future

It is exciting to consider what the future holds for environmentally responsible materials, but with commercial viability most effectively enabled by a demand-led market, the question will be whether the costs outweigh the benefits, and whether clients will be willing to make the investment.

Interesting areas of development to follow include:

- PCMs for more efficient thermal energy storage, utilising sensible and latent heat;

- environmentally responsive 'smart' materials that can vary their properties according to external conditions, such as glazing with a variable light-transmission factor;

- cladding materials that permit heat flow in only one direction;

- electroluminescent plastics that may act as a source of light;

- 'biotecture' and the concept of 'growing buildings' from living materials.

GUIDELINES

1. Take a holistic view and consider materials that may offer more than one function.
2. Undertake a LCA to understand when the environmental impact occurs, ensuring that the boundaries of assessment are clearly defined.
3. Explore the potential to use reclaimed materials, ideally already on or near the site.
4. Evaluate options for off-site construction to reduce site wastage through damage, and to improve health and safety through controlled operations.
5. Introduce tougher measures to help prevent illegal logging of timber; this is most likely to be achieved through stricter sourcing and procurement procedures.
6. The greatest inefficiencies are introduced during design and construction. Design with consideration for deconstruction, in order to reduce the quantity of waste sent to landfill, of raw materials extracted, and minimise the need to recycle.
7. Design out the need for hazardous materials; consider the health and safety implications of materials in production and in use.

Further reading

Addis, B. (2007) *Building with Reclaimed Components and Materials: A Design Handbook for Reuse and Recycling*. London: Earthscan.

Anderson, J. and Shiers, D.E. with Sinclair, M. (2005) *The Green Guide to Specification*. Oxford: Blackwell Publishing.

Murray, R. (2002) *Zero Waste*. Greenpeace Environmental Trust.

Nicholls, R. (2006) *The Green Building Bible*, 3rd edn, Vol. 2. Llandysul: Green Building Press.

Sustainable Homes (1999) *Embodied Energy in Residential Property Development: A Guide for Registered Social Landlords*. Hastoe Housing Association, Middlesex: Sustainable Homes. Available at: http://www.sustainablehomes.co.uk/pdf/Embeng.pdf

Thomas, R. (2005) *Environmental Design*. Abingdon: Taylor & Francis.

(Website accessed 12 February 2008.)

8   WATER

RANDALL THOMAS AND ADAM RITCHIE

Introduction

Water supplies to present-day cities generally come from groundwater, river water and water collected in reservoirs in the regions that surround them.[1] London (and the Thames Valley region), for example, with a high population but relatively low rainfall (740mm/y in the south-east region on average[2]), is representative of expanding urban areas that need to manage precious water resources carefully. It is surprising to find that Surrey, in the south-east of England – a country derided for its rainy climate – is drier than Syria.[3]

The starting point in examining the issue of sustainability is the usual one: can demand be reduced? Another important point is the relationship of the quality of the product to its intended use, for example, drinking-water quality is not needed for flushing WCs. We will return to both but first, a few definitions. Mains water is that supplied from the distribution system and, as the principal supply of 'wholesome' (or potable) water, is subject to strict quality controls – this normally involves treatment, for example, filtration, ozonation and chlorination. Groundwater is normally abstracted from aquifers (permeable underground formations from which water can be pumped via boreholes). Surface water is water that falls to earth as rain and runs off its surface into rivers and reservoirs. The water supply in England and Wales comes from a mix of groundwater and surface water. In the south-east of England over 70 per cent of our water supply comes from groundwater; in the north-west it is only 11 per cent[4] (a map of the principal aquifers in south-east England is shown in Appendix B).

Treatment of water is important for sustainable cities. Groundwater, for example, can be contaminated in many ways, varying from de-icing chemicals used on roads, to acid rain resulting from combustion processes, to chloride and ammonia from the landfill of waste. In many urban brownfield areas (see Glossary) there is often a legacy of land contamination leaching into the groundwater, and this needs specialist consideration.

As discussed in Chapter 4, how to deal with surface water is a field of intense activity and importance. The tendency of urbanisation has been to seal more and more of the surface of the earth, usually with unattractive tarmac (see Glossary). One result of this has been the need to deal with the run-off of large volumes of water over short periods coinciding with rainstorms. Another consequence of so much tarmac has been an increase in the amount of solar radiation absorbed, thus contributing to the urban heat-island. An alternative or, better, a complementary approach is landscaping.

Water and the Landscape

A black impermeable surface will absorb none of the rain that falls on it and very roughly 90 per cent of the incident solar radiation. A park with trees and grass will take in almost all of the rain and most of the solar radiation. The exact amount of the sun's energy absorbed will vary with the ratio of trees to grass and the species involved but, very roughly, the figure might be 80 per cent.[5]

A judicious selection of plants should mean that rainfall alone will suffice for the park provided that one can accept the grass turning a straw-yellow colour in dry summers, as it does regularly now in the South of the UK. During a typical summer (from around May to August), a London park will have an average rainfall of 1.6mm/day. Much of this will be used for evapotranspiration by plants (see Appendix F), resulting in the air being cooled and a feeling of greater comfort in the city.

Water in lakes, ponds and fountains can have the same physical cooling effect; in addition there is often an accompanying psychological benefit and an element of sheer delight. Horizontal water surfaces tend to calm, and laughing fountains excite – the city has a need for both. Water also offers incomparable opportunities for plant and wildlife habitats, and so promotes greater biodiversity.

8.2 Fountain outside the Alliance Bernstein Building, Avenue of the Americas, New York.

8.1 Courtyard pool at the Alhambra, Granada.

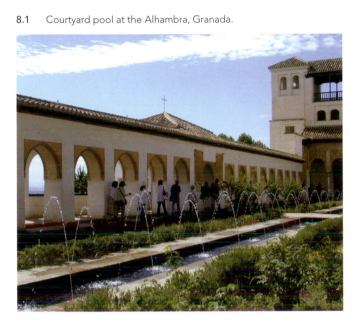

At the Alhambra in Granada, Spain, water from the Sierra Nevada mountains is used to great effect (see Figure 8.1) in these and many other ways. Evaporation from the pool on a hot summer's day in Granada lowers the temperature of both the air and the surrounding buildings. Cleverly designed fountains can improve the cooling effect by promoting evaporation. A notable example is outside the Alliance Bernstein Building on Avenue of the Americas in New York where the passer-by is temporarily enveloped by a cloud of relief from the unyielding summer heat (see Figure 8.2).

Modern urban development has forgotten about water in the landscape; over-zealous risk assessments concerning maintenance and health and safety have conspired against its delight and enjoyment. In London, some of our favourite places (and highest property values) are found alongside canals and the river; addresses with 'Riverside' and 'Waterfront' in the name attract a significant premium. At the city scale, Hamburg, Amsterdam and Venice all owe their character to water in the landscape between buildings.

The proposals for Deptford Wharves (see Chapter 18) recognise the benefit of water and reinstate a section of what used to form part of the Grand Surrey Canal, but had been back-filled. The body of water

simultaneously provides: a history lesson, an amenity, surface-water attenuation, summertime cooling, and it also increases the range of habitat. Its success will rely heavily on ensuring it is not encircled by a metre-high safety fence and by a plethora of warning signs, features which the canals have thankfully managed (so far) to resist, as have the ponds at Bo01 in Malmö (see Chapter 16).

The convergence of ideas of sustainable urban drainage, amenity and cooling gives designers and planners a raft of new design opportunities in the spaces between buildings.

Water and Buildings

The mains water supply is, of course, used (and misused) in thousands of ways. In Japan, local authorities encourage recycling. For example, in Tokyo, for a building with a floor area of over 30,000m² to get planning permission, it must recycle rainwater and have an in-building grey-water treatment system. Definitions vary somewhat but often rainwater is considered as one category, grey water as another and black water as a third. In this definition, grey water means all waste water from domestic appliances with the exception of toilets. Thus it includes discharges from kitchen sinks, washroom basins, baths, showers, washing machines and dishwashers. Black water is all water

8.3   Typical domestic water use.[6]

Garden 4%

Dishwasher 6%

Internal taps 8%

Clothes washing 9%

Shower 18%

Toilet flushing 20%

Baths 21%

Non specific uses 14%

that combines into the foul drain and then into the sewer system. It thus includes all grey water and the waste water from toilets.[7]

If we look at domestic water use, the national average consumption in 2006 was 151 litres per person, per day.[8] However, given that only 28 per cent of the 22 million domestic customers in England and Wales have water meters, the accuracy can be improved upon. Figure 8.3 shows some typical present-day figures for how water is used.

Only about 8 per cent is used through internal taps (for drinking, cooking and hand washing) even though all domestic water is treated to international standards for potable water. It is like using our highest-grade source of energy, electricity, for all power and heating in the home when a lower-grade source, gas, is available. Note also that about one-fifth is used for toilet flushing and that this water could be of a lower quality. There clearly are better ways of meeting our water needs.

As mentioned before, the starting point is to reduce demand. This can be done in a number of ways, including the use of more efficient dishwashers and washing machines, low-volume-flush WCs, taps that aerate the water stream and low-flow showerheads. By actively managing water use, it should be possible to reduce consumption to a figure closer to 100 litres per person, per day (this is the basis for the water use in Figure 1.6, p.7).

Table 8.1 shows the potable water consumption targets (excluding external uses) for the Code for Sustainable Homes.[9] Note that to achieve Level 1 – the least onerous level – the consumption target is significantly lower than the current national average; to achieve level 6 – the most stringent – it is nearly half as much. To reach these targets we will need to examine how rainwater and grey water might be used to save water.

TABLE 8.1

Code for Sustainable Homes: Potable Water Credits		
Water consumption (l/person/day)	Credits	Mandatory levels
≤ 120	1	Levels 1 and 2
≤ 110	2	
≤ 105	3	Levels 3 and 4
≤ 90	4	
≤ 80	5	Levels 5 and 6

Water Harvesting and Recycling

The first candidate for use is rainwater, which is generally considered to be cleaner than grey water and to entail less risk of infection in the event of systems not operating properly. Its quality is generally good but it is contaminated to some extent by the gases, dust and living organisms in the atmosphere and by pollutants on the collection surfaces, typically roofs. In and near urban areas, the emissions of flue gases with CO_2 and sulphur dioxide can result in water of increased acidity and corrosiveness.

Traditionally, rainwater has been stored in a butt and used for watering the garden. The next step could be to collect the rainwater and store it in, say, a basement or underground storage tank made of concrete or plastic. Figure 8.4 shows one such arrangement, now widely available, where rainwater is used for toilet flushing, the washing machine and for the garden. An automatic mains back-up system ensures a water supply when there is insufficient rainfall.

What begins as an individual site collecting rainwater for its own needs can, thanks to the greater density of cities, develop easily into a neighbourhood scheme where groups of buildings connect into a rainwater harvesting network. This can present advantages should an underground tank not be suitable or where the basement is used for another purpose. It normally reduces the cost as well.

8.4   Rainwater collection and recycling system.

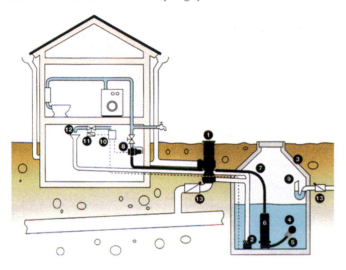

NOTES

1	Vortex underground filter	8	Automatic pump control
2	Inflow smoothing filter	9	Trapped overflow
3	Tank	10	Automatic mains back up
4	Floating fine suction filter	11	Solenoid valve
5	Suction hose	12	Type 'A' air gap
6	Multigo pressure pump	13	Anti-surcharge
7	Pressure hose		

The size of the tank will vary with the demand, the rainfall, the available area of collection surface and the percentage of demand that is to be met from the tank (obviously, a huge tank will protect against severe droughts but will have a cost penalty). One should keep in mind the variability in rainfall with the season.

The cost of such a system for a single home is approximately £2,000–£2,500 (note that installation is generally more economical for 'new-build' rather than as a retro-fit) and at current water prices – that include sewerage charges – it would have an economic payback period of about 50–70 years. The environmental benefits, however, are substantial in that the need for mains water is reduced and the infrastructure demands on both supply of mains water and disposal of surface water are reduced.

8.5   An 'Ecoplay' grey-water recycling system.

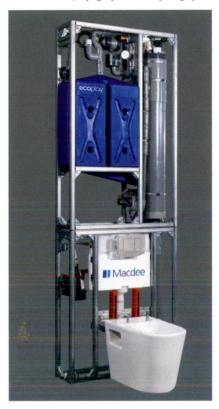

Grey-water recycling is the next step – but which grey water? Bath water and shower water are often considered the next most likely candidates for recycling; kitchen water is less valued because it contains fats and organic materials that need filtering out. Individual systems that collect bathwater and re-use it for a WC are commercially available. The system shown in Figure 8.5 has been proposed in every home at a new development in Chesterfield (see Chapter 9, for more on this project). Alternatively, larger communal systems are possible, located in a basement servicing a residential block. As with rainwater, the merits of distributing grey water on a district basis need evaluating. However, with grey water, good practice is to match supply and demand so that the water is not stored for more than one day or so, lest it go septic.

At Corby Parkland Gateway, a new swimming pool and theatre are being built within 200m of one another. The swimming pool produces an excess of grey water from showers and pool-water dilution, whereas the

8.6   The proposed Queen's Walk grey-water main, London.

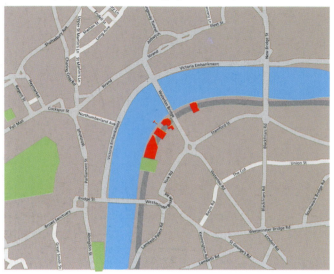

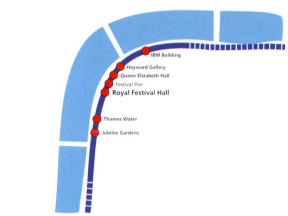

theatre has a large demand for water for toilet flushing. A grey-water main is being laid underground between the buildings to capitalise on this symbiotic relationship. Elsewhere, on London's South Bank, a grey-water main is proposed along the Queen's Walk to allow the re-use of groundwater extracted by the Royal Festival Hall for cooling its auditorium (see Figure 8.6). The water, which is presently discharged into the River Thames, will be used by office buildings for toilet flushing and for the irrigation of local parks.[10]

The key concept to which we return is that of supplying water with a level of treatment commensurate with its intended use. Dual water supplies to buildings, one potable supply for drinking and washing and the other, a lower-quality supply for WC flushing, will become a common feature in new developments and cities of the future.

Heat Recovery from Waste Water

In principle, heat recovery from warm waste water is possible and is occasionally incorporated into projects. It has been used most successfully when the discharge of warm water is coincident with the demand for hot water (this being the case for showers but not baths) so that storage is not required. Maintenance is required in some designs to keep the heat exchangers free from fouling but new designs with simpler heat exchangers are being developed.

In North America, there is considerable interest in recovering heat at a district level from waste water in sewers. At Vancouver's Olympic Village, described in Chapter 19, the low-grade heat in the sewage and waste water will be recovered using specially-designed heat-exchange sewer pipework and then upgraded using a heat-pump.

The Future

On the whole the UK is not short of water, but in regions like the south-east, where the supply and demand are poorly matched, this means water must be conserved, or be transported via a national water grid (as is presently the case with electricity or gas) and at a significant energy cost. The issue of the energy needed to treat, transport and supply mains water – not to mention to process waste water – should not be overlooked. The UK water industry is already responsible for 4 million tonnes of CO_2 (equivalent) emssions[11] (which for a supply of 16 billion litres per day equates to approximately $0.7gCO_2$ per litre). While Sweden, for example, does not consider water conservation to be a priority (see Chapter 16), the carbon footprint of water should mean that reducing water demand is a necessary element of any sustainable urban design.

GUIDELINES

1. Reduce demand.
2. Try to ensure that the quality of the water is as high as required for the use but no higher.
3. Organise the site so that as much of the rainwater falling onto it as possible can be re-used.
4. Even if water recycling is not incorporated at the outset of a project, allow for its incorporation (in terms of space for storage and pipes, dual water supplies, etc.) at a later date.
5. Consider rainwater recycling and bath water recycling for each new project.
6. Choose vegetation that doesn't need irrigation in the summer.
7. Water is physically and psychically nourishing – design with it.

Further reading

Chartered Institute of Building Services Engineers (2005) *Reclaimed Water (CIBSE Knowledge Series)*. Balham: CIBSE.

Department for Communities and Local Government (2007) *Development and Flood Risk: A Practice Guide Companion to PPS25, 'Living Draft'*. London: TSO. Available: http://www.communities.gov.uk/documents/planningandbuilding/pdf/324694

Environment Agency (2007) *Conserving Water in Buildings: A Practical Guide*. Bristol: Environment Agency. Available: http://tinyurl.com/24rtev

Grey, R. and Mustow, S. (1997) *Greywater and Rainwater Systems: Recommended UK Requirements, Final Report 13034/2*. Bracknell: Building Services Research and Information Association.

Water Regulations Advisory Scheme (1999) *The Water Regulations Guide*. Newport: WRAS.

Woods Ballard, B., Kellagher, P., Martin, P., Jefferies, C., Bray, R. and Shaffer, P. (2007) The SUD Manual. London: CIRIA. Available: http://www.ciria.org/suds/publications.htm

(All websites accessed 2 February 2008.)

9 WASTE AND RESOURCE

ADAM RITCHIE

Introduction

The outlook on waste gives grounds for optimism that our future may not be so gloomy. While, clearly, there is no room for complacency – we're only at the start of the journey – indicators between 2003 and 2008 (indeed, between editions of this book) show that behavioural change is possible. In England, recycling rates are up and landfill rates are down.[1] Behind the headlines are nevertheless some alarming trends, which this chapter will try to address.

Our waste is a rich mix of materials and minerals. Its energy content, as well as the methane (a greenhouse gas 23 times more potent than CO_2) that some waste produces when it degrades, has put waste squarely on the climate change agenda. In England, each of us produces about half a tonne of waste per year (excluding waste water) and this amount is rising. Only 31 per cent is recycled,[2] and recycling rates vary dramatically, with metropolitan areas having lower rates than non-metropolitan ones. Clearly we must develop new waste strategies for our cities in order to reduce overall quantity, increase recycling, composting and energy recovery, and put our waste to use as a resource.

Waste in the City and in the Regions – an Overview

Regular refuse collection and municipal drainage infrastructure can engender a certain complacency about the quantity of waste we produce and its method of treatment and disposal. A blocked drain or even a short interruption to refuse collections serves to illustrate our dependence on a waste disposal infrastructure. Figure 9.1 shows a London square piled high with refuse during labour strikes in the 1978–79 'winter of discontent'.

Waste generated in cities is, for the most part, transported to the surrounding regions where cheaper land prices favour landfill or incineration facilities. Sewage-treatment works sometimes employ energy-intensive techniques to treat large volumes of waste water using relatively small amounts of land. These tend to be located in areas

9.1   Uncollected rubbish in Leicester Square during the 1978-79 'winter of discontent'.

where odour and visual impact are lesser concerns, which are more often found in the outlying regions.

Approximately 272 million tonnes of waste are produced per year in England and this amount is increasing, on average at a rate of 0.5 per cent per year.[3] One-third can be assigned to industry, commerce and households, one-third to construction and demolition waste and the remainder is sewage sludge and mining and agricultural waste. People involved with the construction and occupation of buildings therefore have an important role to play in reducing the amount of waste.

There is a philosophical question as to the level (local, city, region, etc.) at which waste should be dealt with. This is a live and emotive issue and one that is likely to lead to different solutions in different communities. As with energy (see Chapter 6), some solutions will involve a combination of several approaches.

9.2   The Waste Hierarchy.

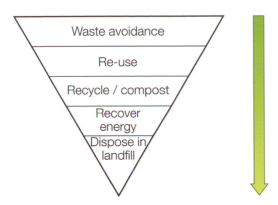

9.4 (a) Typical single dwelling refuse collection in Haringey, London.

9.3   Multi-compartment under-sink bin.

(b) Positioning sketch showing each waste stream.

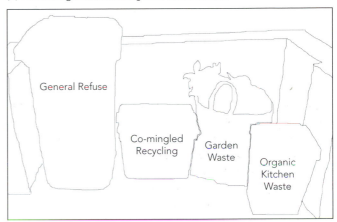

The key element to sustainable urban waste management is to reduce the amount of waste generated in the first place or, to quote Buckminster Fuller, to be 'doing more with less'. In Chapter 8, we examined ways to conserve and recycle water in buildings by using low water-use appliances and grey-water recycling. These simple examples show how, by lowering our water use at the outset, the quantity of waste water requiring transportation and treatment is also reduced. (It also illustrates another part of the complex web of connections described in Chapter 1.)

Waste as a Resource

Resources flow through the environment and through the cities and buildings in which we live and work. We have been accustomed to a linear process of exploitation, conversion, use and disposal with a strong link between economic growth and waste growth. We need to adopt a new sustainable outlook that involves turning this linear process into a cyclic one: making waste re-use and recycling generate revenue and employment, thus contributing to the economy. What is waste to one person can be a valuable resource to another, but barriers such as proximity and lack of information have tended to discourage the uptake of these mutually beneficial relationships.

The hierarchy of waste shown in Figure 9.2 is a valuable tool when thinking about how to proceed. We see here, as we did in Chapter 6 for

energy, the recurring theme – that of conservation – as the starting point. How can we avoid generating waste in the first place? Re-using old buildings, rather than demolishing and then rebuilding them, is an excellent strategy. It is estimated that re-using the Bottle Store building at Stockwell Green, described in Chapter 18, avoided 4,000m³ of crushed concrete waste, not to mention its transport from the site and the raw material needed to replace it. Another strategy is to find as many uses for a single building element as possible. For example, a concrete floor slab can be the structure, can help the environmental control (by means of its thermal mass) and, provided the surface quality is good enough, can be the architectural finish.

Recycling

For construction projects, web-based facilities, such as SMARTwaste[4] can help to identify and categorise material waste, set targets for its monitoring, and put local businesses in touch with one another to re-use and recycle waste (see Chapter 7).

Recycling can be environmentally preferable to the extraction of energy if the energy saved exceeds the recoverable energy (typically 20 per cent for incineration plant[5]) plus the energy used in separating the waste. Concerns regarding dioxin emissions from incineration plant, along with the tangible benefits of recycling such as job creation, must also be included in the equation.

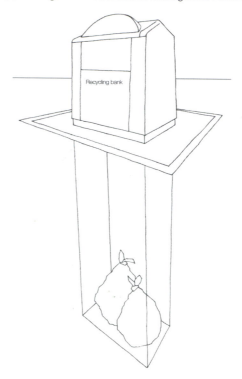

(b) Below ground mechanism for underground refuse stores.

9.5   (a) Underground refuse stores.

Building design can facilitate the sorting process so that waste enters the appropriate waste stream at the outset. Sorting at source is particularly important for waste streams that can contaminate one another such as wet kitchen waste and dry paper and cardboard. Providing (or at least allowing space for) additional or multi-compartment sorting bins (see Figure 9.3) will enable households to easily separate waste at source. Facilities must also be provided at the point of collection, usually in the street outside each building (see Figures 9.4a–b). Separate waste streams take up more space and this factor brings with it some important urban design considerations.

For more dense development of offices and multi-dwelling buildings, waste has traditionally been put in large containers called 'eurobins' or palladins; kept in, or spilling out of unsightly bin-stores at ground-floor level and part of what we have grown used to as 'the "junk" of everyday reality', to quote Graham Howarth (Chapter 14). But new solutions, such as underground refuse chambers[6] shown in Figures 9.5a–b, can help make the street-scape less cluttered. The Malmö Bo01 project, described in Chapter 16, has taken this idea several steps further by providing a vacuum-tube underground waste transport system. This allows householders to send organic and mixed waste separately to central facilities and reduces the need to bring a refuse truck into the narrow winding streets. Similarly, designing separate drainage systems for surface, grey and foul (black) water is also an approach to sorting waste at source.

Energy from waste

A proportion of household waste can be recycled in the form of materials, some of which naturally degrade while others will burn readily without additional fuel. The energy available for release from a material when combusted is described as its calorific value. The calorific values of some waste products are shown in Figure 9.6.

There is a multitude of processes (direct combustion, pyrolysis (see Glossary), digestion, fermentation, etc.) for the conversion of waste

9.6   Calorific values of waste.

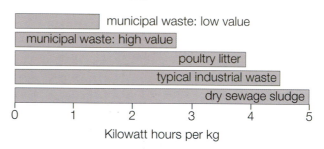

streams into heat and/or electricity or a carbon fuel. Examples already exist at regional, city and local levels and are discussed in Chapter 6 and Appendix E.

In terms of CO_2 emissions, the relative merits of waste processing and avoiding landfill of various materials have been estimated and are shown in Figure 9.7. Waste reduction and recycling, and climate change are clearly interlinked. At different building scales, each solution has its own merits, and individual sites will require careful consideration of suitability and context.

Human waste

Human waste contains organisms that can cause diseases. Any form of human waste treatment must deal with these pathogens and reduce them to safe levels. Treatment must also provide the micro-organisms that break down organic matter with sufficient oxygen without depriving other ecosystems.

9.7 CO_2 benefits of avoiding landfill.[7]

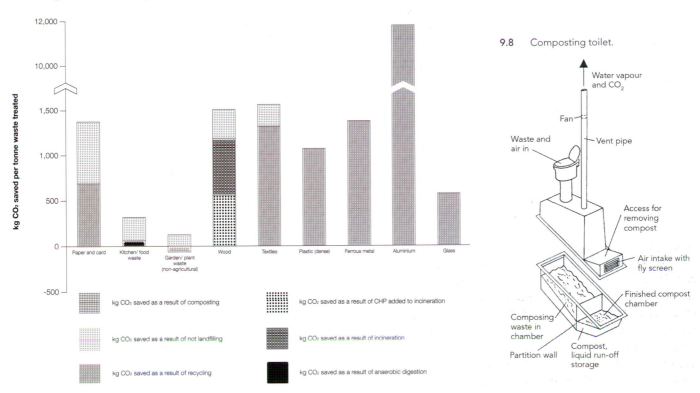

9.8 Composting toilet.

A variety of solutions exists at local and regional levels and some of these are explored below in an urban context. The present urban solution, large-scale sewage treatment works, relies on a complex sewerage infrastructure consisting of pipes, access chambers and pumps, all requiring regular maintenance. It is because of the distances human waste must travel that the predominant use of water in today's foul-water systems is as a transport medium.

The questions that arise are whether we should integrate human waste treatment into the urban environment to reduce the distance travelled by waste and, if so, how can this be done safely? Codes of practice emphasise the undesirability of having many sewage treatment works in a limited area.[8]

One way forward is to stabilise human and other organic wastes to provide valuable nitrogen and organic matter that can be used as an effective soil additive to urban landscape, thus reducing the requirement for other fertilisers.

Aerobic digestion of human waste with a composting toilet (see Figure 9.8) can, given the correct conditions, reduce the volume of waste by 90 per cent[9] through a continual process of breakdown of solids and

evaporation of moisture. A small extract fan draws air from the room through the pan and compost chamber to the outside via a vent pipe. Designed correctly, such a system can obviate the need for additional mechanical ventilation to the room.

Typically associated with single dwellings until recently, these can now serve a block of offices by increasing the volume of the storage chamber and designing a suitable WC layout. Space permitting, the chamber is usually located in a basement or designed as part of the foundations as, for example, at the C.K. Choi building at the University in Vancouver.[10]

Organic kitchen wastes may also be introduced into the system via a refuse chute provided from the kitchen. After a period of 1 to 2 years, the composter is emptied and the compost used in gardens and parks. Depending on the use of additional bulking agents such as wood shavings, liquid compost may be removed at more frequent intervals from the chamber and can be spread on the landscape.

An alternative form of human waste treatment is the septic tank, which is a widely understood technology and has long been used successfully in areas without mains sewerage. A septic tank is a type of settlement tank in which sewage is retained for sufficient time for the organic matter to undergo anaerobic digestion. The processes of solids separation and digestion produce a liquid which requires secondary treatment to produce a high quality effluent that can then be discharged safely into the environment. The sludge collected in the bottom of the septic tank will require emptying from time to time, and much of this is spread on farmland.

Reed beds

Secondary treatment of septic tank effluent can be performed by reed beds instead of, more typically, a below-ground leach field. These are self-contained wetland ecosystems in which complex soil-based microbiological processes promote the degradation of organic and chemical materials. The reeds themselves are necessary for a variety of reasons, one of these being to introduce air via their roots and thereby promote aerobic digestion. The waste water is delivered either over the surface of the reed bed, after which it flows downward (vertical flow), or via a feeder trench at the front of the bed, and then flows horizontally (horizontal flow) as illustrated in Figures 9.9a–b.[11]

Reed beds can be situated locally for a single dwelling or at a central facility for a site that serves, say, 100 people. They require open land area, which is typically at a premium in an urban environment. However, the integration of a reed bed into urban parkland areas could be explored. Approximately 1–2m² of reed bed area per person equivalent is required for correct operation.[12] Important factors in the choice of reed bed size and type are flow rate, organic loading and the required quality of treated effluent. The topography of the site will also determine the type.

In practice, in urban situations, finding space for reed beds is not easy. For example, at the Coopers Road development (Chapter 11), which has 664 occupants on 1.69 hectares of land, providing 2m² of reed-bed area per person would require approximately 8 per cent of the total site area. Such an area could only be found with great difficulty and so this example illustrates the problem with such an approach in some existing urban areas – but that is not to say that it is impossible.

Sustainable Urban Drainage

The integration of urban surface water retention and drainage in the context of the landscape is discussed in Chapter 4.

9.9   Reed-bed waste-treatment systems.

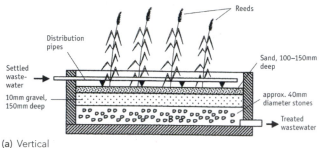

(a) Vertical

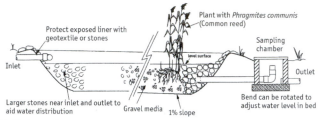

(b) Horizontal

Waste Water Strategies in Practice: The Eco-dome

Situated on the northern outskirts of Chesterfield – on the border of the Peak District in the East Midlands region – the Eco-dome development is a new leisure destination with hotels, serviced apartments, a sports clinic and a water-park. Within the dome's landscape setting are also 250 woodland lodges, lakes and a golf course. The leisure and tourism industry is notorious for the quantity of waste it produces but there is a growing demand for more environmentally-responsible resorts. One of the principal environmental design strategies for the Eco-dome is to use waste as a resource and some of the concepts are shown in Figure 9.10.

The woodland lodges each incorporate a grey-water recycling unit (as shown in Figure 8.5, p.83). Black water from the lodges will be treated on-site by packaged sewage treatment plants, and the treated effluent will be passed through reed beds and then used for irrigation of the golf course. Rainwater falling on the roofs will be collected and stored in underground tanks. Storing water underground keeps it in darkness and at a relatively low and stable temperature of 10–12°C to minimise bacteria growth, and thus ensure reasonable water quality; it is clean but not potable. Rainwater can become contaminated by atmospheric

9.10   The Eco-dome water and waste schematic.

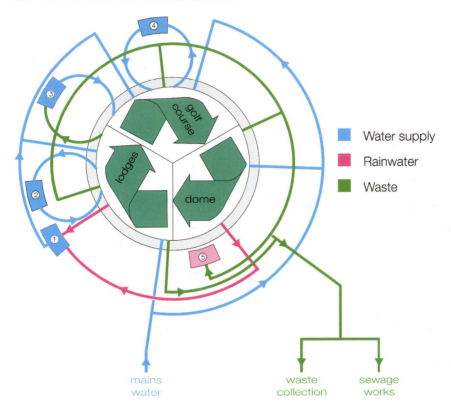

pollution, bird droppings and debris from the dome roof. Since the first flush off the roof contains the highest levels of contamination, a filtration system will divert most of this water to drain before tank-filling begins. The stored water is used for flushing the WCs, for irrigation and for window cleaning.

The site will also have a dedicated waste management and processing facility and an electric-vehicle based collection (no cars are permitted onto the main site). The facility is geared around three streams of recyclables and non-recyclables: organic co-mingled recyclables (glass, paper, metal, card and most plastics) and refuse. In addition to 'operations' strategies for minimising waste (for example, reduced packaging of products for sale), the refuse fraction will be gasified (see Appendix E) by the on-site biomass gasification plant for heat and electricity generation.

Conclusion

It is clear that waste reduction and recycling are key elements in sustainable design. At the building level, a waste strategy should extend beyond the site boundary and consider the opportunity waste offers us for, say, energy generation, or perhaps simply as a rich compost. At the city level, designers and planners are beginning to take the view that an integrated waste strategy, such as that developed in Malmö, encourages beneficial relationships between waste producers and those who can put that waste to good use.

GUIDELINES

1. Minimise demand in order to minimise waste.
2. Follow the waste hierarchy and use waste as a material resource or an energy resource.
3. Minimise water use in transporting and treating human waste.
4. Use the rain falling on the site.

Further reading

Grant, N., Moodie, N. and Weedon, C. (2005) *Sewage Solutions: Answering the Call of Nature*, 3rd edn. Machynlleth: Centre for Alternative Technology.

Grey, R. and Mustow, S. (1997) *Greywater and Rainwater Systems: Recommended UK Requirements, Final Report 13034/2*. Bracknell: Building Services Research and Information Association.

Hogg, D., Barth, J., Schleiss, K. and Favoino, E. (2007) *Dealing with Food Waste in the UK*. WRAP. Available: http://tinyurl.com/2a24dc

Murray, R. (1999) *Creating Wealth from Waste*. London: Demos.

Van der Ryn, S. (2000) *The Toilet Papers: Recycling Waste and Conserving Water*. Chelsea Green.

(Website accessed 2 February 2008.)

10 SUMMARY

ADAM RITCHIE

The complex nature of cities means that the problem of making a sustainable city will require a complex solution: this shouldn't put us off trying, and the preceding chapters have offered a variety of approaches.

We generally look to the past to inform our view of the future, and, in so doing, we need to analyse the ingredients that make a successful 'place' and work with them once again. That is not to advocate, say, a return to Victorian planning, or the Garden City movement, for example, since we are now dealing with modern issues that affect the recipe: a changing climate and the need for more people to live in a more humane city environment.

The planning of our physical environment needs to include a broader range of sustainability-related criteria than is currently the case. Traditional concerns of density, height, highway engineering, and so forth should be treated less rigidly and only as part of a bigger overall picture. We must bear in mind that cities, first and foremost, are places for people.

Some of the best examples cited in this book have resulted from a challenge to traditional or conventional 'wisdom'. Where is the delight if, around every corner, we encounter a predictable and monotonous pattern of streets, buildings and materials?

The main environmental sustainability criteria can be visualised as a triangle of form/density, movement/transport, and buildings/energy (use and production). More compact cities are likely to require less infrastructure and should need less energy for transport. The effect increased density has on building energy consumption is not so straightforward, raising it on the one hand (for lighting) but lowering it on the other (for heating).

We can expect (and should demand) some major changes in government policy. The EU Energy Performance of Buildings Directive (EPBD) now requires all homes and large buildings to have energy performance certificates, and that public buildings display these 'energy labels', much as domestic refrigerators do at present. In the future, the trading of personal carbon allowances seems a likely development of the current European emissions trading scheme for large businesses.

Movement and transport are gradually shifting away from the car and towards walkable communities, bicycles and mass transport. Energy and pollution are not the only driving forces for this shift, which will favour increased densities. Reducing congestion is a third factor. Reliable and well-designed public transport will eventually reverse the perception that public transport is a last resort, especially if it can be made quicker, cheaper and safer than the alternatives. The fourth important factor is the declining level of public health and fitness. Some two-thirds of Britons are overweight, mostly due to poor diet and little exercise. If it is true that the life expectancy of this and future generations will drop as a result, then safe walking and cycling will increase our fitness and have the potential to help reverse the trend.

Landscape will play a vital role in making sustainable cities. The 'space between the buildings' will, among many other advantages, nourish our aesthetic sense, improve the air we breathe and help save us from the deluge. The buildings and landscape will work together, merging seamlessly in many cases. Cities will inevitably be hotter than their surroundings in the summertime but open spaces, planting and water will work to make it more bearable.

Buildings will require fewer resources and will carefully select the ones they do need, taking into account the effects over the lifetime of their use. To this end, Max Fordham has set out a simple, but challenging, agenda:

- A design should aim (in so far as is practical) to provide adequate natural lighting inside buildings whenever the sun is above the horizon.

- The general metabolism of a building from the miscellaneous uses of energy (e.g. kitchen appliances, artificial lighting at night, human metabolism, etc.) must be used to provide adequate heating.

- Surplus energy must be rejected by passive means.

- Any residual demand should not exceed the supply that is available from renewable energy sources.

The major shift in the vision of sustainable cities is the potential of buildings to produce energy. This will entail a whole host of solutions (solar and wind power, geo-exchange, and so forth) that will make cities more interesting as well as sustainable.

Very few urban projects currently address all of the relevant issues and we are in a period of transition. Our knowledge of the possibilities and the interactions is only gradually increasing. Similarly, the idea of professionals such as local authority planners, designers and engineers all working together is only slowly gaining acceptance – and the concept that they would all collaborate with the users of the urban environment and the occupants of its buildings is a novel one, but, as the following case studies show, is becoming more common and helps to form stronger communities. Success will require a great deal of effort at ground level. The days when an architect like Le Corbusier could design a city from an aeroplane are over.

The case studies in Part II illustrate how the general principles discussed in Part I can be applied to real situations. They have been written by people who know that design matters and that it can help create cities of delight. The studies mainly deal with the environmental aspects of sustainability but some also develop the social and economic as appropriate. Each has its own emphasis and approach, and in this reflects the variety of the city itself, as well as its particular local or national agenda.

The discussion of Coin Street (Chapter 13) deals with user participation in the design and management process. BedZED (Chapter 15) covers a host of social and environmental issues, including mixed use in a dense setting and the first large-scale attempt to wean urban development off fossil-fuel-derived energy. Coopers Road (Chapter 11) is a study of the regeneration of an urban community, and Malmö (Chapter 16)

looks at the difficulties of creating a new community to high ecological standards.

These projects, which are all now complete and under occupation, highlight the importance of an ongoing dialogue between designer, constructor and the 'ultimate' client – the occupier – who often is not the design client. Good lessons can be learnt by returning to a project and evaluating the success or otherwise of every part of the design.

How the urban space can be sculpted to respond to the sun is indicated in the Parkmount study (Chapter 12), and the iterative process of design, computer modelling, further design and so forth in order to achieve the optimum access to daylight is described at Stonebridge (Chapter 17).

The importance of imaginative design in creating environmentally responsible and exciting buildings is shown by the study of, for example, the Contact Theatre (Chapter 14). Often one is struck by how local opportunities have been seized upon to strengthen the urban fabric.

Stockwell Green and Deptford Wharves (Chapter 18) describe the importance of embracing the history of urban industrial sites, which to the visitor may seem unremittingly ugly on the surface, but to the community have become an accepted, deeper part of their lives. The size of the professional team developing these schemes illustrates the breadth of knowledge needed to regenerate city-centre communities at much higher densities than before, and, of course, demonstrates the complexity of sustainable urban design.

Our case studies from Canada (Chapter 19) and Sweden (Chapter 16) reinforce the idea that a contextual approach is paramount and gives the valuable perspective that while all developed countries will benefit from fewer cars and better energy efficiency, each has specific problems of its own to address. The UK, for example, must reduce the carbon intensity of its electricity, while simultaneously reducing its reliance on foreign fossil fuel. It is also suffering from a historic under-investment in its ageing Victorian infrastructure (leaking water mains, combined sewers, overcrowded trains, and so forth).

The transition to carbon-neutral cities therefore will not be an easy one, and will undoubtedly involve developing in tandem both the city and the area outside its walls. There will not be one unique solution. Instead, in a way that is similar to the output of photovoltaic panels, we are likely to see many solutions that give us 95 per cent of optimal performance. If this proves to be true, it will be tremendously encouraging because it will favour diversity, a sense of place and a feeling for the particular.

Taken together, the following case studies in Part II, which are drawn from world-wide experience, address the main environmental issues of sustainable urban design. They describe the growing movement to adapt and create cities of the future.

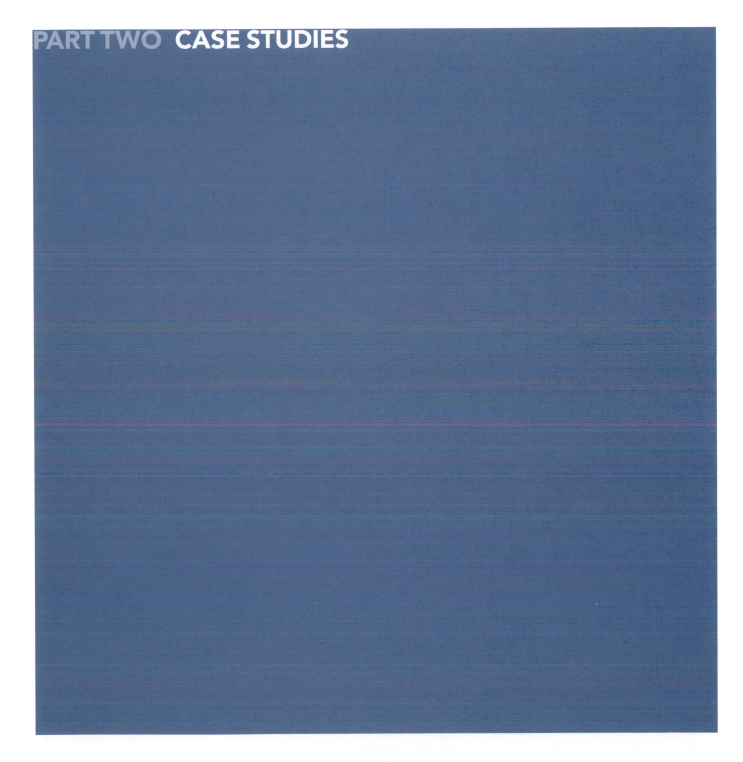

PART TWO CASE STUDIES

11 COOPERS ROAD ESTATE: REGENERATION

DAVID TURRENT

11.1 Aerial view of the existing site.

DESIGN TEAM

Client	The Peabody Trust
Architect	ECD Architects
Landscape Architect	Coe Design Landscape Architects
Services Engineer	Max Fordham LLP
Structural Engineer	Price and Myers (Phase 1)
	Brand Leonard (Phase 2)
Quantity Surveyor	BPP Construction Consultants
CDM Co-ordinator	Philip Pank Partnership

Key Project Information

Programme	Residential and community centre
Site Area	1.69 ha
Dwellings per hectare	138
Habitable rooms per hectare	615

Introduction

Coopers Road was a failing 1960s estate in need of considerable investment; the high-rise deck-access blocks lent themselves to anti-social behaviour and the open space between buildings was poorly used and lacked surveillance (see Figure 11.1). In 1999, in consultation with the residents, Southwark Housing made the radical decision to demolish the estate and re-develop it in partnership with the Peabody Trust. ECD Architects were appointed in 2000 to engage in a process of consultation and prepare a masterplan that would address the key urban design issues of scale, identity, security, ownership of public space and relationship with the surrounding areas. The regeneration project is progressing in four phases (see Figure 11.2). Phase 1 – completed in December 2005 – consists of 74 dwellings for rent. Phase 2 – completed in May 2008 – consists of 80 dwellings, including 33 for shared ownership. Phase 3 (Success House) will provide 46 flats and maisonettes for sale (including 14 shared ownership) and a Youth Club for the use of the local community. Phase 4 will provide a further 50 dwellings for rent. The overall density is 138 dwellings per hectare (615

11.2 Phasing plan.

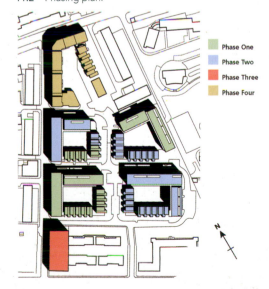

Phase One
Phase Two
Phase Three
Phase Four

11.3   Existing site green space diagram.

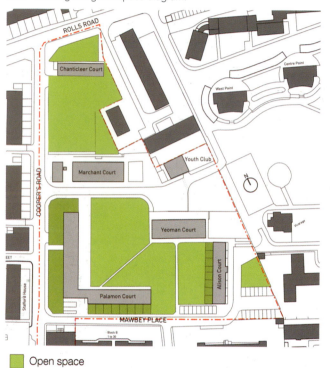

□ Open space

11.4   Consultation with the local residents.

habitable rooms per hectare), similar to the density of the original estate, but in a low/medium rise form. In addition to the new-build housing, the adjoining Kent House has been refurbished by the Peabody Trust. Coopers Road, when complete, will be a model of sustainable urban regeneration providing modern, energy-efficient homes in a secure and attractive environment.

Site Context

Coopers Road is located off the Old Kent Road in south London, a short bus ride from the Elephant and Castle and close to the Bermondsey Spa Regeneration area. Local amenities include a Tesco supermarket and Burgess Park. The surrounding area is dominated largely by council housing estates, with the London Borough of Southwark Astley Cooper estate to the west and the Corporation of London's Avondale Estate to the east, with its three distinctive high-rise towers. The Old Kent Road itself is a busy thoroughfare, effectively the main road into the capital from Europe, bounded, for the most part, by an assortment of undistinguished retail buildings.

The original estate (now demolished) consisted of 196 dwellings in five blocks, varying in height from three to eleven storeys. The existing open space consisted mainly of grassed areas with a few trees. There was no sense of ownership of these large spaces, they provided little amenity value, were intimidating and under-used (see Figure 11.3). The play areas were not well maintained and had limited equipment. The adjoining site, Success House, occupies the site of 419–423 Old Kent Road, adjacent to two existing Peabody buildings, Kent House South and Kent House North. The building which previously occupied the site (office and storage space) was three storeys high with a footprint of 600m².

Project Brief

All homes for rent were to be designed to Lifetime Homes Standards,[1] with some provision for full wheelchair accessibility. The scheme was to be built in phases to allow the gradual decanting and demolition of existing blocks. The client for Phases 1 and 2, the Peabody Trust, required an EcoHomes rating of 'Very Good'.[2]

Consultation

The original estate had a strong sense of community, and its preservation was seen as an important ingredient for the long-term success of the project. The tenants formed a Steering Group with representatives from the Peabody Trust and Southwark Housing, and were closely involved in the development of the masterplan through a series of meetings and workshops.

At key stages during the design process, larger events were held to involve all the returning residents. Tenants were encouraged to record their desires and dislikes on Post-it notes stuck to posters in a mobile 'office'. This wish list informed the initial masterplan proposals which were then presented to the estate at a number of 'fun days' (see Figure 11.4). Neighbouring estates were included in these events to encourage local awareness and good relations.

Areas in which the tenants influenced the design included the choice of heating system for the scheme and the layout of the homes. When asked to choose between individual boilers or a central heating system for the whole estate, the tenants favoured a system similar to their existing district-heating system, the view being that any faults would be repaired quickly as they affect a number of people, not just an individual. The comments received on the plans meant a change to the proposed layout of the two-bedroom dwellings, as it was suggested that the occupants would benefit from separate WCs and bathrooms.

The consultation process has continued through the detailed design and construction phases of the project, and will address future management as well as design issues.

Design Strategy

The new housing is designed around four courtyards (see Figure 11.5). The courtyard form, which evolved through consultation with the residents, encourages a sense of community and engenders a strong sense of identity. Courtyards create a clear hierarchy of private, semi-private and public spaces and provide a good model for urban regeneration.

Each courtyard consists of approximately 40 homes in a mixture of one-, two- and three-bedroom apartments and three- or four-bedroom family houses, providing a balanced community within a composition

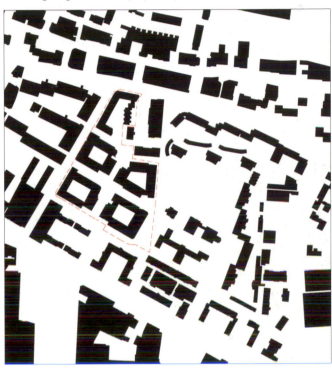

11.5   Figure ground of the proposed estate.

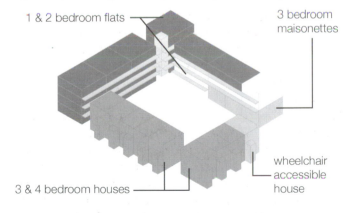

11.6   Different unit types make up the courtyard community.

1 & 2 bedroom flats

3 bedroom maisonettes

3 & 4 bedroom houses

wheelchair accessible house

of four-storey flatted blocks and three-storey houses (see Figure 11.6). This arrangement has been designed to be flexible and in order to meet changing needs and future developments in living patterns.

11.12 Solar access into the courtyards.

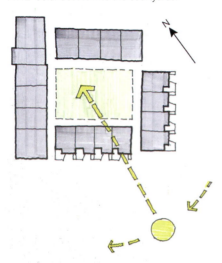

Many of the tenants have lived on the estate or in the neighbourhood for 40 years and, for them, access to private amenity space was a high priority. The communal gardens are secure spaces, each one devoted to its own courtyard block. Gardening clubs and workshops are being organised to encourage and assist tenants who, until now, may never have tended a garden. Within the communal gardens there are places for gardening, cycle storage, composting, children's play, seating and picnics. It is interesting to learn that, in practice, the communal cycle stores have not been popular, and residents have preferred to store bicycles on their private balconies.

Sustainability

From the outset, both client and design team shared a commitment to make Coopers Road a model of sustainable urban regeneration. This meant designing a scheme which would provide good quality appropriate accommodation, not just in the immediate short term but 100 years from now.

Orientation and solar access were foremost in the consideration of the planning of the Coopers Road courtyards (see Figure 11.12). The lower three-storey houses are placed to the south of the higher four-storey flatted blocks, and the roofs are designed to face south wherever possible for the future retro-fit of photovoltaic (PV) panels. By maximising the daylight penetration into the homes, the demand for artificial heating and lighting is reduced.

Flexibility and adaptability have also been key issues for the design team. For example, service risers are located on the outside of the building for ease of access and have been oversized to facilitate the installation of future technologies, such as PV or rainwater recycling, when these become economically viable.

In addition to this, our sustainable strategy is focused on six key areas:

- energy and CO_2 emissions;
- water conservation;
- materials sourcing;
- waste management;
- transport and car use;
- social well-being.

Our aim was to design the buildings in such a way that it is technically feasible to achieve zero CO_2 emissions by 2020 without major modifications to the fabric, services or infrastructure. The first priority was to reduce the demand for energy on site. We then needed to select an efficient system for delivering energy, and finally we had to devise a strategy for the gradual phasing in of renewable supplies so that our target of zero CO_2 emissions could be achieved.

Building strategies

Reductions in CO_2 emissions

Reducing energy demand is principally achieved by good daylighting, passive solar gain, detailing to reduce air infiltration, and high standards of thermal insulation. We considered very high standards of insulation but these proved prohibitively expensive. Instead we adopted a standard which anticipated the 2002 revisions to the Building Regulations (wall U-value 0.3 W/m²K, roof 0.25 W/m²K and windows 2.0 W/m²K). With some additional financial assistance from London Electricity (now EDF Energy), residents have also been encouraged to use efficient A-rated appliances. CO_2 emissions are estimated by SAP calculation[4] to be less than 25kgCO_2/m.yr.

On-site power generation

Community heating with combined heat and power was selected as a suitable way of providing heat and electricity while reducing CO_2 emissions. A detailed feasibility study carried out by Max Fordham LLP (described in Chapter 6) concluded that, despite the higher initial capital cost, the payback period for the system would be less than ten years. The gas-fired CHP engine provides 11 per cent of the heat demand and 12 per cent of electrical demand (see Figure 11.13).

One of the main advantages of a central boiler plant is that it allows future changes of fuel supply. A switch to biomass within the next 10–15 years could significantly reduce CO_2 emissions; so too could a client/community decision to purchase 'green' electricity.

Water conservation

Mains water is conserved by installing low flush WCs, and spray taps in the kitchens. A rainwater harvesting system filters the water which is stored and then used for flushing WCs. Rainwater butts are also provided to some properties with gardens.

Selection of materials

Materials were chosen for their low embodied energy content and impact on the environment when disposed. This meant preference for timber and masonry rather than plastics and steel. In addition, the contractor was encouraged to source materials from within a 50-mile (83 km) radius wherever possible in order to minimise CO_2 emissions released by transport. Construction waste was minimised by the prefabrication of window/cladding elements and the standardisation of components.

The contractor experienced difficulties in sourcing FSC-accredited timber, thereby losing the project EcoHomes credits. However, more suppliers are now adopting the scheme and other timber certifying agencies are now recognised by the BRE, for example CSA and PEFC (see Glossary and Chapter 7).

Recycling

All dwellings have a bin within a kitchen unit, designed to facilitate the separation of household waste, and recycling facilities are provided on site to store the waste from the flats. All houses have an external shelf adjacent to the refuse enclosure for the storage of recycled materials.

Landscape strategies

Soil remediation

A site investigation revealed a low level of site contamination and so the private and communal gardens were excavated and replaced with neutral imported topsoil. The new 300–500mm depth of topsoil was sufficient to satisfy the remediation requirements.

11.13 On-site power generation with CHP engine.

Water conservation

Porous paving was chosen to allow rainfall to percolate through the sub-soil, allowing a degree of natural drainage. The site is both conventionally and naturally drained. The central courtyard gardens and surrounding porous paving act as natural sumps within the core of the site. About half the area of circulation, such as parking bays, uses porous paving, while the tarmac roads are conventionally drained.

Composting and recycling

Residents are encouraged to recycle kitchen waste, which is collected and composted in the communal garden areas. Leaf collection, prunings and grass cuttings from the gardens are also composted and returned to the estate grounds as a soil ameliorant.

Habitat creation

A hedge of native species – willows, elder and hawthorn – is planted adjacent to the eastern and northern boundaries as cover and food for birds and insects. Stands of trees – multi-stem birch and hazel – frame the hedge and generate more cover for the mini-habitat. Standard trees – the native gean (or cherry) – are included within the hedge.

Green environment

Trees are planted within the streets and define the edge of circulation spaces, home zones and car parking. Their location, to the northern

11.14 Future-proofing the scheme with photovoltaics.

side of the blocks, prevents overshadowing and does not limit the passive solar gain to the south-facing elevations. However, the roads and pavements are beneficially shaded during summer months. The street trees have been selected from native species or cultivars of indigenous species, such as hornbeam, ash, pear, and sorbus. Fruit trees and useful plants that attract wildlife are planted in the back gardens and courtyards.

Trees absorb carbon dioxide, emit oxygen, filter dust and contaminants, and support a range of wildlife species, particularly birds and insects. The building elevations and garden walls form a protective edge to the streets and are formed into 'green walls'. Climbers planted at the base of gable walls act as a deterrent to graffiti artists.

Front gardens are planted with a protective hedge to each boundary. Borders are a mix of hardy, drought-tolerant perennials. Dense ground cover is planted at low-level under windows, combined with a mulch layer over the topsoil to help conserve moisture.

Selection of materials

Both materials and planting in the communal gardens have to be robust to withstand year-round use. Within the communal gardens the environment is enhanced with the use of natural materials. The main components of the garden are timber: seats, bollards, planters, tables, decks and edges, either made of sustainable heartwood, green oak or douglas fir. All timber, with the caveat above, is from certified and sustainable sources. Garden boundaries are made from woven willow panels, supplied from long-established willow beds in Somerset.

Resident Feedback

Elaine Davis, tenant of Coopers Road and also Vice Chair of the Coopers Road Consultation Group, wrote the following summary of her experiences of the project:

Our old flats were completely run down both structurally and environmentally. We had a high level of deprivation, anti-social behaviour from the youth and a general feeling of depression in and around our Estate.

We realised early on in the project that attempting to replace our old flats with just new housing was not going to be enough of a change. We had to work on the total regeneration of our environment and that is the way in which we took our project forward. We managed through the process to create a community and that, in our opinion, is the basis for all that we have achieved so far and continue to strive for in the ongoing development of our new homes and community.

The architects, the landlords, the builders and our whole team, which every step of the way has had tenant/resident involvement and representation, all worked closely together and in partnership to create a new and vibrant community, which we are all really proud of. This is still a work in progress but our feedback so far through our monthly meetings is one of positive response from our old and new tenants and residents alike.

We feel secure and safe in our new homes. We researched the design and layout of our courtyards extensively, security was obviously a priority for us because of our old problems with the immediate area, and the problems of anti-social behaviour including graffiti, drugs and general nuisance associated, unfortunately, with inner city living. We are also in the process of working towards providing our new Youth Club, which we hope will be inclusive not just for our youth but people of all ages and we know this will be very warmly received in our area.

This project for me, my family and the entire tenants and residents of Coopers Road, old and new, has transformed our lives. We now know each other personally and socially – this was not the case before the project began. We are no longer isolated or alienated; we are a community and care for each other and our environment.

Conclusion

The aim of the project was to provide a model for sustainable development in an urban context that would be both affordable and replicable. The buildings are capable of developing over time and the servicing strategy is simple, robust and designed to accommodate change. As a theoretical exercise, future-proofing of the scheme (Phases 1 and 2) was tested by calculating the potential contribution from roof-mounted photovoltaics (see Figure 11.14). The potential area of south-facing roof is 450m^2 which, based on the use of monocrystalline PV panels, could generate 45,000 kWh/yr and reduce carbon emissions by 18,900 kg/yr.

Some key points are:

- mixed-tenure sustainable urban regeneration;
- a model of good community consultation;
- courtyard buildings enclosing communal gardens;
- community heating and CHP;
- design strategy to achieve zero CO_2 emissions by 2020.

Further reading
Evans, B. (2005) 'United Estate: AJ Building Study', *The Architects Journal*, 28 April, pp. 26, 34.

12 PARKMOUNT: STREETSCAPE AND SOLAR DESIGN

RICHARD PARTINGTON AND ADRIAN HORNSBY

DESIGN TEAM

Client	The Carvill Group
Architect	Richards Partington Architects
Urban Designer	Llewelyn Davies
Services Engineer	Max Fordham LLP
Structural Engineer	Fergus Gilligan and Partners
Quantity Surveyor	The Carvill Group
Contractor	The Carvill Group

Key Project Information

Programme	Residential
Site Area	0.57 ha
Dwellings per hectare	97
Habitable rooms per hectare	290

I very much welcome the investment in new housing represented by this new and exciting development in the Shore Road area. The transformation of a previously derelict site into a landmark location is a good new story for the area.

Nigel Dodds MP and Assembly member

Introduction

In Belfast, the tentative steps towards a more peaceful and integrated society have yet to be reflected in the physical landscape, which is still marked by the provocative murals, the painted kerb lines, and the oppressive walls that separate communities.[1] Everywhere there are constant reminders that Belfast is a patchwork mosaic of neighbourhoods.[2]

These are the characteristics of the southern end of Shore Road and our site, known as Parkmount. To the south-west is the mainly derelict and notorious Mount Vernon estate, once scheduled for demolition.

12.1 Map of the area to the west of Belfast Lough between the Antrim Road and Shore Road.

Immediately to the east is the Shore Crescent estate, a Protestant community planned in the 1970s around a series of 'secure' dead-end roads and cul-de-sacs, as was the practice for housing layouts of the time. Further to the east is the new motorway, which runs parallel to Shore Road along the edge of Belfast Lough. Figure 12.1 shows a map of the immediate area.

The Brief

In 1997, the Northern Ireland Housing Executive (NIHE), the main public body responsible for delivering housing, established a project team to promote new ideas in housing design with the intention of building these into a demonstration project. The NIHE then looked to private developers, through a tender process, to deliver the project and take the risk for marketing and sales. There was a process of negotiation and discussion with the winning tenderer, the Carvill Group, that clarified at the outset the aims of all the parties and set down the benchmarks for assessing the environmental performance of the scheme.

12.7   Site strategy.

Roof pitch set to
maximise solar potential

PV pilot scheme.
Total area: 70m²

Solar thermal panels

Building acts as a
barrier to road noise

Natural stack ventilation
of access spines

Crescent arrangement of
buildings provides shelter to
courtyard from prevailing winds

N

12.2   LI
an

Site Layout

One of the perceived shortcomings of post-war housing design is the failure to address the issues of ownership and demarcation of space. Landscape areas and open space whose ownership is common or ambiguous are often poorly maintained or vandalised, which in turn has implications for crime prevention and personal security. However, in Belfast, this is not just a question of providing natural surveillance and distinguishing 'front and back' or 'public and private'. Understandably,

12.8   The completed scheme.

The acco
imately 6
sity of 97
Some 46
dimensio

The key c

●   flexi
     and

●   crea

●   a co

●   a log
     phas

●   simp
     run

●   attai

●   good
     and i

12.9   Analysis of daylighting at sketch design stage.

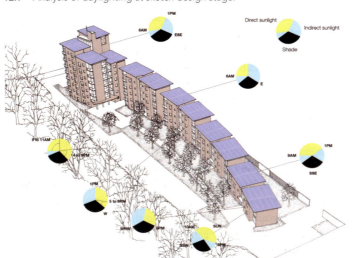

1PM

6AM
ESE

Direct sunlight

Indirect sunlight

Shade

6AM
E

9 to 11AM
E to 6PM

1PM

9AM
SSE

1PM

5 to 6PM
W

WNW

SSW

SUN

house purchasers expect high levels of visible security and active surveillance, and gated developments with security cameras are not uncommon there. We were uncomfortable with the idea that Parkmount might be conceived as a secure 'enclave' – this seemed to contradict the notions of permeability and pedestrian movement that underpin regeneration planning.

Security

At Parkmount, a number of devices are used to establish clear but secure entrances to the project and to delineate the transition from street pavement to dwelling entrance. In Victorian and Edwardian housing, this transition would have been marked by a series of thresholds, each reinforcing the demarcation of private ownership: the gateway, the front garden, the steps up to the front door, the portico or porch, etc. At Parkmount, the single shared space has one secure access point, so it is not a public space, but gaps between the buildings are

placed to give glimpsed views into the courtyard and these are emphasised on the street edge where there are breaks in the low wall and
railings. At these points, paired freestanding brick pillars with small
canopies and lighting suggest gateways and entrances. In the future,
with the emergence of a safer and less troubled society, it will be
possible to connect these gateways directly to the landscaped court
via footpaths.

Solar Design

The roof profile is the distinguishing feature of the project. It helps to
unify the whole scheme so that each of the repeated blocks is seen as
part of a considered whole. The strength and clarity of the roof form
are also a clear architectural representation of the central theme of
solar design, which has influenced every aspect of the project.

Through a series of massing and site studies we examined the possible
forms for the roof-scape and checked there would be no overshadowing. The aim was to maximise the surface area that could
present an optimal inclination and orientation to the southern sky
(within plus or minus 20° of due south). The form of the buildings
responds directly to the 'solar logic' with the lowest roof at the southern end of the site ascending at a constant 5° angle towards the north
and culminating in the nine-storey tower. The development of the
arrangement and massing of the buildings is discussed in a case study
in *Photovoltaics and Architecture*.[5] Figure 12.7 shows the final layout
of the buildings.

Even though the living spaces have various orientations, more than 80
per cent of the apartments have good sunlight penetration and many
have dual aspect living rooms that are ideal for a normal working day,
giving direct sunlight in the morning and the evening. Those apartments in the tower that do not have an ideal solar orientation, because
of the density and the constrained site, have the compensation of the
best views in a north-east direction towards the Lough. Figure 12.8
shows the completed scheme.

The quality of daylight in interior spaces and the potential for passive
solar design seem to be ignored in so much recent housing where
small windows are the norm. Figure 12.9 is a sketch analysis of daylighting for the developing scheme and by paying attention to these
issues, we believe that the quality of the internal spaces and their
marketability has been greatly increased.

12.10 The completed PV installation.

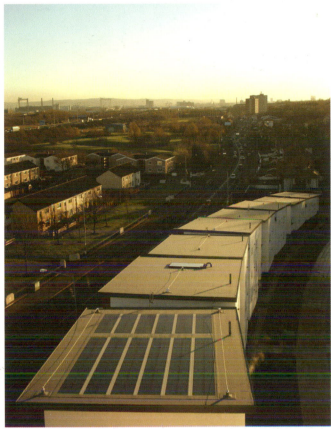

An array of 70m² of grid-connected photovoltaic panels was designed
with an estimated annual output of 4,400 kWh/year, which provides
enough electricity to meet the annual consumption of two of the apartments. The design for this sample roof area (PV fixing, access, cable
routing, inverter design, etc.) can be applied to all the low-rise units in
the future. The scheme uses amorphous silicon modules, factory-
bonded to the single-ply roofing membrane and protected by a fully
weatherproofed transparent polymer coating. The amorphous silicon
can be applied in very thin, flexible layers, which makes it ideal for use
with lightweight roof membranes. On the other half of the same block,
a solar thermal panel provides pre-heating of hot water to one of the
apartments below. One 2.5m x 1.3m panel, with an effective absorber
area of 2.8m², has been installed. Figure 12.10 shows the completed PV
and solar thermal installation.

12.15 Fred and Vivenne Mitchell.

12.16 Sandra Eve.

Postscript and Lessons for the Future

The Parkmount Development (now known as 'Horizon Buildings') has been a success on many levels. Apartment values have more than doubled from an original price of £65K–70K in 2003, in what is still considered a relatively undesirable area. However, this has to be set against the dramatic house-price rises generally seen in Belfast City over the past couple of years. The development is well liked and well looked after – the landscape is maturing, there is no sign of graffiti and even the communal bike stores are well used. The general perception among purchasers and occupiers is of spacious and well-lit interiors (an endorsement of the high daylight levels rather than the apartments' sizes which are, in fact, quite small).

The variety of internal finishes and interpretations of the internal spaces at Parkmount are both unexpected and gratifying. Residents have adapted and furnished the spaces to suit their budgets and needs, accommodating home comforts, home-cinema and home-working, even the symbol of home – a fireplace (Figures 12.15, 12.16 and 12.17 show a selection of internal photographs from occupiers who were pleased to invite us into their personal spaces).[9] The passive design measures would all seem to be contributing to a comfortable and efficient internal environment, and although the large-scale regeneration has yet to be realised, there have been publicly funded projects to improve the streetscape and environment on Shore Road.

The trial area of PV panels has been less successful. No additional funding was ever obtained for the PVs, in spite of the considerable efforts made. The reasons for this stem from a series of complications brought about by the original design decision to use integrated PV, embedded within the roofing membrane, rather than clip-on panels. The thin-film PV technology also promised lower costs with some reduction in efficiency. However, the developer incurred considerable added expense, in part because there were no direct competitors to the specified system, and also because there was only one recognised installer in Northern Ireland. This is often a problem for construction in Northern Ireland where the market is not perceived to be big enough to attract the full range of services and suppliers that we have been used to on the mainland.

The specified array provided 2kWp (see Glossary) of electrical output at a cost of £25–30K (although this has to be offset against the standard roof membrane which could be omitted in the areas where there were PVs). This produced the first disagreement with the funding bodies, who felt that a more reasonable price for a 2kWp installation would be in the region of £12K. The extra cost was attributed to the use of the integrated solar roofing membrane but the fact that the PVs were also providing the waterproofing was not taken into account. In effect, the scheme was disqualified for using an innovative technology rather than an established one. Similar disagreements occurred over the specification and installation of the inverter, which, like the membrane itself, came from a German company (for whom the UK mainland company was a supplier). The inverter was fitted and worked, but the funders demanded a form of guarantee which could not be provided and therefore refused to accredit the German inverter

12.17 Mr and Mrs Baird.

12.18 Sun on the horizon. Taken from a Parkmount apartment balcony.

according to Northern Ireland standards. The lack of funding seriously cut short the ambition for comprehensive monitoring, and although monitoring equipment was installed, there has been no co-ordinated system for collecting data from the PV or solar-thermal along with a number of control apartments. Interested occupiers can monitor output and electricity costs but sadly have no basis for comparison.

If Northern Ireland was the wrong location for innovation with active solar technology in 2002, it would seem that the current situation, according to the media, is very good. Grants are being awarded as part of the DTI's Low Carbon Buildings Programme to cover 50 per cent of the cost together with a top-up of 15 per cent offered by Northern

Ireland Electricity, the regional electricity company. Grants are only available to housing associations, public sector housing providers, schools and public bodies.

Although PVs have not realised the potential that many expected (payback periods greatly exceed the life expectancy of the panels) and there are still frustrating issues with grid connection, we are definitely edging towards a solar future. The fundamental design decisions at Parkmount have been endorsed, i.e. concentrate on the passive, common-sense technologies that give the greatest returns, and future-proof the building form to realise the potential of emerging technology on the horizon (see Figure 12.18).

Further reading

RPA (2004) 'Parkmount Housing'. Available:
    http://www.rparchitects.co.uk/publications/RPA parkmount housing.php.
Young, E. (2004) 'Sunny side up', *RIBA Journal*, August, pp. 40–49.

(Website accessed 15 December 2007.)

13 COIN STREET HOUSING: THE ARCHITECTURE OF ENGAGEMENT

GRAHAM HAWORTH

13.1
(a) Mission Street, San Francisco - the 'junk' of everyday reality.

(b) Manhattan - even 'designed' cities cannot deliver the abstract certainties desired by design professionals.

(c) Manhattan - 'the seventh investigation', 1969, by billboard artist Joseph Kosuth explores the non-art context of the public realm and the disorder of the urban environment.

DESIGN TEAM

Client	Coin Street Community Builders/ Coin Street Housing Co-operative
Architect	Haworth Tompkins
Landscape Architect	Camlin Lonsdale
Services Consultant	Atelier Ten (Coin Street)/ Max Fordham LLP (Neighbourhood Centre)
Structural Engineer	Price & Myers

Key Project Information

Programme	Residential and community centre
Site Area	1.2 ha
Dwellings per hectare	79
Habitable rooms per hectare	334

Introduction

The architect's role in the development of the sustainable city is often ambiguous. Traditional concerns of architectural style, taste and composition preoccupy most good architects. The resulting designs, while visually provocative, are often problematic, unable to survive the closer scrutiny of wider socio-economic, environmental and cultural imperatives.

Equally, a simple commitment to social well-being through technology, as prescribed by orthodox modernism, avoids those situations where architecture has to engage with less precise areas of reality. Architecture, as taught and published, often deals only with abstract certainties, and this 'retreat' is becoming increasingly unsustainable. The potential benefit of good architecture is denied to the wider population, and the product that we all get excited about in the media actually probably influences less than 5 per cent of all global construction, leaving the question of who is responsible for the remaining 95 per cent unanswered.

To be truly sustainable, architecture should be able to meet more objectives, satisfy more needs, be more appropriate, and achieve more relevance. If it is to contribute to meaningful improvements in the urban environment it must engage with the 'junk' of everyday reality and establish key values; values that are often generated as much by economics, social goals and politics as they are by design (see Figures 13.1a–c).

Frank Gehry identified this in an early article entitled 'Getting tough with economics',[1] where he observed a discordance between designers' aspirations and the reality of the context they were working in:

If you walk out on the street there are lots of cars, lots of dumb walls – this other thing called Design is a sort of forced attitude, it demands to be made of fancy not reality – the values are wrong.

As an architecture studio engaged in producing built work, our methods naturally focus on ways of contributing to a more sustainable urban environment. Embracing technology is essential, but we are sceptical of the reductive fetishisation of technology. Similarly, to predicate sustainable working practice exclusively on quantifiable indicators is over-simplistic, for the true measures of sustainability are also qualitative and cultural. We are interested in the pursuit of a humanistic culture, one that encompasses not only architecture, visual arts, literature and philosophy, but also the common activities of daily life.

Establishing key values can take many different routes, but what increasingly interests us are those ideas away from mainstream thinking that exist on the periphery – 'in the margins' – ideas that can by-pass the 'style, taste and technology debate'. We are interested in extending the context of our work to engage with a range of cultural values, recognising the potential for architects to engage with the various agencies involved in creating the urban environment in order to achieve more sustainable results.

Consider shelters for the homeless in New York, for example, designed by Michael Rakowitz, an 'artist, instructor, designer and activist' (see

13.2   The paraSite shelter for the homeless by Michael Rakowitz.

13.3   Gemini GEL by Frank Gehry - 'adaptable, low-cost, low-tech cut and paste'.

Figure 13.2). Michael built his first structures from garbage bags and contact cement while a graduate student at MIT, and has recently developed an ongoing customised shelter project he calls 'paraSite'. These temporary, inflatable structures provide life-sustaining warmth and shelter by taking in the waste exhaust heat of air ducts and steam vents, and cost only £2.50 ($5) to make. As Rakowitz points out, his work should not really exist and the shelters should disappear along with the problem. 'In this case, the real designers are the policy makers and the ones who are capable of organising bureaucracy.'[2]

An early Frank Gehry project for Gemini GEL – a company that produces fine art graphics – takes the idea of the simple stucco box of neighbouring light-industrial buildings, with their flat roofs, packaged air

13.4
(a) Jae Cha's low-cost community projects in Honduras (left) and Bolivia (right).

(b) A Will Bruder makeover in Arizona - £5/m² 're-wrap' maximum space for minimum cost - a sustainability maxim.

conditioning and chain link parking lots, and hacks it around, creating a low-cost dynamic urban environment, responsive to future replenishment, addition and change. Gemini was originally two small buildings which Gehry remodelled and clad with a new façade in grey stucco. A 500m² (5,000ft²) two-storey gallery and workshop were added subsequently and the car park was later developed as a restaurant (see Figure 13.3).

Jae Cha's low-cost work in Bolivia and Honduras uses the simplest of materials – timber and polycarbonate sheeting – in poetically beautiful ways. The results are extraordinarily powerful, demonstrating an exemplary understanding between architect and community (see

Figure 13.4a). In Arizona, Will Bruder's radical remodelling of a typical suburban house regenerates an existing structure through an economic lightweight 're-wrap' and is a perfect model for inventive sustainable urban regeneration (see Figure 13.4b).

What is inspiring in this kind of work is that, while it concerns both aesthetics and technology, the key innovation, or the starting point for the idea, is often economic, social or political. We have recently undertaken several projects in London which deal with similar issues and which have helped us focus more laterally on ideas about sustainability and what it really means. This has clarified our thinking on how the process of making architecture can enhance sustainability, particularly in an urban environment, and how essential it is in providing both the catalyst for change and the 'glue' that binds the results of the change together.

One of these projects, a development for Iroko Housing Co-op, is explained in depth here as a way of illustrating the complex issues at play in sustainable urban regeneration, and how certain criteria that architects often consider peripheral can positively influence the design. The project also demonstrates the necessity for projects to

13.5   Aerial view with the overall Coin Street area outlined and the Iroko site highlighted within.

13.6   Bangra workshop at one of Coin Street's summer community festivals.

evolve and change direction in response to external factors such as development economics, funding and changes in circumstances. This is the opposite of 'single vision' Modernist master planning and represents a more 'loose fit' and diverse approach to urbanism.

Coin Street: The Iroko Project

Since completing the first phase of the Iroko development in London in 2001, we have had the benefit of watching the first residents settle into the scheme and have been able to examine which aspects of the design work well and which might benefit from some adjustment. These include management issues as well as the physical architecture. We have also been progressing with a further phase of the project but funding will presently only allow part of the overall proposal to go ahead. This second phase, the Coin Street Neighbourhood Centre, completes half of the remaining unbuilt site area, and forms a key part of the overall concept and social infrastructure.

Iroko represents one stage in the development of a group of sites, totalling approximately 35 hectares, on the South Bank of the River Thames in London. The client, Coin Street Community Builders (CSCB), is a non-profit-making company, which aims to provide affordable

homes in the centre of the city, and over the past decade it has transformed this part of London.

Located immediately behind the National Theatre – one block back from the river – the Coin Street area has become a model for community-led urban regeneration (see Figure 13.5). There will eventually be some 600 homes at Coin Street, of which 55 per cent will be 'affordable', owned and managed by five separate housing co-ops, together with arts, sports and community facilities, shops and workshops, cafés and restaurants, a park and riverside walkway.

CSCB are genuine 'community builders' – constructing the framework for a sustainable community on the South Bank. Importantly, they are not just looking at the physical design of housing in isolation, but also exploring the socio-economic structures needed to allow residential accommodation to integrate with other uses. These range from local initiatives: festivals, education, sports and community activities (see Figure 13.6), to forging links with prominent cultural institutions such as the National Theatre, the Hayward Gallery, the Royal Festival Hall and Ballet Rambert, together with new major employers such as London Weekend Television and Sainsbury's supermarkets.

13.7 Various configurations for housing layouts at Coin Street.

(a)

(b)

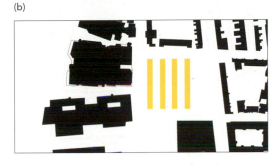

(c)

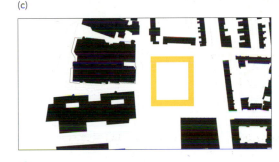

(d)

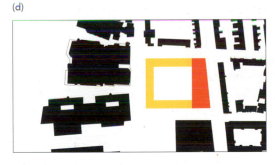

(e)

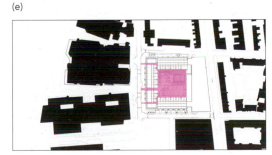

The Iroko project, which we won through a limited entry competition in 1997, provides a total of 59 dwellings and includes 32 family houses, which can each accommodate up to six people; the balance of accommodation is made up of a mix of flats and maisonettes. All dwellings are for rent and are managed by a housing co-op formed by the residents. The total site area is 1.2 hectares, with 0.8 hectare for housing, and the remaining 30 per cent of the site area used for communal activities; the Coin Street Neighbourhood Centre constitutes 15 per cent of this and we are currently developing the design brief for the remainder, which should complete the project by 2010. Thus, the whole urban block will be completed within a 13-year time-frame.

The site was one of the few in the area that could accommodate large family homes in the form of individual houses with adequate levels of outdoor amenity space. Initial designs indicated that 50–70 dwellings, of which 30–40 were houses, might be achievable. Conscious that social housing tends to be fully let, and that an excessive number of children on estates has been shown to create problems, CSCB emphasised the desire for a spread of dwelling sizes, confirming that its prime concern was quality of accommodation and environment rather than maximum density.

We were also conscious that the status of the inhabitants of European cities had undergone a sea change in the previous decade. Urban dwellers are no longer marginalised, deprived or socially excluded; they are confident, creative and self-assured. However, in parallel with the rise in confidence of the individual, there has been a corresponding collapse of collective confidence in the community, which we felt could be addressed in the design.

City-centre housing also proves to be something of a paradox. A sufficient scale of architecture is required so that the buildings can fit comfortably into a metropolitan context, but this must also provide a setting for small-scale domestic activity. Therefore, finding an appropriate scale of response to the site environment was the main starting point for the design. The balance between the monumental and the domestic was examined as a way of creating a specific sense of place and community, with a unique identity, through an architecture that had sufficient scale and presence to respond to the exposed urban context. At the same time, the design should create high levels of privacy and communal amenity for the residents. We believed that on this site a strong typology was needed, one that could easily be

13.8 Traditional use of a hollow square form with access galleries on the inner courtyard face.

13.10

(a) Busy traffic adjacent to Bonnington Square communal garden in Vauxhall.

(b) The communal garden at Bonnington Square in Vauxhall.

13.9 Stanley Gardens in Notting Hill.

'read' and understood by both the public and the residents; a form that established very clear signals distinguishing between public and private.

We explored various configurations for housing layouts, including traditional street patterns and individual housing blocks, most of which proved unable to provide the right level of defensible space. The final form we adopted was the hollow square model. This helped to redefine the urban block as a whole and provided the right level of external enclosure, leaving the internal space open as a central communal amenity. The dwellings are arranged around an open courtyard, which allows communal space to be maximised in the form of a large land-scaped garden with play areas, bounded on three sides by residential accommodation and on the fourth side by the Coin Street Neighbour-hood Centre (see Figures 13.7 a–e). This form is used most frequently for multi-storey apartment buildings where the habitable rooms of the dwellings face outwards to the street and where access takes place on the internal face (see Figure 13.8).

The use of a hollow square for single family dwellings or town houses is less common, but some of the best examples are in the garden squares of Notting Hill in London, where private gardens open onto a communal garden shared by occupants from opposite ends of the site (see Figure 13.9). This model has proved very successful and the central space becomes a focus for shared ownership and interaction. We were also interested in the calming effects of landscape and planting in the inner city (see Figures 13.10a–b).

The scale of the design proposals is a response to the inner city environment, which demands a particular massing and density to maintain the metropolitan buzz. The fact that the project is constructed over a concealed basement car park with 265 spaces adds to the urban concentration. The central landscaped courtyard over the car park pro-vides a tranquil communal area, sheltered from the noise of the street and designed to cater for a range of activities and age groups (see Fig-ure 13.11). Pathways, large planting beds and profiled concrete walls divide the space into four main areas: a large sloping lawn area,

13.11 Communal courtyard garden over basement car park.

13.12 External brick enclosure to Iroko, placed within the busy metropolitan urban context.

13.13 Rear elevation of the Neighbourhood Centre clad in timber, and deep window reveals.

a seating terrace focused on a specimen tulip tree, a toddlers' play area with play equipment, and a sunken ball game area with a stepped seating platform. The housing has a very direct relationship with the Coin Street Neighbourhood Centre, which effectively closes off the courtyard on the south side. While the two uses are physically separated and private, both housing and community facilities visually address each other and it has been possible in the detail design to maintain the privacy of the dwellings while allowing the Neighbourhood Centre to benefit from the visual amenity and sense of space provided by the courtyard garden.

The elevational treatment of the houses acknowledges their dual aspect, addressing the public streetscape on the outside, and the private landscaped garden space in the centre. Figures 13.12 and 13.13 show street elevations expressed as a simple brick screen with deep window reveals, and on the courtyard garden side a more informal timber cladding – from sustainable sources – has been chosen to slowly weather and mature with the landscaping (see Figure 13.14).

13.14 Courtyard garden creates a quiet oasis in the centre of the city.

13.15 Aerial view of Iroko courtyard with site of Stamford Street Neighbourhood Centre outlined in red.

The proposals embody many of the principles of sustainability relating to spatial planning and solar access; each dwelling has roof-mounted solar thermal panels for the production of domestic hot water and the specifications of insulation levels, ventilation systems and materials have been chosen to have minimum environmental impact. Each dwelling is fitted with mechanical background ventilation; the ventilation rates can be modified and heat is recovered from the exhaust air to preheat the supply side of the system.

The density of the housing in the project was predominantly design-led, although it did coincide with government guidelines of that time, set out in PPG3 which proposed higher housing densities on urban brownfield sites to protect London's greenbelt.[3] The overall density is 334 habitable rooms per hectare (291 habitable rooms in total) compared to Lambeth's planning guideline of 210 habitable rooms per hectare, an increase of 59 per cent. The development was not let at full capacity and the occupancy on completion was 260 occupants, of which 140 were children under the age of 16. If fully occupied, this would rise to 360 occupants.

The integration of other mixed uses with the housing is an important part of Coin Street's sustainable development strategy. As well as providing formal closure to the courtyard form and completing the urban block, the Neighbourhood Centre responds to some very specific local needs (see Figure 13.15).

The Coin Street Neighbourhood Centre

There are very limited indoor facilities that specifically serve the needs of Coin Street's growing residential community. In addition, employment in the area's traditional industries, such as the docks and the printing industry, has been in decline and is now being replaced by opportunities in the new growth industries of leisure, arts and media. However, many inner London residents fail to find employment in these growing industries because of inadequate training.

A 1999 MORI survey of local residents and businesses, sponsored by South Bank Employers' Group and CSCB, highlighted inadequacies in affordable childcare, youth and family support, learning and enterprise support, sports and social facilities, and a general lack of community facilities in the local area. The immediate target area is shown in Figure 13.16.

This need was actually exacerbated by the completion of the Iroko housing, which quickly highlighted the inadequacy of local community facilities including schools, indoor and outdoor sports facilities, childcare and out-of-school programmes. The need for learning and enterprise support was also indicated in the MORI survey, e.g. 30 per cent of working-age local residents had no formal qualifications – well above national levels – and employers had significant difficulties recruiting staff.

13.16 Catchment area of Stamford Street Neighbourhood Centre.

13.17 Stamford Street entrance façade of Neighbourhood Centre.

CSCB's response formed the brief for the Coin Street Neighbourhood Centre, which houses an unusually wide mix of functions within a single building, making it prototypical in many ways. Facilities include a 70-place neighbourhood nursery and crèche, spaces for out-of-school, youth and family support facilities, a neighbourhood café, offices for CSCB/Coin Street Group, and a learning and enterprise support centre for up to 300 delegates. A restaurant/retail space, rented on a commercial basis, has also been included to enliven Stamford Street and contribute to revenue funding (see Figure 13.17).

The aim was to create a welcoming, informal environment where each constituent part of the accommodation reinforced the others and where there was the maximum opportunity for cross-over and discovery. Just as importantly, the building needed to announce its unique purpose and communal values clearly to the neighbourhood, while maintaining a sympathetic response to the complexity and variety of the surrounding urban context. The Neighbourhood Centre had to respond architecturally to the listed Georgian terrace opposite and the noisy Stamford Street in a very different manner to the private realm of the Iroko housing and its garden.

In parallel to the organisation and appearance of the building, the design team addressed issues of sustainability by developing a hybrid system of natural and assisted ventilation that has helped to generate the primary form and texture of an architecture to deal with relatively hostile environmental conditions.

The southern façade to Stamford Street is noisy, dirty and potentially hot, so there are no opening windows on this elevation. Instead, a series of rectangular solar 'chimneys' are arranged along the façade, establishing a second façade layer within the building. Figure 13.18 shows how these chimneys drive the natural ventilation system by pulling air in from the cooler, fresher garden side, and across the internal spaces, before exhausting it at roof level. The idea of a sustainable low energy building is further developed by using the exposed concrete ceilings for night-time free cooling of the first and second floors.

The massing of the project also responds to the scale of the Iroko Housing (the height of the building is similar to that of the upper ground terrace of Iroko) and has been designed to protect the Iroko garden courtyard from traffic noise and fumes.

13.18 Natural ventilation solar 'chimneys'.

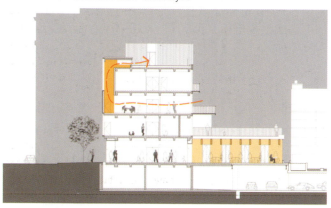

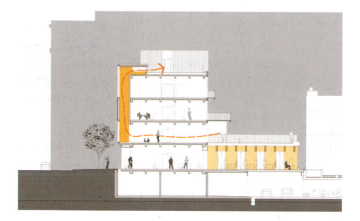

13.19 Neighbourhood centre closes off the courtyard, protecting it from traffic noise and provides a degree of passive surveillance to the housing.

The concept of the Iroko courtyard as a series of terraced spaces of varying levels continues into the Neighbourhood Centre. Indeed, the garden extends to the roof where a high level terrace for the learning and enterprise support centre gives excellent views over London while maintaining privacy for the Iroko residents (see Figures 13.19 and 13.20).

Iroko Housing: Lessons

While the Neighbourhood Centre was completed in September 2007, the housing component of the scheme had been fully occupied five years earlier, and the architecture has proved to be robust and capable of taking some knocks. The design of the dwellings has been successful: people like them. Had the budget allowed, more storage within the

dwellings would have been desirable. The private gardens, balconies, roof terraces and high-level walkway access are all very successful (see Figure 13.21). However, the mechanical background ventilation system has proved problematic. It seems that it is difficult for most tenants to understand, to the point that most people don't use it correctly, showing that further training and information are required.

There has also been an interesting shift in occupancy since the project was initially occupied. Current figures indicate a significant drop in numbers with 203 adults and 65 children under the age of 16, which is the result of some adult separations, children growing up and a decline in new births.

The communal areas now appear to have settled into an accepted operational 'form of life' after some teething trouble. The residents initiated some modifications themselves that were not in the original scheme such as the introduction of CCTV, something that has evolved holistically and would probably have been resisted if it had been the landlord's initiative.

The main issues on Iroko, and they are not particularly problematic, are mainly managerial and social. It appears too much for the residents to take on some aspects of the project such as the external pavement

13.20 Ground and first floor plans of the Neighbourhood Centre.
(a)

(b)

areas and the landscape maintenance, and there are proposals for CSCB to take the lead. The underlying issue of maintenance is covered by the lease agreement: CSCB are responsible for the building fabric and the co-op have responsibility for the common parts; the co-op want to set the rental levels as low as possible, while CSCB want to protect their investment. The result is a sort of compromise. The building fabric is largely self-cleaning, particularly the brick and metalwork, but the pre-cast concrete steps and untreated timber cladding has not been cleaned of dirt in five years and clearly a shorter cleaning cycle should be implemented for these elements.

The soft landscape is also showing signs of wear, but this is the result of heavy use, which is a positive sign. Surprisingly, it has been used

primarily by children rather than adults. There is a strange dynamic at work here, where adult members of the community are not willing to intervene with the supervision of others' children to avoid conflict, so the default position is that the courtyard becomes a child and teenager territory. There are signs that this will change as the average child age increases and the space eventually is used more by the adult members of the community.

All hidden corners in the courtyard, particularly the re-entrant corners, have attracted abuse in various forms and these are likely to be closed off and given over to extended private gardens. The children tend to damage the soft landscaping, not maliciously but through overenthusiastic play. The completion of the first phase of the Neighbourhood Centre will provide an element of passive surveillance, which should prevent this happening.

Background to Coin Street Community Builders

The origins of CSCB illustrate that true community involvement in both the planning process and urban regeneration initiatives can lead to more sustainable urban design. CSCB came out of a campaign that ran during the 1970s and 1980s and two year-long public enquiries overseen by the then Secretary of State, Michael Heseltine.

The Coin Street area was in a state of decline, large employers like Boots, WH Smith and Her Majesty's Stationery Office had moved out and their premises lay empty. The city as a whole was in a state of flux, with high unemployment in traditional industries and the decline of the Greater London Council.

It is easy to forget the mood of that time. Riots in Brixton and Hackney and the voice of disenfranchised youth were perfectly captured by punk music which saw 'London Burning' – a wasteland of abandoned warehouses, tower blocks, heroin, police and thieves; the popular attitude was one of 'direct action'. Although it was run-down, the surviving residents did not find the area threatening or menacing; there was still a strong sense of community. They sought to resurrect the neighbourhood rather than move to another area, and felt deep scepticism that displacing the local community with a commercial development was a sustainable long-term option.

Instead of a clear statement on the planning needs of the area, the policy had been one of waiting to see what the market came up with.

13.21 Personalisation of the garden spaces by residents.

13.22 Original Coin Street protestors in the 1970s.

13.23 Ernie - a local resident and CSCB committee member, recently awarded an MBE for services to the community.

Such vagueness seemed to be the antithesis of good planning. Local residents, alarmed at the closure of local schools and shops, the loss of housing and the prospect of further office development, decided to get directly involved in the planning process (see Figure 13.22).

The sites became the subject of two separate planning applications, the more dramatic of which was designed by Richard Rogers for Greycoat Estates. Rogers' scheme was an ambitious 'single vision', a master plan for a necklace of tall new buildings along a covered galleria, one-third of a mile long, stretching from Waterloo Bridge to the OXO Tower.

As a formal piece of urbanism, it had great design integrity, but relied on over 100,000m² of commercial space to be viable. It also proposed demolition of the OXO Tower Wharf and the creation of a new pedestrian bridge link over the Thames. The scheme was aimed at a new city-wide public as an extension of the South Bank public amenity, but many felt that it neglected local issues.

An alternative scheme put forward by The Association of Waterloo Groups, later to evolve into CSCB, avoided the grand statement and concentrated instead on a range of smaller ideas, starting with the needs of the indigenous community, reinstating the original street pattern of urban blocks and retaining OXO Tower Wharf.

Notwithstanding the differences in architectural approach, the issues were really about the mix of scale and use, the choice between a city-focused commercial scheme with an element of residential (Greycoat) or a locally focused residential scheme with an element of commercial (Coin Street). There followed one of the country's longest planning battles which resulted in both schemes being granted planning permission.

Although the strength of opinion favoured Coin Street, local community groups would have been unable to afford to purchase the sites (which now had the benefit of planning permission for office use) without the direct intervention and support of the local authority which, after much lobbying, imposed covenants on the sites. These restricted the purchaser to only building fair-rent housing and light industrial/shopping space in accordance with the community planning permission, which reduced the value of the site to a fraction of its potential commercial market value, making it an unattractive proposition for commercial developers.

Every planning authority has such powers to intervene directly but seldom uses them. This controversial change to the Unitary Development Plan and the subsequent land sale by the disbanding GLC, ended in the development of 'the capital's most valuable piece of real estate' being undertaken by a local community group whose scheme flew in the face of market forces.

At the time, Coin Street was very controversial but before long most people were beginning to wonder what all the fuss was about as the community scheme proved to be so right for the area. The sustainability lessons from this episode, which can be applied to other city centre sites, are quite simple.

It is possible to achieve social goals through new development and for a community to positively harness the power and support of the elected local authority to implement positive change. Clearly the involvement of the local groups in planning and development early in the process resulted in a more complex range of options being considered. The involvement of the local community provides an invaluable source of local knowledge, history, and cultural memory; the seed bank from which more sustainable urban communities can grow (see Figure 13.23).

The evolution of Coin Street also demonstrates that it is possible to avoid rigid, 'single vision' master planning and replace it with a more holistic approach to urban planning which, rather than force through one big idea, advocates the synthesis of lots of small ideas into a whole. Master planning can be diverse and provide a menu of projects that can be implemented by different architects as and when money and land become available. It is still possible to start out with a wide vision, but which is capable of being broken down into more manageable phases. This is more organic – it can adapt to change as communities evolve and develop differently from what was originally envisaged.

Coin Street also demonstrates the need for defined management and organisational structures that enable the initiative to develop and

survive. The main board of CSCB sets the overall development guidelines for the area and forges educational and employment links with local institutions and businesses. A commercial management group within Coin Street runs the infrastructure, rents out the commercial space, and organises festivals and cultural events. It even has its own team of gardeners to maintain the parks, riverside walks and other public areas.

In general, the affordable housing is self-managed and the co-op system works well. Each element of the residential is run by a specially formed housing co-op and there are currently four in existence, all of which, optimistically for an urban setting, are named after species of trees: Palm, Redwood, Mulberry and Iroko. A housing co-op is a group of people who jointly own their homes and control the way the housing is run. The properties belong to the co-op as a whole and members pay rent to it.

The co-op is non-profit-making, so any surpluses go back into improving the housing. This keeps management costs and rents down, particularly if members do some of the day-to-day work themselves on a voluntary basis. The co-op system also provides on-site management so that the usual problem areas of high density social housing, such as supervision of communal spaces, lifts and stairs can be adequately controlled. CSCB provide a training programme which helps the residents to understand their responsibilities as co-op members and so feel confident in carrying them out.

Unlike most social housing groups, CSCB have developed a team with a range of skills which enable them to exploit the huge potential of the sites and their location to provide opportunities to cross-subsidise the housing. The OXO Tower contains two large up-market restaurants and a series of craft workshops, a coffee bar, florist and gallery spaces. The car park beneath Iroko has been leased to NCP and provides spaces for local office workers and visitors to the South Bank. There are also strategically placed advertising hoardings and illuminated billboards which bring in much-needed revenue.

Some people find it difficult to understand why a not-for-profit company like CSCB should want to entertain these commercial activities, leasing a restaurant to Harvey Nichols that serves fairly expensive food to wealthy people and providing spaces for commuter parking when they should be discouraging the use of cars in central London.

The answer is purely pragmatic. They make money from the commercial parts in order to fund those other parts such as maintaining the parks and gardens, having festivals and cross-subsidising the housing. The commercial reality of the cross-subsidy is essential to subsidise the affordable housing, as building high density inner city housing is on average 100–150 per cent more expensive than traditional two-storey housing.

Further phases of Coin Street, which by necessity push even harder to generate a commercial revenue stream, are currently at the planning application or early development stage. The Doon Street Swimming and Indoor Leisure Centre, for example, located across the street from Iroko, will cost more that £20 million to build and, so that no one is excluded from using the facilities because of price, will require some further £400,000 per year in revenue subsidy. Neither Lambeth nor Southwark Councils has the money to build and operate such a facility in the area so most of the funding will have to be generated by the commercial housing element elsewhere on the Doon Street site. The current absence of an affordable housing component in the scheme has led to criticism from some quarters, and demonstrates the difficulty CSCB face in maintaining a sustainable balance of uses in the face of commercial pressures, which to date they have been so adept at manipulating.

What can we learn from Coin Street? Primarily, for us, it is another example of 'working in the margins' – challenging conventional wisdom on the role and practice of architecture. Several characteristics of CSCB's approach establish valuable yardsticks for other sustainable urban communities:

- the origins and background to CSCB itself;
- positive involvement of the local community in the planning process;
- adoption of neighbourhood master planning;
- co-op-based structure of the organisation and community involvement in the design process;
- creative use of cross-subsidy and funding;
- commitment to high quality specification and high initial capital investment;
- diversity of design;

- high density and mix of use;
- low energy demand and use of renewable energy sources.

We envisage a series of similar scale initiatives that draw inspiration from Coin Street and its achievements in bringing about positive change. The process is in a constant state of flux, particularly the question of the social management and maintenance of the architecture when it is completed, and this – and the associated human energy and commitment needed – should be factored into any truly sustainable design proposal. But perhaps the biggest challenge to the success of sustainable communities in future is not to lose sight of the 'key values', which, as discussed earlier, are often generated as much by economics, social goals and politics as they are by design. The commitment to social housing in the light of commercial pressures, which was the starting point of the Coin Street initiative, is something that they are having difficulty sustaining in the latest phases of the development and which, if it is not addressed, can only be detrimental to the sustainable community they have successfully created.

The design of future sustainable communities will have to face these pressures head on. They will probably be different in scale, materiality and diversity, and there is likely to be more emphasis on improvisation, on the temporary and the provisional in the city. We are experiencing this shift already and are becoming increasingly involved in an examination of found or 'undesigned' space as a source of sustainable working methods. Our low-cost student housing at Newington Green (see Figure 13.24), explores these possibilities and uses the sheltered garden site to provide a naturally ventilated scheme with a strong fenestration pattern, giving an architectural presence that belies the project's low build cost; our temporary theatre for The Almeida Theatre at Kings Cross (see Figure 13.25) uses found space as a starting point.

In addressing contemporary issues of sustainability, the poetry of the temporary and the improvisational becomes increasingly attractive, encouraging an architecture that borders on 'non-design', provisional, economic, open to addition and change. An urban architecture is evolving that celebrates ambiguity and improvisation, underpinned by humanistic values, a type of 'post-internet' vernacular.

Current projects that we are working on are following the trend set out in this chapter, and tend to be predicated on driving down capital cost while enclosing the maximum amount of space. They increasingly have

13.24 Newington Green low-cost student housing.

diverse mixed-uses and briefs that require flexibility and the ability to change easily and quickly. This leads to simple, adaptable and robust containers, which can be modified over time as functional demands change.

The main challenge for architects in all this, their unique contribution to the sustainable city, will be how to balance the force of this inevitable change with the more qualitative and poetic values of cultural memory and history.

13.25 The Almeida Theatre, Kings Cross.

Further reading
Abrahams, T. (2007) 'Coin Street Neighbourhood Centre', *Blueprint*, December, pp. 50–54.

A+T Civilities (2008) Coin Street Neighbourhood Centre.

A+T-DENSITY IV (2003) 'Iroko Housing - London Haworth Tompkins'.

A+T-DENSITY New Collective Housing (2006) 'Iroko Housing - London Haworth Tompkins'.

Coin Street Community Builders (2007) *Coin Street SE1 Neighbourhood News*. London: CSCB. Available: http://www.coinstreet.org/upload/documents/Publications 143.pdf

Davis Langdon & Everest (2002) 'Coin Street Housing', *Building*, 15 March, pp. 76–81.

(Website accessed 12 February 2008.)

14 SUSTAINABLE DESIGN IN AN URBAN CONTEXT: THREE CASE STUDIES

ALAN SHORT

DESIGN TEAM (Contact Theatre)

Client	Contact Theatre Company
Architect	Short and Associates
Services Consultant	Max Fordham LLP
Structural Engineer	Modus Consulting
Quantity Surveyor	Dearle & Henderson

Key Project Information

Site Area	0.21 ha
Programme	Theatre

Determinism in Sustainable Design

Fifteen years ago it seemed as if passive solar design, as a conscious intent, was forcing building form into mono-pitched prisms all oriented south. Rigorously applied 'heliotropic' site planning organised groups of prismatic objects parallel to each other and spaced apart to maximise solar exposure. Try as one might, it was very difficult to induce such a strategy to make a recognisable urban environment. In the 20 years we have spent trying to design sustainable buildings, the majority of which have been in some kind of urban context, we have discovered, slowly, that with the application of ingenuity and imagination one can transform a building of almost any shape and orientation into an effective functioning passive solar object. This chapter tracks the development of our thinking, principally in plan form, from the wide-frontage, narrow-section buildings of that period, to the deep and condensed plans we have been developing more recently. Figure 14.1 maps this slow development. Seventeen years ago, while developing the plan of the New School of Engineering and Manufacture for Leicester Polytechnic, we speculated that the strategy developed to enable a building to interact more directly with its 'natural' context in order to reduce its consequent carbon dioxide emission, might simultaneously help to embed the building more meaningfully into its physical, urban context. The new school, later to become the newly incorporated De Montfort University's Queens Building, is a 10,280m² laboratory building, a type for which the twentieth century prescribed a standard diagram of a deep-plan, cubic building, with three or four floors of double-loaded corridors, enclosing a larger, central volume, all sealed and mechanically ventilated and cooled, and largely artificially lit. As a prompt, upon appointment, we were shown by the then Head of Engineering drawings of such a building recently completed in Sweden. We were intrigued as to how the application of a particular environmental strategy could help to dissolve this rather large building and its unforthcoming standard plan type into its complicated context. As we were completing the Queens Building, the opportunity arose to consider the integration of a sustainable theatre into yet denser urban fabric.

CASE STUDY 1:

The Contact Theatre, Manchester: The Context in 1993

In 1993, the Contact Theatre Company was a full producing house, operating on a shoestring with a company strength of 65 people in two buildings separated by 100 metres of windswept temporary university car park. The simple rectangular auditorium building with an exceptional stage width of 17 metres was built in 1963. It had very thick load-bearing masonry walls but a lightweight roof of channel-reinforced woodwool slabs, felt-covered. Its roofline pitched gently up along the longitudinal axis of the auditorium, and some sort of operating height was recovered economically over the stage without any distinct discontinuity in form. The side cheeks of the tilted mansard were faced in copper. A small foyer on two levels was contained within the rectangular envelope to the south of the main auditorium across the full width of the rectangular plan, and a band of tiny dressing rooms and a sub-stage completed the north end of the box. A scene dock projected to the east with a large dock door. The blank scene dock formed, in effect, the main approach elevation to the theatre (see Figure 14.2).

on the temperature and information about the levels of CO_2 received by the building-management system from sensors in each occupied space.

Synchronising cultural and environmental intent

The entrance elevation to the Contact (see introductory image on p. 134) is built up from cantilevered overlapping zinc screens that enclose the upper level bar and foyer. The patterns are derived from the embroidered hangings and banners that have been brought out for many generations to dress festivals in southern Mediterranean parishes. Our theory is that the shapes of the banners are derived from architectural moulding profiles supplied by local stonemasons. This is certainly the case in Malta where we found the stonemasons consulting Vignola's treatise to inform their stone-cutting technique. Fresh air is drawn up behind each projecting layer and taken through a simple heater box with a diverter, providing fresh air to that end of the foyers. The two vertical borders at either end clothe extract chambers.

CASE STUDY 2:

Coventry University Library: The Context in 1996

While the Contact was under construction, the practice won the opportunity to design a large (11,000m²) library on an inner-city site. Coventry University is a post-1992 university developed out of Lanchester Polytechnic and associated colleges. The new publicly incorporated institution has had to develop its newly acquired university infrastructure very rapidly. One of the key components in this ambitious restructuring has been the construction of a Library and Learning Resource Centre, completed in August 2000 to replace the existing Lanchester Library (see Figure 14.8). The concept of the building is somewhat different from that of a traditional library in that it is an important teaching venue as well as being a repository for books and place for scholars engaged in private study. It is densely provided with computers and the prognosis is for yet denser provision. A Learning Resource Centre contributes many of the broader student support requirements called for in contemporary University Charters. It is not simply the new politically correct jargon for a traditional library. All of which is to say that the internal environment is potentially noisy, that students are allowed to talk, and that a certain amount of teaching happens on the principal floors in and among the IT provision and the books.

The client's requirement for a deep plan

The Chief Librarian and his staff insisted on a deep-plan square building, the inverse of the type diagram that we had hitherto drawn,

14.8   Aerial view of the new library.

which attempts to dissolve a large programme into sequences of narrow sectioned elements coiled around each other. We wondered if it might be at all possible to make such a deep-plan building, 50m by 50m, naturally conditioned, which was also a much-emphasised ambition of the original brief. The Coventry inner ring road, elevated at this point, grazes the site, and a major interchange is adjacent at ground level. Furthermore, the need for security, and to discourage a latent temptation to throw books out of library windows for later collection, introduced the requirement to lock all the windows. We generated six alternative diagrams, all of which placed a large atrium in one part of the plan, a type plan of the last 30 years. The Institute of Energy and Sustainable Development at De Montfort University tested each plan type and we discovered that the introduction of a large atrium delivered a well-lit and reasonably well-ventilated but very narrow zone around the major void, and that the rest of the floor plate, apart from a narrow zone adjacent to the external elevations, was poorly served.

The development of a strategy to naturally condition a deep floor plate

It occurred to us that this large void could be redistributed to make fields of useful floor plate, alternating with smaller penetrations, so that one would redistribute and alternate this well-lit, well-conditioned perimeter zone. The more dimly lit spaces between became reasonable locations for book stacks. A simple and economical square grid,

14.9 First-floor plan, Coventry.

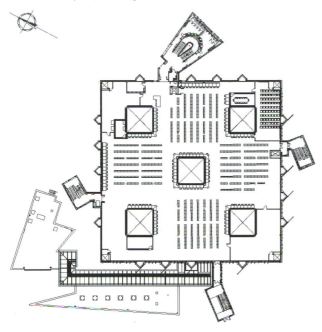

14.10 Section showing routes for air entry into the library.

14.11 Section showing exhaust routes.

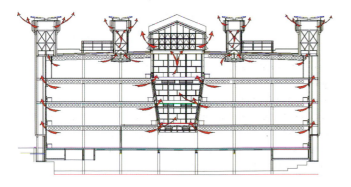

14.12 Studying around an air-intake court.

optimised at about 7 metres, set the rather crude rhythm of floor plate and void (see Figure 14.9). The next proposition was to draw fresh air beneath the principal floor and above the lower level through a continuous plenum, exposed to all four principal elevations, introducing fresh air into the building up through the four atria (see Figure 14.10).

This idea would deliver natural light and fresh air, warmed when necessary, to the readers and computer users and their tutors. The next proposition was to draw the warm air out through a large central atrium and perimeter stacks (see Figure 14.11). An effective and well-sealed damper was developed specifically for the project. A high level of local control is achieved by a fine grid of zones and close groupings of dampers. There are some 200 dampers in the building. This strategy provides a level of close, tight control, driven by the sophisticated building-management system considerably beyond that provided in our earlier buildings. As we worked through the logic of what is actually a very simple configuration, additional refinements were introduced. A glass lens was placed below the greenhouse tops of the intake atria to protect them from direct solar gain. A similar lens was placed at the base of the central atrium with a damper below soffit level, to choke the extract from the ground floor. The device enables library users to stand in the middle of the ground floor in the deepest part of the building and look up and see the sky. This has become a popular periodical-reading place (see Figure 14.12). The strategy seems to exclude traffic noise satisfactorily. If anything, the library floors are a little too quiet. There is no plant noise. There are no reports of the library being troublesome to clean. Particulate matter does not seem to be admitted into the building in any greater quantity than is expected by cleaners who attend to mechanically ventilated buildings.

14.13 Thames Valley University first-floor plan.

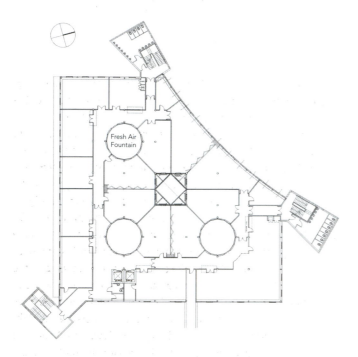

14.14 Thames Valley University roof plan.

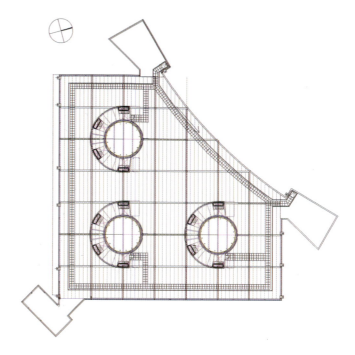

The construction type and detail

There are no applied finishes to the walls or the concrete soffits and the ceiling heights are prodigious. The building assembles itself into a substantial urban palazzo and we pursued this analogy with enthusiasm. A contemporary illustration of the Palazzo Strozzi under construction was very useful; it shows how a principal elevation can arrive at a corner and fold back onto a much more utilitarian elevation, under which service rooms are stacked up at twice the rate of the principal floors. The Coventry north elevations double-bank inexpensive aluminium windows in a vague recollection of this principle. The 9-inch brick masonry modelled to the south-west and south-east elevations is in Flemish Bond and the principal window openings are protected by a brise-soleil embedded in the modelled masonry skin, formed out of cast-stone cills and brick piers. There is no need to make large frames of lightweight sun shading for these orientations at this latitude. They are the result of a particular set of aesthetic preferences.

The extract terminations

The rotated stacks between the window bays model the elevations at a coarser grain. The terminations to the stacks are taken well above obstructions on the roof and the converted motor-car factories nearby and develop into another type of termination. Split tubes of extruded aluminium are ranked, layered and displaced relative to one another to disrupt an incoming air stream while enabling a free discharge of air

on the leeward side. We rather enjoyed the accidental evocation of a car radiator grille, given that the building is in the heart of the declining Midlands motor industry. Fortunately the Coventry public, who retain a deep affection for motor cars, have taken to this imagery. The strategy is effective and we were interested in developing it. The opportunity came in the form of a commission to make a highly adaptable Learning and Teaching Building for Thames Valley University in 2001.

CASE STUDY 3:

Thames Valley University New Learning, Teaching and Central Services Building: The Context in Late 2000

Thames Valley University is located in Ealing and Slough, just west of London, and is an amalgam of various former colleges. It is one of the principal exponents, with the City University, of the UK Government's intention to widen access to higher education in Britain. This is an extremely challenging task on the resource base allowed to new universities. It requires high levels of managerial agility and responsiveness as subject areas variously prosper or ebb away. The university's portfolio of curriculum offerings has been dramatically overhauled in the past few years and now it specialises in Health and Community Studies (funded by large Health Trust contracts), Business Studies, Media and Music. It inherited a large and valuable campus alongside the A4 motorway in the middle of Slough comprised of 1960s buildings suffering familiar construction inadequacies: the

14.15 Detail of exhaust object, section and elevations.

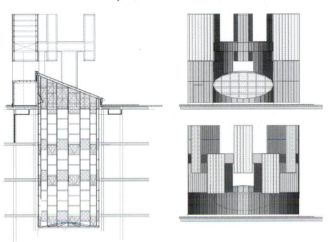

incorporation of asbestos, failing flat roofs and decaying lightweight cladding in the shadow of one of the principal landing and take-off flight paths to and from Heathrow Airport.

The university's restructuring strategy proposes to dispose of a large component of the site and consolidate its learning and teaching accommodation requirements in a new building, with very high levels of inherent flexibility, on the residual site adjacent to the Paul Hamlyn Learning Resource Centre.

The strategy

This commission enabled us to develop the idea of a multi-storey, deep-plan flexible building and refine the original Coventry diagram. The Thames Valley building is broadly triangular and deploys three glazed penetrations, circular in plan, to extract stale air and deliver light deep into the building.

Fresh air is introduced from the perimeter, and from the centre through a device we have come to call the 'fresh-air fountain' (see Figure 14.13). The fountain is fed by ducts at ground level and below the slab from each of the principal elevations. The budget is somewhat lower than that for the Coventry building. It has a simple steel frame, pre-cast concrete plank floors, a secondary steel frame along the perimeter with studwork infill, external insulation and, variously, render or cedar cladding.

The atria tops are developed into tiara-like semi-circular H-pot arrays (see Figures 14.14 and 14.15). All services are thrown outside of the principal plan area, which can be configured as completely or partly cellularised with large open-plan areas for administrators or computer suites, or as completely open floor plates. The south elevation filters solar gain seasonally through an external mesh sun-shade screen in which finer mesh panels trace the sunpath diagram, through the over-heating months, onto the elevation behind. However, as higher education develops, it will require what the university already describe as 24/7 accommodation. Much of its occupancy and use will be in the dark during the evenings with teaching predicted to happen until 9.00 p.m. The optimisation of the artificial-lighting scheme in the building will be as important as its ability to distribute good levels of natural light. Again, as at De Montfort, this new university is very interested in its own branding. Its students are busy people with full- and part-time jobs, making tremendous personal sacrifices to acquire higher education, many of them living in a nocturnal world at speed. A fascinating contrast in interests and priorities with the ancient universities, this institution has embraced the anticipated kudos of owning a new research level, green building.

Conclusion

Throughout the past decade, our clients have coaxed us into modifying our rigid ideas of an optimal diagram for an environmentally responsible public-scaled building. By chance, they have all been in city centres, except for the first. We have grappled with demands for particular plan types, unpromising orientations, and harsh acoustic and air-quality conditions. We have discovered that one cannot simply clip devices onto existing 'business-as-usual' building types; a more fundamental contribution is required. We also suspect that 'greenness', as an intent, aligns itself directly with a contextual intent in the broadest sense, and that fineness in detail and response offers the greatest rewards.

Further reading

Anon (2001) *Celebrating Innovation: Innovation and Integration in Design and Construction*. London: Commission for Architecture and the Built Environment, pp. 36–39.

Garnham, T. (1999) 'Building study', *Architecture Today*, June, pp. 25–31.

15 BEDZED: BEDDINGTON ZERO-FOSSIL ENERGY DEVELOPMENT

BILL DUNSTER

DESIGN TEAM

Client	The Peabody Trust
Environmental Consultant	BioRegional Development Group
Architect	The ZEDfactory – Bill Dunster Architects
Services Engineers/ Building Physicist	Ove Arup Partners
Structural and Civil Engineer	Ellis & Moore
Quantity Surveyor/ Construction Manager	Gardner & Theobald

Key Project Information

Programme	Residential, workspace, community centre
Site Area	1.65 ha
Dwellings per hectare	50
Habitable rooms per hectare	164

Introduction – the Aspiration

BedZED is a new community of 82 homes, 18 work/live units and 1,560m² of workspace and communal facilities built in 2002 for the Peabody Trust in the London Borough of Sutton. In putting together our designs and proposals for BedZED, the team tried to reconcile a higher-quality, affordable lifestyle and workstyle in an outer London dormitory suburb, with a step change reduction in carbon footprint.

Our definition of zero-fossil energy development (ZED) is an excellent passive building envelope that reduces the demand for heat and power to the point where it becomes economically viable to use energy generated on site from renewable resources. At BedZED, we have attempted to generate enough renewable energy over the course of a year to meet the new community's total annual heat and power demands. This means

exporting electricity to the grid in summer, when demand is lower, and importing from the grid in winter, when demand is higher.

The quantity of renewable energy imported from outside the site's boundary should not exceed each citizen's fair allocation of the limited quantities of national communal renewable energy resource. The ZED-factory team, working with carbon footprinting team Best Foot Forward, used this recommendation to develop the concept of the National Biomass Quota – recognising that the national reserves of green grid renewable electricity and renewable biomass are extremely limited and capable of meeting no more than 30 per cent of current national energy consumption.[1] This study calculated that there was only 250 dry kg/person per year of biomass available at a residential density of under 50 dwellings per hectare – applicable to 70 per cent of the UK – and around 500 kg/person per year available above this density, all assuming no net loss of agricultural land to energy crop (see Table 15.1 and Figure 15.1). Recognising that the proponents of 'offsetting' – whose supposedly low-carbon developments try to outsource their power generation problems to another location – were going to run out of national renewable generating capacity very quickly, has made us increasingly aware of the importance of combining both load reduction and building integrated micro-generation. Recent government energy targets suggest a maximum contribution from offshore wind of around 15 per cent of national electrical demand, suggesting this is the maximum practically achievable with 2MW turbines spaced on a 500m grid on the limited areas of reasonably accessible continental shelf (i.e. in waters less than 50m deep). Similarly, uranium ore supplies at sufficiently high concentrations to make extraction sensible from a carbon-saving point of view, are limited to the first 15 years of an international nuclear renaissance.[2]

The challenge at BedZED was to show that it is possible to provide a holistic living/working community enjoying a high overall quality of life, while limiting its consumption of scarce national resources, such

TABLE 15.1

Analysis of the UK biomass quota				
	Land Use (Mha)	Usable yield per hectare*	Total yield	Resource availability per capita
		0dt/ha/yr	Mt	0dkg/person/yr
Straw	0- waste product		7.5	125
Forestry	0.25	10	2.5	42
Other energy crops	2.6	10	26	433
Subtotal (fuels for heating and power)	2.85			
		Litres/ha/yr	MI	Litres/person/yr
Biofuel (based on oilseed rape)	1.15	1139	1310	22
Waste vegetable oil	0- waste product		176	3
Sub total (transport fuels)	1.15			25

*Estimates take into account efficiency losses

as brownfield (see Glossary) land and biomass, to the quotas available if these resources were fairly allocated to each UK citizen. Many contemporary projects claim carbon neutrality by using many times their fair share of the national biomass resource. All this has achieved is the squandering of limited communal reserves, and the exposure of these new communities to future fuel-poverty as prices rise through global and national scarcity.

A Local Response to a National Problem – the Wider Context

A study[3] by Brenda and Robert Vale showed that an average UK family's annual carbon emissions were spent in the following way:

● one-third for heating and powering their home;

● one-third for private car use, commuting and land-based travel;

● one-third for 'foodmiles' (see Glossary), with the average UK meal having travelled over 3,200 km (2,000 miles) from farm to dinner plate.

This clearly shows that energy-efficient building design is important, but no more so than the other key factors determining everyday life in the UK today. The idea was to try and use both the architectural form and the masterplan to make it easier for the new community to work on site, play on site, share childcare, share vehicles, share water treatment and power plants, and share organic food deliveries from local farms.

BedZED tries to show that it is possible to substantially reduce a typical household's carbon emissions, and hence reduce its overall ecological footprint, at the same time as increasing overall quality of life. We found that the contemporary lifestyle in a conventional suburban home is so dysfunctional that it is possible to rethink each of these daily activities and reduce its carbon emissions while simultaneously providing quantifiable benefits to each individual. Encouraging this process of 'enlightened self-interest' could then become the fastest way of reducing the environmental impact of the UK volume house-building industry.

This is important because we are no longer appealing to the niche green consumer, but proposing alternative lifestyles that can be adopted by a wider market, while still making substantial progress towards creating a carbon-neutral urban infrastructure in the UK. We replace our urban fabric on average at around 1.5 per cent, per year,[4] which shows that, if ZED standards became common, we could as a nation wean ourselves off our addiction to fossil fuels by the start of the next century, while still retaining historic buildings and attractive city centres. However, much of our ordinary built fabric has little value and does not rise to the environmental challenges of the new millennium. Figure 15.2 shows the current area of urban sprawl, which will eventually cover 11 per cent of the UK by 2016.[5] To avoid house prices rising, we are told we need an additional 3.8 million new homes by 2021,[6] (not allowing for an increase in population) and it is hard for key workers, such as teachers and nurses, to find affordable homes in the South-East of England.

15.1 UK energy consumption.

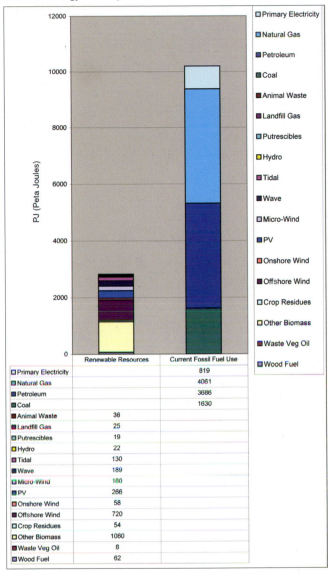

	Renewable Resources	Current Fossil Fuel Use
☐ Primary Electricity		819
▦ Natural Gas		4061
▦ Petroleum		3686
▦ Coal		1630
▦ Animal Waste	36	
▦ Landfill Gas	25	
☐ Putrescibles	19	
☐ Hydro	22	
▦ Tidal	130	
▦ Wave	189	
▦ Micro-Wind	160	
▦ PV	266	
☐ Onshore Wind	58	
▦ Offshore Wind	720	
☐ Crop Residues	54	
☐ Other Biomass	1080	
▦ Waste Veg Oil	8	
▦ Wood Fuel	62	

Legend (right of chart):
☐ Primary Electricity
▦ Natural Gas
▦ Petroleum
▦ Coal
▦ Animal Waste
▦ Landfill Gas
☐ Putrescibles
☐ Hydro
▦ Tidal
▦ Wave
☐ Micro-Wind
▦ PV
☐ Onshore Wind
▦ Offshore Wind
☐ Crop Residues
☐ Other Biomass
▦ Waste Veg Oil
☐ Wood Fuel

15.2 Shaded areas show extent of urban sprawl in England and Wales.

■ Urban Sprawl

In the UK, we import between 60–80 per cent of our food,[7] and increased global competition for healthy organic food (currently 70 per cent imported) will become more intense as developing countries raise their expectations, and as the world's population continues to rise. Competition for food, fossil fuels and water leads to conflict, and results in the need to invest substantial military and trade resources in order to ensure supply. BedZED shows how almost all the new homes could be built on existing stocks of brownfield land, while still providing each household with a garden, and enough workspace on site to provide future employment opportunities to all resident working adults. Saving agricultural land from urban expansion will become a priority as the number of refugees to the UK increases due to accelerating climate change, and the tradable global agricultural surplus dwindles as international cereal production is disrupted by drought.

The Masterplan – How Do We Create a Compact City Where People Want to Live?

At BedZED, almost every flat has a small land- or sky-garden and a double-glazed conservatory, integrating the two features most desired by many suburban households. The original design intent was to reconcile Ebenezer Howard's suburban garden city concept with the UK Urban Task Force's[8] agenda to substantially increase residential densities and reduce urban sprawl. But how do we reconcile higher densities with better amenities than are found on traditional urban templates?

The central block of four terraces at BedZED (see Figures 15.3 and 15.4) achieves residential densities of over 116 dwellings per hectare, including live/work units. This provides approximately 400 habitable rooms per hectare and 200 jobs per hectare, at the same time providing 26m² of private garden and 8m² of public outdoor-space per home. Even allowing for the entire BedZED site, including playing field, parking, CHP plant and community buildings, a density of around 50 dwellings per hectare is achieved. If these standards were commonly adopted, it would be possible to reduce UK urban sprawl to about 25 per cent of its current footprint over the next century, while staying within a three-storey development template capable of retaining high levels of private garden provision. This means that almost all of the new homes could be provided by brownfield-site regeneration, saving valuable agricultural land and green-belt for biodiversity, leisure and locally produced organic food.

How do a new building-physics model and low environmental impact cultural priorities inform a new urban typology? There has been much

15.3   Perspective section through BedZED.

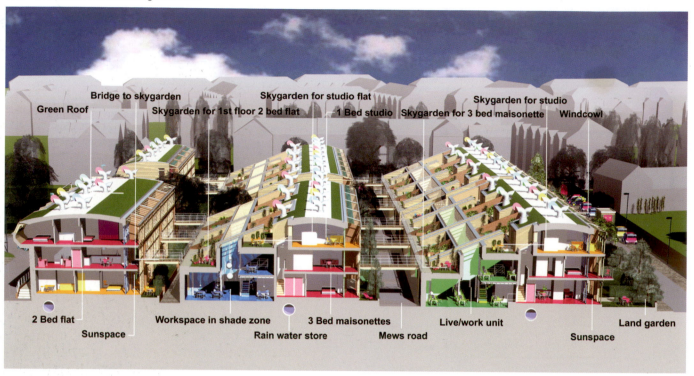

Green Roof
Bridge to skygarden
Skygarden for 1st floor 2 bed flat
Skygarden for studio flat
1 Bed studio
Skygarden for 3 bed maisonette
Skygarden for studio
Windcowl

2 Bed flat
Sunspace
Workspace in shade zone
Rain water store
3 Bed maisonettes
Mews road
Live/work unit
Sunspace
Land garden

15.4   Slice plans showing ground level to roof.

architectural debate among traditional urban designers about the visual effect of south-facing terraces on our existing urban landscape. At BedZED, we have composed the gable ends to create a new type of

street elevation (see Figures 15.5 and 15.6) and we would argue that this type of solar urbanism is as valid as the more conventional urban strategy where buildings are designed simply to face the street. The currently fashionable perimeter block layouts with parking courtyards make it difficult to achieve meaningful contributions from building-integrated solar micro-generation. The idea that workspace is placed to the north, and that a mixture of energy efficiency with renewable micro-generation (as well as urban convenience) must inform new low-carbon communities, contradicts many established urban Codes. ZEDfactory is working on a new set of Design Codes that facilitate the achievement of high targets for building-integrated micro-generation.

As climate change accelerates, preventing summertime overheating becomes much easier when employing south-facing, double-skin façades with sunspaces. With 50 per cent of the outer glazed screen openable, the winter sunspace becomes a balcony in the summer. The balcony also shades the internal glazed-screen below (see Figures 15.7 and 15.8). A popular misconception is that the adoption of east- and west-facing façades minimises solar gain through the large areas of glazing required to achieve daylight levels in high-density, deep-plan urban developments. This has a tendency to maximise low-angle solar gain on west elevations towards the end of the day when all passive-cooling potential from the building's thermal mass has been exhausted.

15.5 Long section through BedZED.

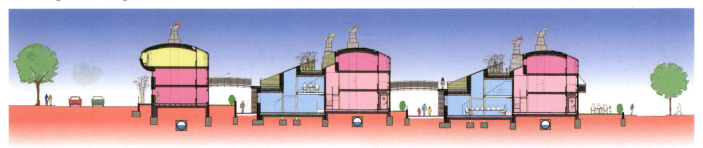

15.6 London Road elevation.

15.8 Sunspace bathed in sunshine.

15.7 The living room glazing is shaded by the sunspace balcony.

The problem of summer overheating is more difficult to solve by design, and often leads to a solar-shading solution that results in occupants having to resort to artificial lighting.

How do we socially integrate this lifestyle within existing communities? BedZED effectively combines an office park with a housing estate, at the same time integrating communal sports and leisure facilities. This doubling-up of land-use offers potential developers more income than would a conventional single-use approach, while respecting the normal planning restrictions on storey heights. Potentially, this additional revenue could fund the increased costs of a carbon-neutral specification, enabling carbon trading to be integrated as part of the planning-approval process. This is exciting because local communities can use the democratic UK planning process to increase the financial yield from sites within their jurisdiction and allow environmentally benign development to take place, without relying on central government carbon-emission legislation, which will always be held back by the volume housebuilders' lobbying power and resistance to change.

15.12 The CHP plant room and clubhouse.

3. pedestrian-only mews with gable-end entry workspace and a café/shop;

4. covered arcade with housing/nursery and health clinic. (The glazed roof on the arcade was omitted as a cost saving in the realised project.)

These four building-blocks, each with different subdivisions creating a variety of flat-types, could enable the BedZED system to be replicated on other sites. The scheme approaches the highest density of naturally lit, mixed-use urban grain, capable of benefiting from useful amounts of solar micro-generation, while providing each household with an out-door space. Early studies undertaken by Ove Arup & Partners showed that passive solar gain contributed up to 20 per cent of a zero-heating-specification home's annual space-heating requirements, although it should be noted that some homes at BedZED are more shaded by adjacent blocks than others, and therefore the contribution varies somewhat.

Building the Community – From 'Eco-slob' to 'Eco-saint' in One Generation?

The original concept behind BedZED was to create a mixed-use development that could be adopted by almost anyone, whether motivated by environmental issues or not. We believe this is important as there are many eco-village communities globally that intentionally celebrate their contrast with everyday life continuing around them. At BedZED, the social and income mix is varied, with the residential tenure

15.13 The 'ZEDwheel'.

approximately one-third social rented, one-third shared ownership, and one-third private. All workspace is rented from the Peabody Trust. Now, five years after occupation, the overall take-up of most of the green lifestyle activities, including the car pool and local food-sourcing, has proved disappointing (despite considerable, and well-funded promotional efforts by BioRegional), although a very gradual upsurge has been noticeable over time. This process tends to irritate the more enthusiastic and self-conscious environmentally-aware members of the living and working community, and friction can occur. For example, a successful community bar/café (built and funded by ZEDfactory, and operating on Friday nights from shared workspace fronting onto the village square) was dismantled and moved to the clubhouse due to curmudgeonly objections citing noise, security, and the need for a proper licence if opened to the public. Having moved from the centre of the community, and thus removing the opportunity for casual encounters as people crossed the village square, the bar effectively closed and now only opens for organised functions. This process could have been avoided by placing the community clubhouse, or village hall in the centre of the development. The local authority, however, required this to be placed adjacent to the playing field on low-value 'metropolitan open land' that could never be used for

15.14 Super-insulated walls.

15.15 Environmental strategy diagram.

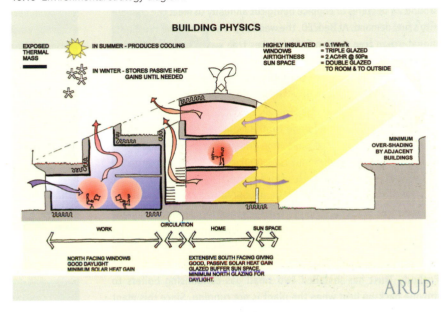

residential or commercial use. This 'checklist' approach to sustainable development cannot replace '*joie de vivre*', and frequently the environmentalists' tendency to take themselves too seriously creates an unpalatable and divisive social force. We believe it is important to provide the community with an infrastructure that promotes and facilitates more environmentally benign lifestyles, but allows people to adopt these initiatives willingly and at their own pace – avoiding accusations of social engineering or eco-fascism. BedZED is an experiment that will take many years to mature, increasing in relevance as climate change and accelerating environmental degradation provide the incentives to implement the original community vision (see Figure 15.13).

Energy Strategy – Limiting Demand so that Renewable Energy Sources Work

BedZED incorporates a minimum of 300mm insulation (see Figure 15.14), triple-glazing, south-facing glazed sunspaces, thermally-massive floors and walls, good daylight, and passive-stack ventilation with heat recovery, and has energy-efficient lighting and the latest 'A-rated' appliances. The environmental strategy is shown in Figure 15.15.

Importantly, by combining workspace with housing, the community's energy demand matches the heat and electricity output of the CHP, which is often not achieved with single-use residential schemes. If, to generate sufficient electrical energy over the course of the year to meet the annual demand, the CHP provides more heat than is needed for summer domestic hot water, the heat produced from renewable energy will be dumped and wasted.

Developer-led, high-profile zero-carbon projects frequently adopt this strategy, even arguing for reduced insulation levels to reduce heat dumping. This reduces the capital cost of the renewable-energy installation, enabling developers to make higher bids for land, but at the expense of future residents' running costs, especially as biomass becomes an increasingly scarce resource. A common strategy at present is to install increasingly large biomass-heating or CHP plant without considering other, more expensive, renewable energy installations. These projects are effectively 'stealing' national biomass reserves, and will probably be uneconomic to inhabit in the early 2020s.

A 135kWe output (see Glossary) CHP plant will consume 850 tonnes of woodchip per year at 30 per cent moisture content. This requires an

15.22 The sky gardens.

15.23 The sunspaces facing onto the vehicle mews.

Conclusion

Perhaps the most important message is that the wholehearted approach to sustainable design is more cost-effective than simply tacking on a few green initiatives to a standard volume housebuilders' product. The quantity surveyors for the project have calculated that the same amount of money per dwelling is simply spent in a different way, allocating more funds for super-insulated walls and glazing at the same time as reducing the central-heating budget to two finned-tube radiators in each home.

Apply this logic to the whole project, and barriers to sustainable development begin to disappear. The strongest objections to the BedZED concept tend to come from volume housebuilders who see any short-term increase in construction costs affecting the value of their existing large land-banks. These organisations frequently promote green lifestyles in place of more expensive low-carbon infrastructure, claiming that foodmiles, aviation and private car use take priority over energy efficiency or renewable energy micro-generation on site. This is a short-term and irresponsible strategy to adopt, as government legislation on carbon footprints and personal carbon allowances is virtually guaranteed, making it critical that we use the last of the fossil fuel to create a low-carbon national infrastructure that no longer relies on fossil fuel or nuclear power. It is also essential that developers do not achieve carbon neutrality at reduced capital costs (thus enabling them to win competitive land bids) by increasing the consumption of limited biomass reserves.

It is important to note that the Peabody Trust funded the entire construction from start to finish, and, as owner of the freehold, manages the community maintenance and infrastructure. BDA worked without fees for nearly five years to research and realise the project, and in the past two years applied the generic Hopetown urban concept to the BedZED site. Being a charity, BioRegional obtained a modest grant towards their promotional effort from the WWF. Both the engineers, Arup, and quantity surveyors, Gardiner and Theobald, provided their support in the early stages of the project free of charge. It is inconceivable that the project would have been sufficiently convincing to the Peabody Trust funding board without the donated time, input and enthusiasm of the original project partners.

A considerable amount has been learnt from both the sales and procurement process. Contractors consistently overpriced tender packages due to unfamiliarity with the construction details and specification, and an accelerated programme (with an open-ended construction management contract) made it hard to meet the original and ambitious cost plan. At the same time, rapid overheating of the construction industry around the Millennium caused serious labour shortages for traditional trades – at one stage we had to bring carpenters to site from Reading, some 80 km (50 miles) away.

All ZEDfactory projects since BedZED use similar details, but by using Design and Build contracts, and the physical presence of the BedZED village to demystify the zero-heating-specification construction process. Most of the increased cost of the gardens and sunspaces also

15.24 Elevated view of the BedZED from the south-east.

enhances the sales value (see Figures 15.22 and 15.23). Resident surveys indicate that these features are far more important than the energy-efficient low-carbon specification. It appears that the market will only adopt energy-efficient homes if they genuinely offer a higher quality of life, and provide a better product to the volume house-builders' alternatives currently filling the estate agents' windows (see Figure 15.24).

Future ZEDs – ZED in a Box

We have now developed the BedZED concept into a range of standard house-types, with the integrated ZEDfabric supply chain,[11] pre-negotiated volume discounts and the perceived higher-risk, 'green' technological elements already priced and performance-tested. There-fore, we can source local materials, suppliers and contractors for the structural frame and fabric of the base-build, but still have the benefit of the specialist environmental modelling and innovative components that would ordinarily be unaffordable for most sites. But, most impor-tantly, we can provide planners and local councils with detailed environmental performance projections before a site has even been purchased. This enables the environmental performance to be traded as planning gain within Section 106 Agreements (see Glossary). It is hoped that these initiatives will substantially remove many of the barriers to change that are currently obstructing large-scale carbon-neutral developments of this type in the UK. We hope to show that these benefits create added value for the developer that will exceed the additional construction costs, and we believe that, in time, the market will simply 'vote with its feet' and request ZED developments in preference to conventional alternatives.

Further Reading

Dunster, B (2007) *The ZEDbook*. Abingdon: Taylor & Francis.
Twinn, C. (2003) 'BedZED', *The Arup Journal*. 1. Available:
http://www.arup.com/ assets/ download/download68.pdf

(Website accessed 2 February 2008.)

16 BO01 AND FLAGGHUSEN: ECOLOGICAL CITY DISTRICTS IN MALMÖ, SWEDEN

EVA DALMAN AND CECILIA VON SCHÉELE

DESIGN TEAM

Client	City of Malmö
Masterplan Architect	Klas Tham in collaboration with City of Malmö Planning Office

Key project information: Bo01

Programme	Mixed use
Site Area	22 ha
Dwellings per hectare	59

Key project information: Flagghusen

Programme	Residential
Site Area	4 ha
Dwellings per hectare	157

Introduction

To many people, Malmö in Sweden is synonymous with sustainable urban design. Some 3,000 building-design practitioners and students per year make the pilgrimage to Västra Hamnen (the Western Harbour) to visit the experiment begun for the 2001 Swedish Housing Expo. Its first phase, Bo01 (see Figures 16.1 and 16.2), has now become part of both the Malmö psyche and also its skyline, with the completion of the Turning Torso tower by architect Santiago Calatrava in 2005. This case study charts the growth of this area and how the lessons learnt from Bo01 are being applied to the area's latest development, Flagghusen (the Flag Houses).

From industrial wasteland to a leading ecological area

Bo01 – the City of Tomorrow – is an entirely new, ecological district, which today is home to 1,908 inhabitants in 1,303 apartments on a land area of 22 ha. It is the first development stage of Västra Hamnen, one of Malmö's growth areas. The area is typical of the redundant, contaminated industrial urban land that has afflicted the environment, but

16.1 Vastra Hamnen (the Western Harbour area).

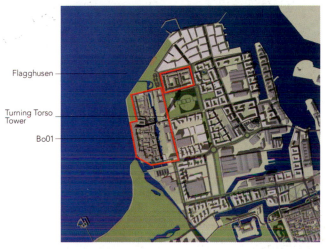

16.2 The Bo01 area.

16.11
(a) Estimated and observed total energy consumption.

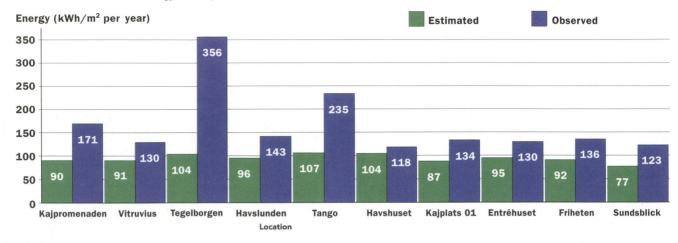

(b) Estimated and observed heating energy consumption.

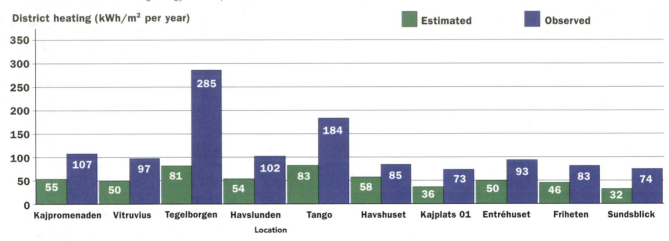

- a part of the garden left to grow naturally;
- a courtyard containing at least 50 Swedish wild flowers.

Other points bring landscape architectonic qualities to the courtyard or facilitate rain and surface water drainage. Rainwater is dealt with locally (see Figure 16.10) by open channels in the landscape that connect to holding areas, such as ponds and canals, which discharge into the sea. The water is cleaned and treated in a surface run-off system.

IT and the Environmental Performance

IT is used to improve the environmental performance of the area and also to facilitate a lower-energy, more environmentally-friendly daily life for residents. IT helps to measure, control and regulate different sub-systems as well as monitor and charge for residents' energy use.

Road information technology systems are being used to inform the public and to control traffic in the area. Public transport vehicles are given priority at intersections controlled by traffic lights, and bus shelters feature real-time information displays that show when buses will arrive. Opportunities for remote work from home and e-commerce also reduce residents' needs to travel out of the area.

Different initiatives are needed to meet the communication and documentation needs of the district. A dedicated website[4] and environmental web-TV channel are less conventional forms of communication used to inform, engage and influence the public.

Energy performance

Detailed measurements of district heat and electricity were taken during the period 2002–03, the second full year following the occupation of ten properties selected for monitoring. Figure 16.11 compares

16.12 Model of Flagghusen 1:100 scale.

the estimated and observed total energy demand (a) and heating energy demand (b) and shows that observed energy consumption is generally in excess of the initial estimates.

The principal reason for the discrepancy is thought to be space heating demand, which is due in varying degrees to unsatisfactory insulation, thermal bridging and poor air-tightness. Less obviously, the energy performance calculations are, with the benefit of hindsight, underestimates as a result of: (1) unreliable heating contributions from solar gains (and the slow response of the underfloor heating system to these gains); and (2) the assumption that room temperatures would be 20°C when observations show it to be 22°C on average.

The study recommended the following in terms of setting future benchmarks:

- Estimating cooling energy demands, even if cooling plant is not installed.
- Limiting allowable electricity demand to 35 per cent of total energy to penalise the use of electricity for heat.
- Weighting energy use for larger and smaller dwellings, not simply by m².
- Refining the definition of floor area such that it is not open to interpretation.
- Using a more realistic indoor temperature of 22°C in calculations.
- Applying a mandatory air-tightness standard of less than 1 air-change per hour at 50 Pa test pressure.

16.13 Flagghussen viewed from the park. November 2007.

The Next Generation of Sustainable Urban Design at Västra Hamnen: Flagghusen

If Bo01 is first-generation sustainable urban design in Malmö, then Flagghusen (The Flag Houses) represents the second. In 2004, the decision was taken to develop a 4 ha area north-east of Bo01 (see Figure 16.1). The mission given to the city planners by the politicians of the city of Malmö was to create a new housing district with affordable rents and a high level of sustainability.

The planning context for Flagghusen is distinctly different from when Bo01 was conceived. For Bo01, the Swedish Government allocated a 250 million SEK (€ 27 million) fund from which the city and developers could apply for money to cover the extra costs that sustainable building then implied. Added to this, Bo01 was a national housing expo, which meant developers were striving for the best results since it offered great marketing potential. For Flagghusen, however, there is no

extra money; simply market conditions. There is no longer a housing expo either; it is a site like any other. Flagghusen heralds the move from the extraordinary to the 'ordinary' at Västra Hamnen.

Sustainability goes mainstream

An important theme throughout the planning process was that if the concepts practised in Bo01 could be repeated and multiplied, then collectively they would make a real difference to the environment. The starting point was to learn from the Bo01 experience. One lesson was that in order to attain ambitious goals a written contractual agreement is not enough: more trust is needed between developers and planners. In March 2004, a project entitled 'The Creative Dialogue' was initiated whereby the city invited all interested developers to participate at a very early stage in the planning process. The idea was to reach a consensus on plans, architecture, environmental and quality issues through dialogue and consultation. Thirteen developers took part and worked together in workshops every other week for two years. The plan adopted (see Figure 16.12) is ultimately an agreement between planner and developer rather than a diktat.

The agreement

The agreement addresses the three core aspects of sustainability: social, economic and environmental. The following are some of its constituent points:

- Two-thirds of the apartments will be for rent at a reasonable cost (on average, the rents will be 27 per cent lower than an equivalent private apartment at Västra Hamnen);

- Variability should be a key part of the architectural design;

- Low energy consumption (120 kWh/m²y);

- Healthy indoor environment. The buildings should include moisture control (to prevent problems of mould growth), and the use of hazardous substances in building materials should be minimised;

- All homes should be no more than 75 m away from waste disposal and recycling facilities;

- A 'Better for Everyone' plan will ensure that apartments can still be used throughout a person's lifetime;

- Safety. A checklist will ensure that the environment is safe and secure;

- Meeting places. The plan offers three very different meeting places: a square, a park and a playground;

- Use of the green-point factor (as described above).

At the time of writing, two of the blocks at Flagghusen, some 62 apartments, are complete and occupied. The other eleven blocks are under construction and will provide a total of 626 apartments by 2009 (see Figure 16.13). Two developers are building houses to a PassivHaus[6] standard on their own initiative.

Making sustainability at the same time both mainstream and affordable continues to prove a challenge for the city planners. For example, not all of the 'features' of Bo01 have been incorporated on cost grounds, among these the vacuum waste collection, and the provision of 100 per cent renewable energy. In other words, a balance between the three core aspects of sustainability is proving harder to attain than anticipated. Reaching higher economic and social standards has ultimately meant cutting back on the environmental standards, but it is a necessary compromise to ensure truly sustainable development. The Creative Dialogue was a way of arriving at the agreement that made 'mainstreaming' sustainable design possible, an agreement which will now be used in other projects in Malmö.

Further reading

Persson, B. (2005) *Sustainable City of Tomorrow BO-01 – Experiences of a Swedish Housing Exposition*. ISBN: 9154059496.

Lewis, S. (2004) *Front to Back: A design agenda for urban housing*. Oxford: Architectural Press.

Palmer, S. and Seward, A. (2005) *Innovation in Sustainable Housing*. New York: Edizioni Press.

17.3   Ernst May's diagrams from the 1930 article 'The Evolution of the Urban Block'.

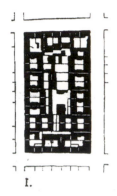
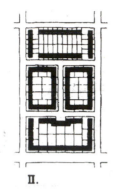
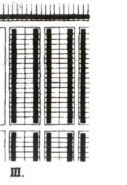
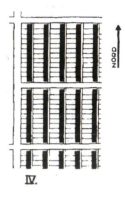

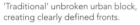

'Traditional' unbroken urban block, creating clearly defined fronts.

Fruitful hybrids possible in the middle of the spectrum.

'Modernist' linear blocks optimise orientation for daylight and sunlight.

housing. Needless to say, cyclical destruction and redevelopment is a particularly wasteful way of making cities. Therefore, unlike the first time round, physical and social renewal have been carefully co-ordinated, in the hope that the current housing stock and city layout can prove more enduring than the last.

In 2005, one of the last remaining sites in Stonebridge was put forward for the Europan architectural competition[1] won by Witherford Watson Mann Architects, with a scheme for elegant, clearly organised residential blocks either side of a vivid, diverse public park. Subsequently, we were commissioned by Stonebridge HAT and Hyde Housing Association to prepare an outline planning application for a smaller but more complex site. The new scheme followed certain basic principles set out in the competition-winning scheme, but was required by the constraints of the site to develop and demonstrate ambitions in relation to sustainability.

The site lies between a busy high street (Hillside) to the south and a new park (Fawood Park) to the north, and is irregular in form and long on its east–west axis but relatively shallow north–south. A watercourse runs through it in a culvert, part of the water supply to the Grand Union Canal. The brief is to provide 122 dwellings comprising 11 three-bed and 111 one- and two-bed apartments on a 0.81 hectare site, giving a density of 380 habitable rooms per hectare (hrh), an increase on the 1997 masterplan maximum density of 245. As well as the significantly higher densities, the introduction of private market accommodation into an area overwhelmingly composed of social housing has brought different challenges to the earlier phases of the estate renewal.

Our design brings together two different ideas for making the city, combining the 'traditional' closed perimeter urban block with the permeable, linear organisation of Modernist city design. The perimeter block is the predominant structure of London's (and indeed Europe's) traditional urban structures, with buildings constructed to the edge of the plot, creating clearly defined fronts and backs, streets and private interior gardens; the Modernist, linear approach is based on the optimisation of orientation for daylight and sunlight.

Figure 17.3 is an illustration from a 1930 article[2] on the evolution of the urban block by Ernst May, director of planning and architecture of the City of Frankfurt, which shows these approaches as polar opposites. It describes the 'evolution' from a 'traditional' unbroken urban block, which clearly defines and shapes the street but makes little or no reference to orientation (I), to an arrangement driven by a 'Modernist' approach to orientation and which provides little definition of the street (IV). This last arrangement shows all dwellings oriented in the same 'ideal' arrangement. The terraces run north–south and are positioned to the east side of the plot, which enables all dwellings to have west-facing living rooms and private gardens in order that they receive afternoon and evening sun. The definition of front and back is blurred, and the private gardens create a more varied cityscape than the traditional street lined by blocks on either side. What May presents as an evolution, we see rather as a spectrum, with a great variety of fruitful hybrids possible in the middle. It is these hybrids that appear to us to have the potential to achieve high environmental standards while supporting street-based sociability.

17.4 A view of the model, taken from the south-west.

17.5 A site plan with typical floor arrangements.

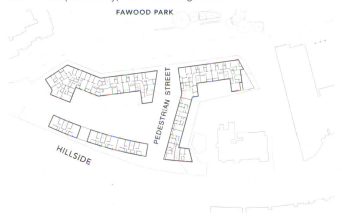

FAWOOD PARK

PEDESTRIAN STREET

HILLSIDE

17.6 Pedestrian street.

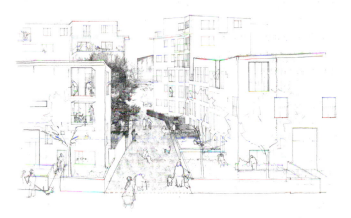

Perimeter Organisation and Permeability

Our scheme is a perimeter block, but is formed primarily by two linear blocks running east–west on the northern and southern edges of the site. These define between them a communal garden at the heart of the scheme. A new pedestrian street bisects the site, connecting the new and existing park. A nine-storey tower is proposed at the western end of the site (see Figure 17.4).

The design in the form of a perimeter block relates, in part, to the principle of 'defensible space', which has been adopted throughout the renewal of this previously troubled estate. The high-rise 1960s estate has, over the past ten years, been demolished and replaced by low-rise housing in perimeter blocks in a fine-grained network of

streets, and we have, broadly speaking, continued this logic. Just as importantly, the site forms the edge of three open spaces: the ecological park along an existing watercourse, the new Fawood Park, and the old park south of the high street. In our view, these loosely contained open spaces around the high street required a consistent frontage to be maintained to contribute to the clear definition of the open space and of the main street, Hillside. Fawood Park, to the north, is like a London square in its dimensions and planting, bordered by terraces of a certain height and formality.

The pedestrian street running north–south opens up a new visual and pedestrian link between the high street and Fawood Park, and between the distinct areas of North and South Stonebridge. As illustrated in

17.13 North terrace, with built corners.

17.14 Broken block with lower linking sections Somers Town, North London.

17.15 Cutting out the tight internal corner, Housing Den Haag, A. Siza.

17.16 Reverse external corner, Housing Den Haag, A. Siza.

consideration of the issues of privacy and of front and back within a development.

On Fawood Park, where the front is relatively quiet, the upper-level corner apartments have good aspect and privacy. At ground level, we have maisonettes on the corners with no bedrooms at street level or a raised ground floor, which gives some additional privacy to bedrooms facing the street. The privacy required across the internal corners is provided by locating staircases in this position or planning the apartments around the corner, as an L-shaped flat (see Figure 17.13).

Others have found different ways of manoeuvring the corner while trying to maintain some physical definition of the built blocks, by thinning or cutting away part of the block. The corners of the blocks in nineteenth-century Somers Town, north of Kings Cross in London, are formed from a pin-wheel plan of lapped blocks with a high one-storey wall on the building line where the blocks break away from the corner (see Figure 17.14). Alvaro Siza, in his 1980s social housing in Den Haag

17.17 A view from a living room overlooking new Fawood Park to the north.

17.18 Lightscape model.

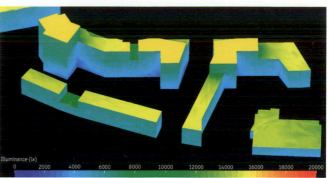

in the Netherlands, deals with corners of this urban block either by cutting out the tight internal corner or removing part of the external corner to form a reverse corner (see Figures 17.15 and 17.16).

Conclusion

A number of design solutions, which are too often considered unnecessary or uneconomic, have been made possible, or even inevitable, by conditions specific to this project. The social problems of the 1960s estate led to a determination on the part of the client to avoid quick-fix economies (deck or corridor access apartments), the failure of which can be devastatingly wasteful, and to arrive at a socially sustainable layout. These attitudes translated into support for the open perimeter block layout and the use of stair access throughout the design. Equally, the combination of the planning authority's housing quality guidelines and the dimensions of the site led to block depths much shallower than is common. A greater emphasis on the long term than the current housing market and political climate would generally permit has clearly benefited the project, as it would do others.

Our design responds to a number of fundamental challenges of contemporary city-making: security, density (driven both by land values and the sustainability agenda), and the specificity of climate and cultural traditions. Working between the paradigms of enclosed perimeter blocks and linear blocks of optimum orientation has enabled us to respond to these issues, reconciling high standards of environmental performance with the principles of street-based sociability (see Figure 17.17).

Postscript: Computational Daylight and Sunlight Evaluation

A three-dimensional model of the proposals was used to evaluate the distribution of daylight on all surfaces of the development. The output is a colour representation of each façade, shaded to indicate the amount of light it receives (see Figure 17.18). The results were used to define points which receive least daylight and sunlight, and which could then be subject to a more detailed examination.

Stereographs are a combined two-dimensional representation of the annual movement of the sun and the level of 'interruption' of the whole sky vault by adjacent buildings. The path of the sun for the whole year is marked out by a series of curved lines, labelled by month and hour. The shaded area indicates where the view of the sky from the test point is blocked. Where the sun path and the shaded area coincide, the sun is blocked at that point in time. The area blocked in a one-month strip represents the sunlight lost in that month. Repeating this process for each month gives the fraction of the total sunlight hours lost annually.

The results from the stereographs were compared to guidance documents to ensure the buildings achieved the recommended access to daylight and sunlight, and that they would cause no noticeable loss of light to adjoining existing buildings. This information was also used to evaluate minor reorientation of façades and adjustment internal flat layouts to achieve maximise internal daylight and sunlight levels.

Further reading

Anon. (2006) *Europan 8: European Results Book*. Editions EUROPAN.

18 'MADE IN STOCKWELL' AND DEPTFORD WHARVES

KATIE TONKINSON AND ADAM RITCHIE

DESIGN TEAM

Client	City & Provincial Properties plc
Architect	Hawkins\Brown
Services and Sustainability	Max Fordham LLP
Structural Engineer	Price & Myers
Planning Consultant	Savills Hepher Dixon
Traffic Consultant	WSP
Rights of Light	Schatunowski Brooks
Socio-Economics	Savills Research
Ecologist	CSa
Hydrologist	Halcrow
Archaeology	MoLAS
Historic Research	WHH Van Sickle
Contamination	WSP Environmental

Key Project Information: Made in Stockwell

Programme	Mixed-use
Site Area	1.2 ha
Dwellings per hectare	241
Habitable rooms per hectare	695

Key Project Information: Deptford Wharves

Programme	Mixed-use
Site Area	4.5 ha
Dwellings per hectare	229
Habitable rooms per hectare	671

Introduction

From an architectural perspective, we think of sustainable urban design as a moving target. We must constantly reassess our approach and pioneer new technologies to remain ahead of the field. A well-known, successful company often talks about 'the best' for their developments: 'the best sweet shop, the best pub and the best fish and chips'. In much the same way, our architecture must continue to better itself; to meet higher standards and to be more relevant in order to make tangible improvements to people's everyday lives. We try to reach beyond pure design values to develop a thoughtful architecture – engaging with social, political, economic, cultural and environmental agendas.

Recently, in the context of architectural practice and sustainability, the Greater London Authority and the Mayor of London have adopted an influential role. The Mayor has encouraged us all to reduce our carbon footprint, to cycle to work and to flush the toilet less. In 2004, he published 'Green light to clean power', in *The Mayor's Energy Strategy*[1] which requires major new developments to reduce their carbon emissions by generating energy on-site from renewable sources. It set out an approach to be lean, green and clean:

- Use Less Energy (be lean)
- Use Renewable Energy (be green)
- Supply Energy Efficiently (be clean)

This is all happening in the context of increased public awareness of sustainability. Renewable energy technologies are becoming more readily accessible. One can pop into a local home-store to pick up one's very own turbine or solar collector – decentralised energy at a truly domestic and tangible scale. Estate agents tell us that making our homes more energy-efficient, and making demonstrable green adaptations will add to their value. Politicians have attempted to gain control of the green agenda by 'green-washing' their houses with micro wind-turbines. Even the planning system in England has been simplified to allow householders to retrofit small-scale renewable technologies to their homes without planning consent.

The public's awareness is starting to be reflected in business attitudes. For example, there is mounting pressure on retailers to make London

18.7   View of the existing ground floor prior to work commencing on site.

18.8   View of typical compartmented commercial unit.

variety of end users. From an environmental perspective, the exposed-concrete soffits would help to keep the building temperature more stable, particularly in summer, in conjunction with a night-cooling ventilation strategy and supplemental comfort cooling on the hottest days.

Density

The accessibility of a site is determined by the time taken to walk to existing public transport nodes and is measured with a PTAL (Public Transport Accessibility Level) rating[2] (see Figure 18.1). *The London Plan*[3] recognises that sites with higher PTAL ratings can support higher residential densities, and therefore endorses the densification of well-connected, urban, brownfield sites.

The site density for this PTAL 4 site (241 dwellings per hectare) was in line with the Mayor's *London Plan* guidelines and was supported by much-enhanced amenity. The client had committed to high quality architectural design, as well as (through a Section 106 Agreement – see Glossary) making contributions towards new social 'infrastructure' such as schools, healthcare, and public transport improvements.

Urban design and architecture

The site is steeped in a history of breweries and bottling plants. Hence the proposal to preserve a part of Stockwell's heritage in part of the

18.9   View of typical open plan floor.

building called The Bottle Store itself would create a real sense of place and a link with the past.

The surrounding context is of greatly contrasting scales and styles, but all generally domestic in use. There are tight-knit terraced houses to the west, local authority slab blocks to the north, point blocks to the east and west and to the south is the Stockwell Green Conservation Area with its nineteenth-century houses. A contextual approach to the

18.10 View of main scheme frontage onto Stockwell Green.

architectural design and chosen palette of materials was taken to ensure an appropriate and sensitive response. For example, glazed bricks were proposed to 'anchor' the base of the scheme and act as a unifying feature. Further datums were established to create a vertical urban grain through a change in format and scale of the cladding to the upper floors. In addition, the proportions of windows, recessed terraces, staggered joints, and the colour of the ceramic rainscreen all have reference to the surrounding architecture (see Figure 18.10).

The design prioritises good-quality public realm by removing the existing boundary wall along Stockwell Green, and realigning the south elevation to frame the front of St. Andrew's Church. The reinstatement of a building frontage along Lingham Street was designed to create a meaningful urban edge and an overlooked street (see Figure 18.11).

Two principal streets have been established. The first provides controlled vehicular access to the commercial uses while the second

18.11 Site plan.

18.15 Site plan showing building uses.

18.16 New Wharves axonometric.

The mixed-use allocation in the emerging Local Development Framework suggests that the site should deliver a significant proportion of new dwellings but also requires employment-generating uses to create a balanced community. The site is largely without existing context. We have traced historic maps in order to look at previous development and to understand the heritage of the site. The boundaries of the old wharves offered the best clue and have helped us to establish a new urban grain. Each of the new wharves (see Figure 18.16) is functionally, formally and materially distinct, recalling the eclectic nature of the original wharf buildings. The articulation of built form within the new wharves will abstract the sense of solidity, mass and protective enclosure offered by traditional wharves to create a new and relevant typology. Each new wharf will work to a mixed-use programme, delivering a diversity of residential types and tenures as well as non-residential uses (see Table 18.3).

Urban design principles

The Grand Surrey Canal still leaves a strong imprint in the site and its neighbouring context. The route of the old water body is revisited as a new heart for the entire development in the form of a twenty-first-century wharf (see Figure 18.17). This impressively scaled body of water will provide physical and visual amenity and environmental benefits. It has potential as a setting for new bars, restaurants and waterside homes, a promenade, a centre for ecology as well as a lido and rowing course. It will also offer opportunities for storing heat and 'coolth' for the buildings and for dealing with a 1 in 1,000 year storm-event. The water body links all of the new wharves and will provide a means of orientation for pedestrian and vehicular traffic around and across the site (see Figure 18.18).

TABLE 18.3

'Deptford Wharves' Key Project Data			
Land use	Gross area (m²)	Residential units	Habitable rooms
Non Residential			
Business	11,327	/	/
Community	1,971	/	/
Hospitality and retail	2,488	/	/
Leisure	846	/	/
Flexible	5,994		
Residential			
1-bed apartment		341	682
2-bed apartment		490	1,470
3-bed apartment		150	600
4-bed apartment		59	295
TOTAL	122,136	1,040	3,047

18.17 Urban design concept – water body.

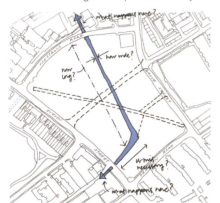

18.18 View of scale model – water body.

18.19 Urban design concept – diagonal axis.

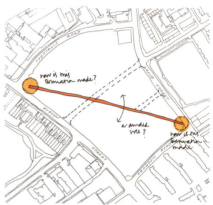

Water across the site – an overview. ▲

It reinstates a historical feature of the site. It is a bold gesture that could become a focus or 'gift' to the site. It could provide much needed amenity to the neighbourhood. By reinstating the whole canal the site is divided into further small plots. What would its reinstatement mean? Is it a nostalgic gesture without meaning for the 21st Century? How would it 'join up' at the side of the site? Could recreate a more relevant and fitting body of water that provides amenity / focus / sustainability / leisure – could it act as a 'path' from Deptford Park to Convoys Wharf. What scale does the water need to be to suit its new purpose? Does it need to look to the past?

Connection across the site - an overview. ▲

It creates a direct, visual link between Convoys Wharf and Deptford Park. It is a bold gesture that seems to be at odds with the existing urban grain. It 'divides' the site into two triangular plots. What does it offer to the surrounding streetscape? It seems like an aggressive gesture - 'I need to get from A to B in the most direct route possible, regardless of context'. It feels very out of place and not connected to this part of Deptford - it divides rather than joins. Are there other ways that we can achieve the same connection?

The end points of this axis define the gateways to our site and create landmark opportunities, both at the junction with Evelyn Street and the proposed Convoys Wharf site (see Figure 18.19). The diagonal axis is marked with tall buildings and associated areas of new public realm. These spaces will act as social gathering points for users of the site and important interfaces between the development and the surrounding context (see Figures 18.20 and 18.21).

A mixed-use brief

The site is large enough to accommodate a mix of housing types (see Figures 18.22–8.24). The urban framework that has gradually evolved focuses on the quality of accommodation and environment and is not an example of a blanket density approach. We have therefore been able to create:

- flats in towers with superb views across London;
- traditional street pattern with family homes and private gardens;
- courtyard development with communal amenity;
- urban lofts set above retail and studio units;
- core community clusters;
- individual blocks forming the fourth elevation to Pepys Park.

The capacity of the site to accommodate non-residential floor space has been tested by socio-economic consultants with an emphasis upon the 'deliverability' of new jobs, retail uses and community infrastructure, which is critical to the economic and social sustainability of large-scale regeneration schemes.

18.20 View of scale model – landmark opportunities

18.21 View of scale model – landmark opportunities.

18.26 Potential routes for connection to SELCHP.

18.27 Diagram to show variation in wind speed at height.

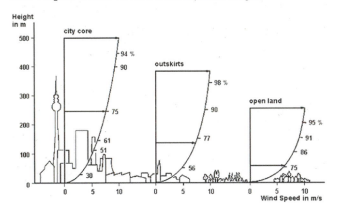

to look at a site's characteristics to understand risks and develop solutions to mitigate against these. The philosophy is to exceed regulatory requirements and define best practice through a design-led approach. The risk of flooding has been assessed in accordance with 'Planning Policy Statement 25'.[7] Parts of the site sit within a 1 in 1,000-year flood-risk zone, which considers, among other simultaneous catastrophes, a scenario where the River Thames barrier is not operational. The masterplanning process has sought to manage the residual risk by making site levels below a certain datum resilient to flooding. For example, the design ensures that vulnerable uses such as habitable

rooms, community uses and electrical substations, as well as services penetrations and car park entrances, are all sited outside of these zones.

The Sustainable Urban Drainage Strategy (SUDS) includes areas of soft landscape and green roof space to slow surface water run-off, with further attenuation provided by spare capacity within the water body during storm events.

The latest forecast

The masterplan forecasts that the regeneration of this urban block will deliver around 1,000 new homes and 1,200 new jobs over the next seven years. This has helped the London Borough of Lewisham prepare their trajectory of delivery of housing and employment over a 15-year period. As part of the planning process upon which we are about to embark, we will look at new models in our approach to design at the planning stage to add diversity and richness. It is our intention to form a design panel and to use this as a mechanism for collaboration with other architects and artists. The panel will explore creative concepts, test ideas and develop detailed design proposals for specific areas of the site. The end result (see Figure 18.28) will be an eclectic new neighbourhood, rooted in the common aim which is the creation of a high-quality environment through sensitive place making.

18.28 The vision - rendered axonometric.

Further reading

Commission for Architecture and the Built Environment (2000) *By Design: Urban Design in the Planning System: Towards Better Practice*. London: CABE. Available: http://www.cabe.org.uk/AssetLibrary/1818.pdf

Commission for Architecture and the Built Environment (2003) *The Use of Urban Design Codes: Building Sustainable Communities*. London: CABE. Available: http://www.cabe.org.uk/AssetLibrary/2178.pdf

Commission for Architecture and the Built Environment (2004a) *Creating Successful Masterplans: A Guide for Clients*. London: CABE. Available: http://www.cabe.org.uk/AssetLibrary/4027.pdf

Commission for Architecture and the Built Environment (2004b) *Design Reviewed Masterplans: Lessons Learnt from Projects Reviewed by CABE's Expert Design Panel*. London: CABE. Available: http://www.cabe.org.uk/AssetLibrary/2160.pdf

(All websites accessed 2 February 2008.)

DESIGN TEAM

Client	Millennium SEFC Properties Ltd.
Architect	Gomberoff Bell Lyon Architects
	Merrick Architecture
	Borowski Lintott Sakumoto Fligg Limited
	Lawrence Doyle Young & Wright Architects Inc.
	Nick Milkovich Architects Inc.
	Robert Ciccozzi Architecture Inc.
	Walter Francl Architect Inc.
Green Building Consultant	Recollective Consulting
Landscape Architect	Durante Kreuk Ltd.
Mechanical Engineer	Cobalt Engineering
Structural Engineer	Glotman Simpson

Key Project Information

Programme	Mixed-use
Site Area	7 ha
Dwellings per hectare	157

Introduction

Vancouver's Southeast False Creek (SEFC) is a 32-hectare former industrial brownfield site being redeveloped as a 'model' sustainable community. The first phase of the development, a 7-hectare site known as Millennium Water, has been designated as the Athletes' Village for the 2010 Winter Olympic Games being held in Vancouver. As such, it must be completed by October 2009, while the remainder of the site will be redeveloped over the course of the subsequent decade. This chapter describes the evolution of the vision for the area, and the phased process that will transform the site from industrial yard to Athletes' Village, and finally to a waterfront community based on principles of environmental, social and economic equity.

19.1 Aerial photo of Vancouver City with SEFC site highlighted.

Vancouver's Urban Context

Over the past decade, Vancouver's waterfront has been rapidly redeveloped. The city's present-day skyline is awash with high-rise residential towers (up to 48 storeys), which, along with notions of density and liveability, have become synonymous with Vancouver's urban form, distinguishing it from the typical sprawling North American city that encroaches endlessly on its surrounding region. High density at the city's centre is the result both of its geographical location – the ocean and mountains being natural boundaries – and of the vision of local developers and planning officials. The trend in Vancouver to build upward instead of outward has given rise to the term 'Vancouverism', which has become synonymous with hyper-dense, mostly residential 'downtown' urban centres (see Figure 19.1).

Another concept associated with development in Vancouver is Eco-Density.[1] This term relates to a planning initiative launched in 2006 by

19.2   The SEFC masterplan.

Master Plan

the City of Vancouver that aims to create greater density throughout the city in a way that reduces environmental impact, ensures the necessary physical and social amenities, and supports new and different housing types as a way to promote affordability. The whole SEFC development is part of this initiative, being a medium-density mixed-use mixed-income development, and is situated in a prime waterfront location across the sea-inlet from downtown Vancouver (see Figure 19.2). The site required extensive environmental remediation to remove contamination, the legacy of years of industrial activities, which included sawmills, foundries, shipbuilding, metalworking and salt distribution. SEFC is the last remaining large tract of undeveloped waterfront property close to Vancouver's city centre, and Millennium Water has been dubbed 'Vancouver's last waterfront community'; its prime location is arousing considerable interest from investors.

Planning Process and Chronology

The first structural foundations for Millennium Water were poured in the spring of 2007, marking a milestone in the long redevelopment process. In 1991, the City of Vancouver directed that SEFC be redeveloped as a residential community which would be a model of sustainable urban design. The City held a series of consultations, at which the public was invited to contribute its views to the proposed future

development of the site. Following the consultation, the SEFC Policy Statement was drafted, in which environmental, social, and economic aspects of building a sustainable community were addressed. The Policy Statement was subject to formal public review before being adopted by City Council in 1999.

Based on the outcome of the public review, the City of Vancouver put together the Official Development Plan (ODP) for SEFC, which was adopted as a bylaw in July 2005. The focus of the Plan was the development of a complete community that would serve as a learning experience for the application of sustainability principles to large-scale neighbourhood design. According to the ODP vision, the area will be transformed into a community 'where people live, work, play and learn in a neighbourhood that has been designed to maintain and balance the highest possible levels of social equity, liveability, ecological health and economic prosperity'.[2]

The ODP described general land-use parameters and regulations under which the project could proceed, and mandated a set of environmental standards to govern the site's redevelopment. This included a Green Building Strategy[3] with specific design principles for form and landscaping (see Figures 19.3 and 19.4), and targets for urban agriculture,

19.3   The ODP parameters for building heights.

19.4   The ODP parameters for land use and landscape.

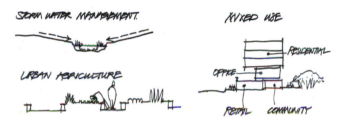

water and energy efficiency, alternative transportation, and waste management.

Millennium Water: Design Concept
Housing and amenities

Millennium Water will offer 130,000m² of commercial and residential space in low- to mid-rise buildings up to a maximum of 12 storeys. After the Winter Olympics, the neighbourhood's 1,100 dwellings will be converted to permanent residential housing, ranging from studios and one-bedroom suites to family-oriented accommodation. Approximately 730 of the dwellings at Millennium Water are being sold as market housing, 120 will be rental housing, and the remaining 250 will be affordable (subsidised) housing.

By 2020, the redevelopment of Southeast False Creek will be complete and its projected 7,200 residential dwellings are expected to house between 12,000 and 16,000 people (approximately 225 dwellings per hectare). The neighbourhood's approximately 560,000m² of development will include a community centre, a non-motorised boating facility, three to five licensed childcare facilities, an elementary school, an inter-faith spiritual centre, five restored heritage buildings and 10 hectares of parkland.

Canada's low carbon energy supply

Canada has an abundance of natural resources. To give but one example, 59 per cent of national electricity demand is met from hydro-electric plant, and in British Columbia (BC), in 2005, hydroelectric plant generated as much as 94 per cent of the regional total. One consequence of this is that the need for carbon reductions from the efficient use of electricity has been less pressing in Canada, and particularly in BC, essentially because of its much lower carbon-intensity at 0.22 kgCO$_2$/kWh[4], compared with approximately 0.42 kgCO$_2$/kWh in the UK. This fundamentally affects the judgement as regards the comparative merits of using electricity versus, say, natural gas, to heat buildings. In Canada, the 'drivers' for carbon reductions are often found to have tangible air-quality, public health and cost benefits rather than being directly linked to climate change mitigation. It will surprise many to learn that, while it is recognised that increasing efficiency has an important role to play, Canadian municipalities do not have the power to impose energy efficiency upon development in the way that Building Regulations can in the UK. In Canada this type of legislation is handled at the provincial level, not federally. On 15 April 2008, BC introduced Bill 27 which requires local governments (municipalities) to incorporate greenhouse gas emissions targets into their community plans and growth strategies.

Passive design strategies

In order to minimise energy demand in buildings, passive design strategies were prioritised over mechanical systems as a means of improving energy efficiency. Energy efficiency is optimised through the construction of high-performance envelopes. Walls have a U-value of 0.35 W/m²K (R-15) and roofs a U-value 0.19 W/m²K (R-30) to reduce energy loss and control heat gain, while protecting the building from deterioration due to changeable climatic conditions. Unusually for Vancouver, façades respond to their specific orientation. Many recently built condominium developments feature floor-to-ceiling, fully glazed façades in response to the consumer demand for the best possible view. And yet, occupants then complain of temperature extremes, often drawing their blinds most of the summer to keep the sun out, and to keep the heat from escaping in winter. The Millennium Water team favoured a 70:30 glass to solid wall ratio in an effort to allow both views and sunlight, while respecting the commitment to energy efficiency. Stairwell glazing is designed to bring natural light through the stairwell and into the corridors, as opposed to conventional fire escape stairs that are normally enclosed. The corridors are also widened to

19.5   Sketch design for optimisation of natural lighting.

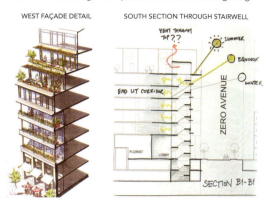

19.6   'Capillary' heating installation in the ceilings.

19.7   Green roofs with Olympic motifs.

encourage a more pleasant indoor experience, improve circulation, and decrease elevator use. Ventilation shafts, 'through' apartments and external corridors encourage natural ventilation, providing fresh air for occupants. Heat gain is controlled through the use of shading devices and deep balcony overhangs (see Figure 19.5).

Heating and cooling

Millennium Water will use a Neighbourhood Energy Utility (NEU) to distribute heat recovered from an adjacent sewer system. The system uses electrically-driven heat pumps to upgrade low-grade heat to high-temperature water (with an average coefficient of performance of 3 [see Glossary]), which is then distributed to buildings throughout the site. It will be the first use of this technology in North America (one of only three similar applications worldwide). The NEU will supply the majority of heating requirements for buildings and will rely on gas-fired boilers during peak load on the coldest days of the year. Within each building heat is distributed in what will be North America's largest radiant 'capillary' heating and cooling installation, comprising narrow-bore pipework coils mounted above the ceiling (see Figure 19.6). Capillary heating and cooling was preferred by the design team as it provides the added benefit of improved indoor air quality due to a reduction in the airborne dust and allergens often associated with turbulent airflows created by conventional mechanical ventilation systems.

Water and landscape

The landscape at Millennium Water is being designed to thrive without the need for potable water for irrigation, to manage stormwater, to enhance native habitat, and to provide opportunities for gardening. All buildings will have a minimum of 50 per cent green roof coverage, with plantings arranged into motifs to celebrate the Olympic Games theme (see Figure 19.7). Urban agriculture is incorporated into the landscape design, the intention being to create opportunities for on-site food production and distribution.

On average, Canadians use approximately 340 litres of potable water per person per day, which is roughly twice the per capita consumption in the UK. While Canada has no regulation controlling WC flush volumes or appliance flow-rates, dual-flush (6 L/3 L) cisterns, low-flow taps (3.8–5.7 L/min) and showerheads (5.7–7.6 L/min) have been specified throughout the project. As a result, the development aims to reduce the use of potable water by at least 30 per cent of conventional levels.

Stormwater run-off will be reduced by 25 per cent through a site-wide system of green roofs, swales and retention ponds. Rainwater is harvested from roofs and stored in underground tanks, treated, and then circulated around the building for irrigation and toilet flushing. Cooling ponds containing collected rainwater will contribute to passive design strategies through evaporative cooling (see Figures 19.8 and 19.9).

Green Buildings: Leadership in Energy and Environmental Design (LEED™)

All buildings at Millennium Water are being designed to a LEED™ Gold green building standard. The developer, through an agreement with the City of Vancouver, was granted higher development density in return for a commitment to achieve LEED™ Gold certification, thereby exceeding the ODP requirement of a LEED™ Silver rating. The LEED™ program is the foremost green building certification system in North America. LEED™ is a voluntary rating system for developing high-performance, sustainable buildings. Buildings are rated according to a set of criteria which determine the level of certification, ranging from Certified, Silver, and Gold to Platinum.

The system was developed by the United States Green Building Council and the number of LEED™ certified projects has grown exponentially

19.8   Rainwater harvesting diagram.

19.9   Potential effects of cooling pond.

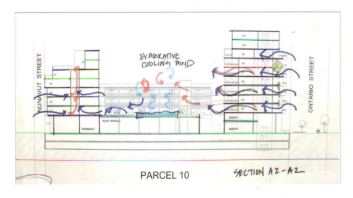

since the program's inception in 2000.[5] LEED™ has expanded to address new construction, major renovations, commercial interiors, 'shell and core', operations and maintenance, homes, neighbourhoods, retail, campuses, schools, healthcare facilities, laboratories and lodging.

Of particular interest to the urban design community is LEED™ for Neighbourhood Development (LEED-ND), which began as a pilot program in 2007.[6] LEED-ND integrates the principles of Smart Growth,[7] New Urbanism,[8] as well as environmental building design, into a new standard for sustainable neighbourhood design. The program was conceived as a joint venture of the Congress for the New Urbanism, the US Green Building Council, and the US Natural Resources Defense

19.10
(a) Finished apartment.

(b) 'Overlay' fit-out.

Council. The SEFC development is participating in the pilot study along with roughly 250 other developments across Canada and the US. The study will evaluate neighbourhood development against a number of criteria under the following categories:

- 'Smart' Location and Linkage/Connectivity;
- Neighbourhood Pattern and Design;
- Green Construction and Technology;
- Innovation and Design Process.

The Athletes' Village

Millennium Water will house approximately 2,800 athletes for the duration of the Winter Olympic Games. The project's design team was responsible for meeting the requirements of the Olympic Village 'overlay', an additional specification set by Vancouver's Olympic Organising Committee (VANOC), which applies to a six-month 'exclusive-use period' around the event. The overlay includes additional provision for temporary housing, dining, fitness, health care facilities and security.

Adaptability of design was paramount for the Olympic Village, since buildings had to meet VANOC's requirements in addition to the sometimes conflicting conditions of the ODP. The design team had to find flexible solutions for creating buildings that would serve two distinct purposes: accommodating the event, and also after the event, leaving a useful legacy. Since the dwellings will be pre-sold and fully fitted out

prior to VANOC's exclusive use period (beginning October 2009), all the interior furnishings and appliances will be in place when the athletes move in. It was therefore necessary to make provisions for temporary protection, including sealing off kitchens and installing temporary floor coverings to preserve hardwood flooring.

The team is exploring various environmentally responsible design strategies to this end, and one example is the option of installing carpet tiles or rubber floor tiles throughout the apartments during the overlay period. Floor tiles are the preferred environmental option since many contain high recycled content, they produce less waste when fitted to diverse floor areas, and, because tiles are modular, they can be replaced piecemeal. The team is also investigating second-hand markets for the floor tiles after the Games.

A temporary panelling system will be installed to protect kitchen surfaces and prevent access to the in-built fixtures. An innovative approach being explored is to print original artwork on aluminium panels (see Figures 19.10a–b). The design team is working with a local artist who is commissioning a number of First Nations artists to collaborate on the project, with the hope of creating limited-edition motifs that celebrate the spirit of the Olympics while also evoking the traditions of Canada's native communities. Panels will be decorated and installed in the kitchens for the duration of the Olympic Village occupancy, after which time they will be cut to size and mounted in recycled wood frames for sale as original, limited dition artwork.

Building Durability and Adaptability

Millennium Water is being built to meet criteria set by the SAFER Home™ Certification Program, a home building standard that provides safety, comfort and adaptability for people of varying ages and abilities, roughly equivalent to the UK's 'Lifetime Homes' criteria. This voluntary standard improves accessibility for people with diverse needs and provides the opportunity for 'aging-in-place'. SAFER Home™ is linked to the principles of Universal Design[9] (Design for All), allowing homes to be used by as many people as possible, without adaptation or specialised design.

The SAFER Home™ program supports sustainability in communities. Canada, like many other countries in the developed world, is experiencing an unprecedented demographic shift; people are living longer than at any other time in human history. By the year 2030, 75 per cent of Canadians will be over the age of 65; each with a variety of physical abilities and limitations. While the social effect of this shift is of obvious significance, the impact on the environment is itself considerable. The Canada Mortgage and Housing Corporation estimates that, in order to keep up with the needs of an aging market, 50,000 homes per year in Canada will require renovation, retrofit or rebuilding. This circumstance would entail a substantial strain on resources; however, it is one that is preventable as long as the design community starts planning today for the needs of tomorrow – future-proofing by design.

Net-Zero Housing

The concept

In Canada, the term 'net-zero' is used to describe buildings that are designed to produce as much energy as they consume on an annual basis. Millennium Water will feature Canada's first net-zero multi-unit residential building (Figure 19.11). The design team is working with the City of Vancouver and Canada Mortgage and Housing Corporation to support this project. The proposed building is a 68-unit social-housing project for seniors. There will be eight street-level townhouses, and the remainder of the units will be located above in a five-storey configuration with exterior access ways. The building will include 83m² of amenity space and extensive roof gardens that will be accessible to the public.

Objectives

Net-zero housing is a design approach that integrates five key principles of sustainable design: Health, Energy, Resources, Environment

19.11 The net-zero site at Millennium Water.

and Affordability. The Millennium Water net-zero project will be a test-bed for the promotion of practical, cost-effective energy efficiency and on-site energy production measures in a way that is transferable to future projects. The aim is to reduce environmental impact, target net-zero energy and greenhouse-gas emissions, and increase liveability, while at the same time trying to work with a conventional project budget.

Design strategies

The net-zero building required an intensive and integrated design process in order to meet its objectives. The building will substantially reduce energy consumption through the application of advanced building technologies and passive-design techniques. Enhanced envelope design including triple-glazed windows, walls with a U-value of 0.28 W/m²K (R-20) and roofs with a U-value 0.19 W/m²K (R-30), will regulate the flow of energy between the building's interior and exterior. Passive design minimises the need for mechanical heating and eliminates mechanical cooling. The building is equipped with mechanically-assisted natural ventilation (with the mechanical system activated only when necessary). As with the whole development, appliances and plumbing fixtures are specified to reduce energy and water consumption.

In conjunction with its reduced energy load requirement, the building will rely on renewable energy systems to provide its own supply of clean, 'green' power. It is proposed that the heat loads will be met

19.12 Shadowing study for a roof-top.

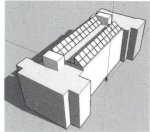
45° March 21 noon

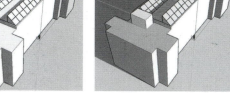
45° December 21 noon

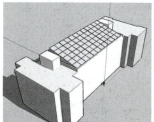
15° March 21 noon

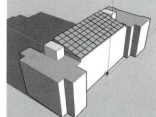
15° December 21 noon

19.13 Estimates of energy balance during the year.

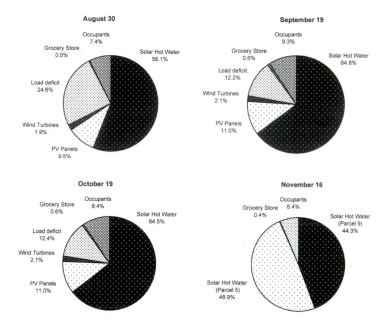

using waste heat from an adjoining supermarket. For the remaining energy requirements, the project team undertook considerable research into renewable energy systems, looking at a range of technologies, local suppliers, efficiencies and cost, microclimate studies, and effective installation options and techniques (Figure 19.12). Throughout the design process, the design team kept an ongoing energy balance sheet, estimating building energy loads and exploring the most efficient combination of energy sources to offset the expected demand (see Figure 19.13). One combination specified the use of roof-mounted evacuated-tube solar-thermal collectors, a photovoltaic array on the roof of an adjoining building, and wind turbines located on nearby public lands on the waterfront.

Monitoring and evaluation

Following regular occupancy, building energy performance will be extensively monitored and documented in order to evaluate the success of the project. The information will be collected and publicly disseminated as a case study to inform future developments.

Building occupants will be educated about the building's systems and design so that they are aware of the goals for the building as well as how their individual choices can influence the building's performance. Suites will include metering devices that provide feedback on per unit energy consumption as well as the associated costs. Awareness programs as well as metering devices within dwellings can persuade users to reduce their consumption rates by up to 20 per cent.[10]

Conclusion

The vision for Southeast False Creek and Millennium Water required a level of commitment to sustainable urban design that is unprecedented on this scale in Vancouver. Meeting this commitment presented a considerable challenge for the design team, one that was made more acute by the strict deadline imposed by the timeframe of the Olympic Village overlay. In order to rise to the challenge, the design team had to make a concerted effort not only to meet established targets, but also to approach the design process from the perspective of sustainability from the earliest stages of concept design.

19.14 Aerial view of site construction January 2008.

The integrated design approach was successful and produced two notable results. First, it established strategies for meeting sustainability targets that were achieved (and some exceeded), and, second, team members, regardless of their level of expertise in sustainability, all learned a great deal from the experience about the interplay between buildings, energy systems and the environment, and, in addition, that sustainable design means 'smart' design. Once the project is completed, it is hoped that the neighbourhood will continue to be a source of learning and inspiration to designers, to the City of Vancouver and to its residents (see Figures 19.14 and 19.15).

19.15 Millennium Water artist's impression.

APPENDIX A
SOLAR ENERGY, TEMPERATURE AND PHOTOVOLTAICS

Solar data

As can be seen from Figure A.1, annual irradiation is similar in much of northern Europe (sometimes referred to poetically as 'the cloudy North').

A.1   Solar irradiation over Europe (kWh/m²y).[1]

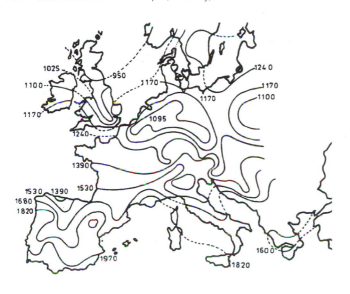

Figure A.2 shows the pattern of the sun's movement across the sky and Table A.1 gives data for a latitude of 52°N.

A.2   Solar paths.

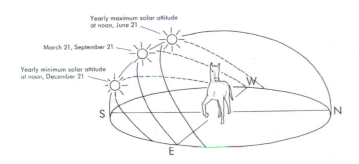

TABLE A.1

Approximate solar altitudes and azimuths at 52°N[2]		
Date and time	Altitude (degrees)	Azimuth (degrees)
21 December		
09.00	5	139
12.00	15	180
15.00	5	221
21 March and 21 September		
08.00	18	114
12.00	38	180
16.00	18	246
21 June		
08.00	37	98
12.00	62	180
16.00	37	262

Temperature data

Figure A.3a gives air and ground temperatures at Falmouth in 1994[3] and Figure A.3b gives air temperatures on a warm day (10 July 1994) in Garston, north of London.

A.3   (a) Falmouth; (b) Garston, 10 July 1994.

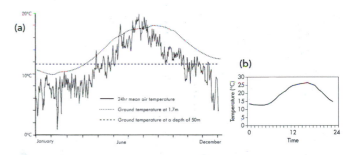

Photovoltaics

PV systems convert solar radiation into electricity. They are not to be confused with solar thermal panels, which use the sun's energy to heat water (or air) for water and space heating.

The most common PV devices at present are based on silicon. When they are exposed to the sun, direct current (d.c.) flows as shown in Figure A.4. PVs respond to both direct and diffuse radiation (see

A.4   Diagram of PV principle.

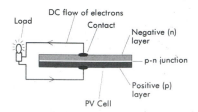

A.5   Direct and diffuse radiation.

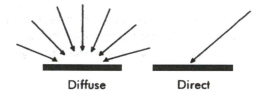

Figure A.5) and their output increases with increasing sunshine or, more technically, irradiance.

Common PVs available are monocrystalline silicon, polycrystalline silicon, thin-film silicon. Hybrids also exist. A typical crystalline cell might be 100 x 100mm. Cells are combined to form modules.

Table A.2 shows a number of current different types of PV cell and their approximate efficiencies.

TABLE A.2

PV efficiencies[4,5]				
	Thin film	Polycrystalline	Monocrystalline	Hybrid (i)
Module efficiency	5–7%	12–14%	13–15%	16–17%
Area needed per kWp	15.5m²	8m²	7m²	6–6.5m²
Annual energy generated	50–52 kWh/m²	100 kWh/m²	107 kWh/m²	139–150 kWh/m²

Note:
i.   'Hybrid' PV combines both monocrystalline and thin-film silicon to produce cells with the best features of both technologies.
ii.   for south-facing system, 30° tilt in the UK.

Higher efficiencies – of over 30 per cent in some cases – are being achieved using multilayered structures. New materials such as copper indium diselenide (CIS) are being investigated and work is also under way on the use of dye-sensitised solar cells and organic films.

It is also useful to keep efficiencies in perspective. A tree (see Figure A.6) relies on photosynthesis, a process that has been functioning in seed plants for over 100,000,000 years and only converts 0.5–1.5 per cent of the absorbed light into chemical energy.

A.6   A Cambridge tree, near an array of seventeenth-century solar collectors (i.e. windows).

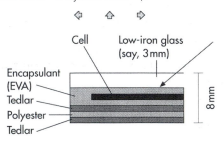

More recently, the UK National Grid has proved only 25–30 per cent efficient in providing us with electricity from fossil fuels.

Crystalline silicon cells consist of p-type and n-type silicon and electrical contacts as shown schematically in Figure A.4. The cells, which are of low voltage, are joined in series to form a module of a

A.7   Typical module construction (glass/EVA/Tedlar™/Polyester/Tedlar™).

higher, more useful voltage. Figure A.7 shows one of many ways of building in PVs.

Modules electrically connected together in series are often referred to as a string, and a group of connected strings as an array. An array is also a generic term for any grouping of modules connected in series and/or parallel. Power from the array (see Figure A.8) goes to a Power Conditioning Unit (PCU), which converts the electrical output from the PV array into a suitable form for the building. The a.c. output from the PCU goes to a distribution board in the building or to the grid if supply exceeds demand.

A.8   Schematic of a typical grid-connected PV system.

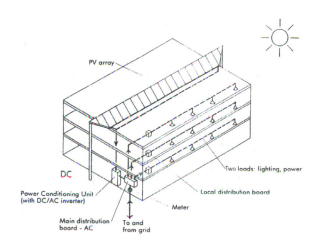

How much energy do PV systems produce? The output from building-integrated PV installations is the output of the PV array less the losses in the rest of the system. The output from the array will depend on:

- the daily variation due to the rotation of the earth and the seasonal one (due to the orientation of the Earth's axis and the movement of the Earth about the sun);

- location, i.e. the solar radiation available at the site;

- tilt (see Figure A.9);

- azimuth, i.e. orientation with respect to due south (see Figure A.9);

- shadowing;

- temperature.

A.9   Tilt and azimuth.

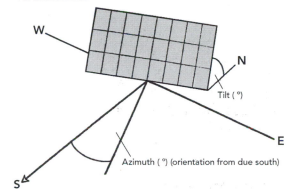

A rule of thumb for maximum annual output is that the optimal azimuth is due south and the optimum tilt is the latitude minus 20° but considerable choice is possible around this 100 per cent point (see Figure A.10).

A.10   Yearly irradiation map for London.

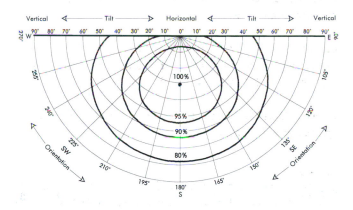

100% corresponds to the tilt and orientation which gives the maximum total annual solar radiation (1,045kWh/m²/y on a surface oriented due south at a tilt of 31°) on a fixed surface in London (51°36' N, 0°03'W)

Table A.2 shows the approximate outputs from different PV materials in London with an azimuth of due south and a tilt of 30°.

For comparison, Table A.3 gives the output of a number of different 50m² arrays.

TABLE A.3

Comparison of array outputs (MWh/y) (London data; unshaded arrays)						
Position	**Thin film silicon**			**Monocrystalline silicon**		
	45° east of south	south	15° west of south	45° east of south	south	15° west south
1. Vertical wall	2.00	2.15	2.13	3.50	3.75	3.72
2. Roof 30°	2.96	3.09	3.08	5.18	5.41	5.38
3. Roof 45°	2.86	3.03	3.01	5.00	5.30	5.26

In urban situations overshadowing can be a key issue. Figure A.11 shows a loss of output due to (continuous strips of) neighbouring buildings.

Potential of a site for photovoltaics

The use of a site's potential for PVs can be evaluated quantitatively. A very simple starting point is to examine the orientation and angle of the roofs and a figure corresponding to the annual solar irradiation of the site. Thus, for example, we may examine the roofs indicated on the housing development illustrated in Figure A.12, a truncated form of Parkmount, transplanted to London.

The amount of solar radiation (expressed as a percentage of the maximum for an ideally sited roof) is determined by using the yearly irradiation map for London (see Figure A.10). Maps such as this exist for a variety of locations. A figure (which may be called the Index of Solar Utilisation) can then be derived using the roof areas and their percentage of solar radiation (Table A.4):

TABLE A.4

The index of solar utilisation				
Roof	**Area (m²)**	**Orientation (° from north)**	**Tilt (° from horizontal)**	**Solar radiation (% of maximum)**
1	86	196	15	96
2	86	196	15	96
3	86	189	15	96
4	86	189	15	96
5	86	183	15	97

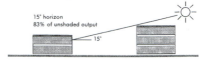

A.11 Shading effects by neighbouring buildings.

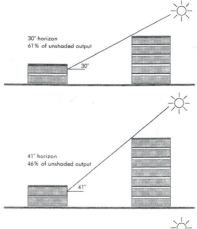

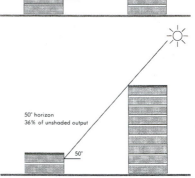

For the roofs in Figure A.12:

Index of Solar Utilisation

$$= \frac{(86 \times 0.96) + (86 \times 0.96) + (86 \times 0.96) + (86 \times 0.96) + (86 \times 0.97)}{430}$$

$$= 0.96$$

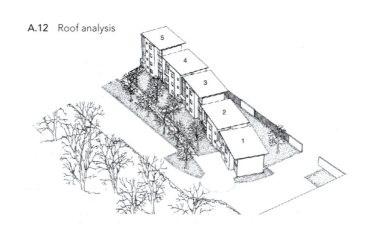

A.12 Roof analysis

APPENDIX B
WIND AND WATER

Wind

Wind energy

Figure B.1 shows the energy in the wind in the UK at a height of 10m in open countryside;[1] the units are GJ/m²/y. Since 1GJ = 278kWh, 3GJ = 834kWh and we see that this is close to the amount of solar radiation falling on a horizontal surface in London (see Appendix A).

Wind turbines

Wind specialists are familiar with the well-known Betz equation:

$$P = 0.645 (A \times V^3)$$

Where P is the power an ideal wind turbine can extract from the wind in kW. A is the swept area of the turbine in m² (i.e. the area within the shape formed by the blades as they rotate, thus, for a horizontal axis machine this would be the circle described by the blades), and V is the wind speed in m/s.

Aerodynamic, mechanical and electrical losses in real machines are likely to reduce this by one-third.[2]

The advantages and disadvantages of different turbines are given in Table B.1.

B.1   Energy in the wind

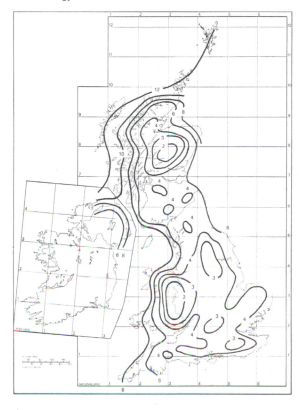

TABLE B.1

Comparison of axis orientation for small-scale turbines[3]			
Type	**Status**	**Remarks**	**Some examples**
Horizontal axis			
Upwind, lift	Large series, proven product	Widely used, mainly in open fields	Inclin, Aerocraft, Bergey, Vergnet, Lagerwey
Downwind, lift	Proven product	Mainly in smaller power ranges, also for open fields; building integration example	Proven
Vertical axis			
Savonius, drag	Proven product	Generally very silent and reliable, storm resistant, low efficency	Windside, Shield's Jaspira turbine (GTi1), Quiet Revolution
Darrieus, lift	Small series	Several subtypes exist, often as prototypes, simple construction, fair efficency; noise and vibration still to be covered	
Combined lift and drag	Prototypes	Simple construction, no external start up needed, low-noise, reliable	Globuan, Solavent
Large turbines	Small series	Low-noise, reliable	AES

Pollutant levels in cities will depend on background levels and local effects, which can be greatly influenced by urban form and the pattern of winds sweeping through the city. Solar radiation will enter areas at different times and will change the pollutant mix.

There will be significant variation with the contaminant studied and generalisation is difficult. Figure C.1 shows NO_2 concentrations in a street canyon in London.[6]

C.1 NO_2 concentration in a London street canyon.

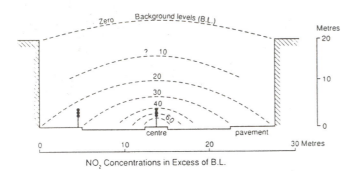

Trees have a positive effect on air pollution as they are capable of intercepting and absorbing CO, NO_X, O_3, as well as particulates under ten microns (also known as PM_{10}). Absorption rates will vary with background pollution levels, weather conditions and species.[7]

In 2007, the city of Freiburg in Germany installed bollards which show real-time (hourly-average) air-quality information (see Figure C.2) as a way of raising public awareness.

C.2   Public information bollard showing air quality measurements.

APPENDIX D
ACOUSTICS

Urban noise levels

Traffic is the main source of noise in the city (Table D.1). Broadly, what one sees is that where the noise level is high in a city, there should be a strategy for sound attenuation.

Figure D.1 shows how the noise from a railway embankment can be modelled to evaluate what attenuation measures may be required for, say, new residential development. Table D.2 gives an indication of the ranges of acceptability issued by the DCLG.[1]

TABLE D.1

Typical urban noise levels		
Location	Noise level dBA	
1.	A quiet living room in the evening with the windows closed	26 – 28
2.	Background noise levels in central London at night	39 – 49
3.	A small urban park with traffic and church bells in the distance and small birds nearby	46 – 47
4.	A street with only occasional traffic	49 – 51
5.	Busy offices	45 – 55
6.	Lively urban area during the day	65 - 75
7.	A very busy street with cars, buses and the occasional motorbike	75 - 85
8.	Underground 'tube' train decelerating into a station	80 – 84
9.	Underground 'tube train accelerating out of a station	84 - 87
10.	Burglar alarm at 1m away	100 to 110

D.1   Calculated noise spectrum from railway embankment.

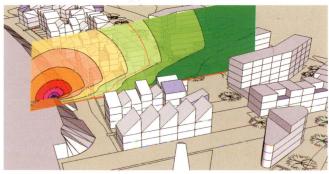

Noise levels day dB(A)

	56 <=	< 56
56 <=	59 <=	< 59
59 <=	62 <=	< 62
62 <=	65 <=	< 65
65 <=	68 <=	< 68
68 <=	71 <=	< 71
71 <=	74 <=	< 74
74 <=	77 <=	< 77
77 <=	80 <=	< 80
80 <=	83 <=	< 83
83 <=	86 <=	< 86
86 <=	89 <=	< 89
89 <=		

TABLE D.2

Recommended noise exposure categories for new dwellings				
NEC	Noise source	Daytime (07 to 23) LAeq,16hrs dB	Night-time (23 to 07) LAeq,8hrs dB	Planning advice
A	Road/ Mixed	<55	<45	Noise need not be considered as a determining factor in granting planning permission
	Rail	<55	<45	
B	Road/ Mixed	55–63	45–57	Noise should be taken into account and protection against noise required
	Rail	55–66	45–59	
C	Road/ Mixed	63–72	57–66	Planning permission should not normally be granted except if protection against noise is provded
	Rail	66–74	59–66	
D	Road/ Mixed	>72	>66	Planning permission should normally be refused

APPENDIX E
FUEL CELLS, TURBINES, ENGINES AND THEIR ENERGY SOURCES

TABLE E.1

Table E.1 Fuel-cell types and characteristics [1,2]					
Item	Fuel-cell type	Operating temperature °C	Fuel	Electrical efficency % now/(target)	Comments
1.	PEM (proton exchange membrane)	30–690	Hydrogen	35/(45)	Units operating at 80°C could be used for vechicles or for CHP in buildings; 'small' units could provide 200kWe – micro might provide 5kWe; high-quality H_2 required
2.	PAFC (phosphoric acid fuel cell)	220	Hydrogen	<42	Well-developed technology; suitable for CHP in larger buildings; in use at Woking; tolerates a less-pure H_2 than for PEMs; some run on biogas; typical output: 200kWe, 200kW thermal
3.	AFC (alkaline fuel cell)	80–200	Pure hydrogen	40–60	Mainly used in spacecraft; occasional terrestrial applications
4.	MCFC (molten carbonate fuel cell)	650	H_2, CO, CH_4, others	47/(60)	Suitable for 200kW – 2MW systems; CHP and stand-alone systems
5.	Solid oxide fuel cells	700–1000	H_2, CO, CH_4, others	47/(65)	Suitable for CHP systems and for combined cycle systems (which combine fuel cells with turbines); 2–1000kW range; CHP and stand-alone systems, a unit that produces 1kW of electricity and 3kW of heat is being tested (see Chapter 6)

There are several ways of providing combined heat and power (CHP): fuel cells, microturbines, internal combustion engines and Stirling engines. All can move the generation of electricity closer to the point of use, and in the case of the smallest units, directly into the home. This is often called decentralised energy (DE).

Fuel Cells
Fuel cells are silent and vibration-free (both important for buildings), produce no or very low levels of pollution, and can be made in a variety of sizes. A fuel cell converts the chemical energy of a fuel directly into thermal energy and electrical energy. Because this process is not limited by the Carnot efficiency (see Glossary), fuel cells can achieve higher electrical efficiencies than conventional combustion processes. Table E.1 shows some characteristics of the principal types. A discussion on fuel cells can be found in Chapter 6.

Microturbines
'Small' gas-turbines come in various sizes from 1–2 kWe (see Glossary) up to 300kWe.[3] They are undergoing intensive development for use both for CHP and standby electrical generation. Gas turbines have a comparatively low level of CO_2 and NO_x emissions and fewer moving parts compared with reciprocating engines.[4] Two 100kWe gas-fired microturbines were installed at the 290 dwelling Budenberg HAUS Projekte project in Altrincham, UK.

Internal Combustion (IC) Engines
The most common form of CHP, an internal combustion engine employs spark ignition or compression ignition (diesel) and is similar to that used in cars and generators. The fuel can be gas, petrol, diesel or a variety of bio-fuels. The gas-fired engine installed at Coopers Road (described in Chapter 11) is shown in Figure 11.13, p.98. IC engines

used for CHP applications are specially adapted to this use. Such an engine running for 5,000 hours is roughly equivalent to a car engine going 250,000 miles at 50mph.[5] Maintenance is a key issue.

Stirling Engines

The engine patented in 1816 by the eponymous Reverend Dr Robert Stirling alternately heats and cools a gas in a confined volume with part of the engine space being kept hot by an external heater. Advances in piston technology are overcoming some of the previous difficulties experienced. Stirling engines are potentially much less polluting than internal combustion engines. Units with an output range of 1–20kWe are commercially available, are undergoing tests or are on the drawing board.

Alternative Fuels and Fuel Extraction Processes

In a future without fossil fuels, we will rely on a range of alternative fuels for the storage and distribution of energy.

Hydrogen

Hydrogen does not exist freely, it must be extracted from other materials and is therefore not a power source in itself. Assuming hydrogen is not produced from fossil-fuel hydrocarbons, the alternatives are to create hydrogen by electrolysing water using electricity from renewable resources, to produce it by breaking down biomass or wastes by gasification, or via photosynthesis or fermentation with algae or bacteria.

Research is ongoing into large-scale solutions for generating (and storing) hydrogen.

Bio-fuel

Plants capture the sun's energy through photosynthesis. Bio-diesel can be made from soybean or rapeseed. Ethanol bio-fuel can be made from corn. The wisdom of using edible crops for conversion into energy is currently the subject of debate and should be researched carefully.[6]

Anaerobic Digestion (AD)

This is a naturally occurring process of decomposition and decay of organic matter under anaerobic conditions. Micro-organisms digest organic materials to produce mainly methane and carbon dioxide. Other by-products include a digestate, which makes a very effective soil improver. The methane can be used to run a gas engine or turbine.

AD plants are currently used at a large commercial scale, however smaller plants exist as shown in Figure E.1.

E.1   Prototype anaerobic digestion plant.

Gasification

Gasification is a type of pyrolysis (see Glossary) and involves the transformation, through partial combustion in the absence of oxygen above 250°C, of a material into a combustible synthetic gas (a mixture of hydrogen, methane and carbon monoxide), volatiles and an ash.

E.2   Prototype gasification plant.

NOTES

1   Introduction

1   Kahn, L. (1969) 'Silence and light: Louis I. Kahn at ETH (Zurich)', in Heinz Ronner, Sharad Jhaveri, and Alessandro Vassella, *Louis I. Kahn: Complete Work, 1935–74*, Institute for the History and Theory of Architecture. The Swiss Federal Institute of Technology, Zurich, 1977, pp. 447–49.

2   UNFPA (2007) *State of the World Population: Unleashing the Potential of Urban Growth*. Available: http://www.unfpa.org/swp/2007/english/introduction.html (accessed 7 January 2008).

3   Cited in Collins, G. and Collins, c. (1986) *Camillo Sitte: The Birth of Modern City Planning*. New York: Rizzoli.

4   Stern, N. (2007) *Stern Review on the Economics of Climate Change*. London: HM Treasury. Available: http://www.hm-treasury.gov.uk/independent_reviews/stern_review_economics_climate_change/stern_review_report.cfm (accessed 7 January 2008).

5   Abstracted from *Bo01 City of Tomorrow: Västra Hamnen, Malmö, Sweden*. Online. http://home.att.net/amcnet/bo01.html (accessed 7 January 2008).

6   In cities, heat is produced by people and equipment and this heat and solar radiation are absorbed in the buildings and streets; there is less heat loss by evaporation, and wind speeds are generally lower so heat is less easily carried away.

7   GLA (2006) *London's Urban Heat Island: A Summary for Decision Makers*. Available: http://www.london.gov.uk/mayor/environment/climate-change/docs/UHI_summary_report.pdf (accessed 7 January 2008).

8   For an alternative view, see Ridley, M. (2001) 'Technology and the environment: the case for optimism', *RSA Journal*, 2/4: 46–49.

9   Abstracted from BERR (2007) *Digest of United Kingdom Energy Statistics (DUKES) 2007*.

10   Commission of the European Communities (2000) *Action Plan to Improve Energy Efficiency in the European Community 2000–2006*. Available: http://eurlex.europa.eu/LexUriServ/LexUriServ.do?uri=COM:2000:0247:FIN:EN:PDF (accessed 2 February 2008).

11   *Digest of United Kingdom Energy Statistics 2007*, p. 13.

12   Available: http://www.merton.gov.uk/living/planning/plansandprojects/10percentpolicy.htm (accessed 1 February 2008) and http://www.themertonrule.org/map (accessed 1 February 2008).

13   Cited in Odum, E. (1971) *Fundamentals of Ecology*. London: Saunders.

14   Mellanby, K. (1975) *Can Britain Feed Itself?* London: Merlin.

15   Pearce, F. (1997) 'White bread is green', *New Scientist*, 6 December, p. 10. Based on 5004kWh/person/year (18,000MJ person/year).

16   See Bolin, B. (1970) 'The energy cycle of the biosphere', in *The Biosphere, Scientific American*, San Francisco: W. H. Freeman.

17   Banister, D. (2000) 'The tip of the iceberg: leisure and air travel', *Built Environment* 26(3): 226–35.

18   Thomas, R. (2005) *Environmental Design*. Abingdon: Taylor & Francis, p. 82. Conversion factor 0.9.

19   Ibid. Conversion factor 0.3 (note that more precise calculations will need to check if this factor has altered significantly).

20   Durnin, J.V.G.A. and Passmore, R. (1967) *Energy, Work and Leisure*. London: Heinemann.

21   Houghton, J. (1993) *Royal Commission on Environmental Pollution, Seventeenth Report: Incineration of Waste*. London: HMSO.

22   World Energy Council (2007) *2007 Survey of Energy Resources*. Available: http://www.worldenergy.org/documents/ser2007 final online version 1.pdf (accessed 24 November 2007). The annual solar radiation reaching the Earth's surface is approximately 3,400,000 EJ compared with the annual primary energy consumption of 450 EJ.

23   Alan Baxter, referring to his practice's work on the flood protection, Bristol. Private communication.

24   Mardaljevic, J. (2001) De Montfort University. 'ICUE: Irradiation mapping for complex urban environments'. Available: http://www.iesd.dmu.ac.uk/ jm/icue/ (accessed 23 November 2007).

25   Anon. (1990) 'Climate and site development. Part 3: Improving microclimate through design', *BRE Digest 350*, Garston: BRE.

26   National Consumer Council (2006) *I Will If You Will: Towards Sustainable Consumption*. NCC. ISBN: 1 899581 79 0.

27   The term 'magnificently equivocal' was applied to American Pastoral by J. Savigneau in 'Une Tragédie Ordinaire', *Le Monde*, 23 April 1999, p. vii.

2   Urban planning and design

1   Urban Task Force (1999) *Towards an Urban Renaissance*. London: E & FN Spon.

2   Ibid., p. 66.

3   Government Office for the South East (1998) *Sustainable Residential Quality in the South East*. Guildford: Government Office for the South East.

4   Ibid.

5   The Prince's Foundation *et al.* (2000) *Sustainable Urban Extensions: Planned through Design*. London: The Prince's Foundation.

6   London Planning Advisory Committee et al. (1998) *Sustainable Residential Quality: New Approaches to Urban Living*. London: Greater London Authority.

7   London Planning Advisory Committee (2000) *Sustainable Residential Quality: Exploring the Housing Potential of Large Sites*. London: Greater London Authority.

8   Ibid.

9   Ibid.

10   Department of the Environment, Transport and the Regions (1998) *The Use of Density in Urban Planning*. London: DETR.

11   Adapted from *The London Plan 2008*. London: Greater London Authority.

3 Transportation

1 Bannister, D. (2000) 'The tip of the iceberg: leisure and air travel', *Built Environment*, 26(3): 229, Table 3.

2 Greater London Authority (2001) *The Mayor's Transport Strategy*. Available: http://www.london.gov.uk/mayor/strategies/transport/trans_strat.jsp (accessed 2 February 2008).

3 The amount of CO2 emitted by aviation is calculated as being that from fuel burnt 'during taxiing and take-off to a height of 1km within the Greater London boundary'. DEFRA, UK (2007) *London Energy and CO$_2$ Emissions Inventory*. London: DEFRA. The UK total is around 550 Mt CO$_2$.

4 Department for Transport (2004) 'National Travel Survey: 2002 (revised 2004)'. Available: http://www.dft.gov.uk/pgr/statistics/datatablespublications/personal/mainresults/nts2002/nationaltravelsurvey2002revi5243 (accessed 2 February 2008).

5 Greater London Authority (2001) *The Mayor's Transport Strategy, Figure 2.11. Note the original source: Informing Transport Health Impact Assessment in London*. London: AEA Technology/NHS Executive London, 2000, and TFL, 2001.

6 World Health Organisation. Available: http://www.who.int/violence_injury_prevention/media/news/23_04_2007/en/index.html (accessed 2 February 2008).

7 S. Stansfeld *et al.* (2003) 'Aircraft and road traffic noise and children's cognition and health', in *Proceedings of the 8th International Congress on Noise as a Public Health Problem*. Rotterdam: ICBEN.

8 Royal Commission on Environmental Pollution (1997) *Twentieth Report: Transport and the Environment: Developments since 1994*. London: RCEP, pp. 19–20.

9 World Commission on Environment and Development (1997) quoted by Department of the Environment (1997) *Planning Policy Guidance Note 1 (Revised): General Policy and Principles*. London: HMSO, p. 3, para. 4.

10 Royal Commission on Environmental Pollution (1997) *Twentieth Report: Transport and the Environment*, op. cit., Table 4.2.

11 Ibid., p. 52, Figure 2.21.

12 Department of the Environment, Transport and the Regions (2001) *Planning Policy Guidance Note 13: Transport*. London: HMSO. See also Department of the Environment, Transport and the Regions (1998) *Planning for Sustainable Development: Towards Better Practice*, Chapter 2 ('Realising the potential of existing urban areas') and Chapter 6 ('Incorporating other sustainability issues: parking').

13 Community Car Share Network (Summer 2001) *The Road Ahead: Community Car Share Network Newsletter*, issue 4.

14 English Partnerships and the Housing Corporation (2002) *Urban Design Principles: Urban Design Compendium*. London: English Partnerships, Table 4.1. Available: http://www.urbandesigncompendium.co.uk (accessed 2 February 2008).

15 Urban Task Force (1999) *Towards an Urban Renaissance*. London: E&FN Spon, Figure 1.3.

16 In Radburn, New Jersey, total segregation of pedestrian and car movement was produced in urban design. This became the ubiquitous approach to urban design in the UK in the 1950s and 60s.

17 Royal Commission on Environmental Pollution (1997) *Twentieth Report: Transport and the Environment*, op. cit.

18 Transport for London (2005) *Central London Congestion Charging: Impacts Monitoring: Third Annual Report*. Available: http://www.tfl.gov.uk/assets/downloads/ThirdAnnualReportFinal.pdf (accessed 2 February 2008).

19 For Home Zones, see Biddulph, M. (2001) *Homes Zones: A Planning and Design Handbook*. Bristol: The Policy Press. For 20mph zones, see Slower Speeds Initiative (2001) *Killing Speed: A Good Practice Guide to Speed Management*. Also Department for Transport, Traffic Advisory Leaflet 9/99 (1999). *20mph Speed Limits and Zones*. For Safe Routes to Schools, see DETR (1999) *School Travel Strategies and Plans: A Best Practice Guide for Local Authorities*. London: DETR.

4 Landscape and nature in the city

1 Champion, T. et al. (1998) *Urban Exodus*. London: CPRE.

2 Welland, S. (2007) Available: http://www.carbonneutral.com/pages/whyweareinbusiness.asp (accessed 15 August 2007).

3 Fitch, J.M. and Bobenhausen, W. (1999) *American Building: The Environmental Forces That Shape It*. New York: Oxford University Press.

4 Lynch, K. (1971) *Site Planning*. Cambridge, MA: MIT Press.

5 Hewitt, M. (2001) 'Can trees cut pain?' *The Times*, 4 September, Section 2, p. 10.

6 Ibid.

7 Wauters, A. (1999) *Homeopathic Color Remedies*. California: Crossing Press.

8 CABE (2004) *The Value of Public Space*. London: CABE. Available: http://www.cabe.org.uk/AssetLibrary/2021.pdf (accessed 2 February 2008).

9 CABE (2005) *Does Money Grow on Trees?* London: CABE. Available: http://www.cabe.org.uk/AssetLibrary/2022.pdf (accessed 2 February 2008).

10 Stiftung Warentest (2006) Available: http://www.stiftung-warentest.de/online/bauen_finanzieren/test/1356200/1356200/1360862/1360865.html (accessed 15 August 2007).

11 Liddell, H. (2006) 'Eco-minimalism – less can be more', in *The Green Building Bible,* 3rd edn, Vol. 1. Green Building Press, p. 102.

12 Stadtentwicklungsbehörde (1997) *Der Grüne Faden*. Hamburg: Environmental Work's Group.

13 English Partnerships and the Housing Corporation (2002) Urban Design Principles: Urban Design Compendium. London: English Partnerships. Available: http://www.urbandesigncompendium.co.uk (accessed 2 February 2008).

25   Lazarus, N. (2002) *Construction Materials Report, Toolkit for Carbon Neutral Developments – Part 1*. Surrey: The BedZED Construction Materials Report. BioRegional Development Group.

26   Addis, W. and Schouten, J. (2004) *Design for Deconstruction: Principles of Design to Facilitate Reuse and Recycling (C607)*. London: CIRIA.

8   Water

1   Sumbler, M.G. (1996) *British Regional Geology: London and the Thames Valley*. London: HMSO, p. 147.

2   Environment Agency (2007) *South East England State of the Environment*. Bristol: EA. Available: http://www.environment-agency.gov.uk/commondata/acrobat/soe07final 1941006.pdf (accessed 1 February 2008).

3   National Audit Office (2005) *Report HC 73, Environment Agency: Efficiency in Water Resource Management*. London: National Audit Office.

4   Environment Agency (2006) *Underground, Under Threat: The State of Groundwater in England and Wales*. Bristol: EA. Available: http://publications.environment-agency.gov.uk/pdf/GEHO0906BLDB-e-e.pdf?lang= e (accessed 1 February 2008).

5   Monteith, J.L. (1973) *Principles of Environmental Physics*. London: Edward Arnold, pp. 65–67.

6   Environment Agency (2005) *Sustainable Homes: The Financial And Environmental Benefits*, Science Report SC040050/SR. Bristol: EA.

7   The DETR defines grey water as water from buildings that can be reused and goes on to say 'light grey water is rain water collected from roofs and used for toilet flushing and non-drinking water applications. Darker grey water is from sinks and baths which can be used for watering plants but would require extensive processing for other uses.' Anon. (1998) *Sustainable Development: Opportunities for Change Sustainable Construction*. London: DETR.

8   OFWAT (2006) 'Security of supply, leakage and water efficiency, 2005–06 report', Table 16.

9   DCLG (2007) 'Code for Sustainable Homes: Technical Guide'. Available: http://www.planningportal.gov.uk/uploads/code_for_sustainable_ homes_techguide.pdf (accessed 28 October 2007).

10   For more information, see http://www.southbanksustainability.org.uk (accessed 9 October 2007).

11   Online: http://www.water.org.uk/home/policy/climate-change/briefing-paper (accessed 1 February 2008).

9   Waste and resource

1   Department for Environment, Food and Rural Affairs (2007) *Waste Strategy for England 2007*. London: DEFRA. Available: http://www.defra.gov.uk/ENVIRONMENT/waste/strategy/strategy07/ pdf/waste07-strategy.pdf (accessed 1 January 2008).

2   Department for Environment, Food and Rural Affairs (2007) *Statistical Release 435/07: Municipal Waste Management Statistics 2006/07*.

London: DEFRA, Available: http://www.defra.gov.uk/environment/ statistics/wastats/bulletin07.htm (accessed 1 January 2008).

3   See DEFRA, Waste Strategy for England 2007, op. cit.

4   Online: http://www.smartwaste.co.uk (accessed 1 January 2008).

5   Houghton, J. (Chair) (1993) *Cm 2181, Royal Commission on Environmental Pollution, Seventeenth Report, Incineration of Waste*. London: HMSO, pp. 39–41.

6   These chambers can typically hold five times more waste than a 'eurobin' but require a special refuse vehicle. For more information, see online http://taylor-ch.co.uk/underground/5/index.html (accessed 29 September 2007).

7   Adapted from Figure 4.1 in DEFRA (2007) *Waste Strategy for England 2007*, op. cit.

8   British Standards Institution (1983) *BS 6297:1983: Design and Installation of Small Sewage Treatment Works and Cesspools*. London: British Standards Institution.

9   For more information, see: http://www.clivusmultrum.com (accessed 29 September 2007).

10   For details of the C.K. Choi building, see DTI (2005) 'Towards a low-carbon society – a mission to Canada and USA', pp. 80–83. Available: http://www.inreb.org/images/backgroundpdf/inreb test.pdf (accessed 27 January 2008).

11   Griggs, J. and Grant, N. (2000) 'Reed beds: application and specification', *Good Building Guide 42, Part 1*. Garston: Building Research Establishment.

12   Centre for Alternative Technology (1998), private communication.

11   Coopers Road Estate: regeneration

1   Lifetimes Homes Standards as defined by 'Meeting Part M and designing Lifetime Homes'. York: Joseph Rowntree Foundation, 1999.

2   Building Research Establishment (2000) Construction Research Communications Ltd, London. In April 2007, the Code for Sustainable Homes replaced EcoHomes for the assessment of new housing in England. The EcoHomes 'Very Good' score is approximately equal to Code Level 3. For further information, see http://www.homezones.org.uk/ (accessed 1 February 2008).

3   A home zone is a street for group of streets designed primarily to meet the interests of pedestrians and cyclists rather than motorists, opening up the street for social use. Legally, neither pedestrians nor vehicles have priority, but the road may be reconfigured to make it more favourable to pedestrians.

4   SAP = Standard Assessment Procedure. The SAP 2001 rating system is a method of predicting total energy requirements for dwellings irrespective of location or usage; the end result is a normalised energy rating for comparison purposes. The method is based upon the BREDEM energy model produced in 1985. The method produces a rating on a scale of 1–100 for Building Regulations purposes, although in reality

values of over 100 can be achieved. Note: the SAP scale was revised in SAP2005 where 100 now represents zero energy cost. It can be above 100 for dwellings that are net exporters of energy.

12 Parkmount: streetscape and solar design

1 Peace lines, as they are euphemistically known, have been built on the edges of the polarising sections of Belfast's northern and western neighbourhoods and extend in sections up to a kilometre long. Though started as impromptu barricades, they now form permanent walls demarcating the sectarian boundaries that have been drawn with increasingly harder lines since the escalation of 'The Troubles' in 1969.

2 McHale, S. (1999) 'Terror, territory and the Titanic', *Cambridge Architecture Journal*, Scroope 11. The patchwork of neighbourhoods has created urban characteristics that are highly unusual in the British Isles explaining in part, the Province's ambivalent attitude towards UK planning policy and guidance. The Belfast Urban Area Plan 2001 describes the city as 'neutral territory' and proposes a commitment to only 50 per cent of development on brownfield land. In Belfast, there are areas of undeveloped land which act as buffers between the communities and so there is question as to whether this blighted land, often in the shadow of the peace line walls can be included within a definition of brownfield land.

3 See Chapter 11, note 2.

4 Refer to 'Area Development Plans – Sustainable Cities Programme', produced by Napier University, which highlights the positive impact of public transport corridors, interchanges and railheads on overall energy efficiency and urban sustainability.

5 Thomas, R. (2001) *Photovoltaics and Architecture*. London: Spon Press.

6 See Chapter 11, note 4.

7 Brewerton, J. and Darton, D. (1997) *Designing Lifetime Homes*. York: The Joseph Rowntree Foundation.

8 Poundbury and Knottley Green, the exemplars of housing and planning guides up and down the country, supposedly hail a new era, but in the image of each and every historical period (except our own) all are thrown together to form incongruous housing 'theme parks'.

9 For feedback and comments of new occupiers, see RPA (2004) Parkmount Housing. Available: http://www.rparchitects.co.uk/publications/RPA_parkmount_housing.php (accessed 15 December 2007).

13 Coin Street Housing: the architecture of engagement

1 Soukler King, C. (1982) 'Getting tough with economics', interview with Frank Gehry, *Designers West*, June.

2 Chen, A. (2001) 'Tent City', interview with Michael Rakowitz, *I.D. Magazine*, February.

3 Department for Transport, Local Government and the Regions (2000) *PPG3, Planning Policy Guidance note 3, Housing*. March, London: DETR.

This provides guidance on a range of issues relating to the provision of housing. It was replaced by *Planning Policy Statement 3: Housing (PPS3)* in November 2006. Available: http://www.communities.gov.uk/publications/planningandbuilding/pps3housing (accessed 19 January 2008).

14 Sustainable design in an urban context: three case studies

1 David Suchet to Stephen Daldry, and copied to Max Fordham, in a letter of 21 June 1996.

2 Tim Lewers of Cambridge Architectural Research.

3 Edwards, A. (1990) 'The Design and Testing of Wind-assisted Gas Venting Headworks: Project Report', School of Physics and Materials: Lancaster University.

15 BedZED: Beddington zero-fossil energy development

1 Dunster, B. (2007) *The ZEDbook*. Abingdon: Taylor & Francis.

2 Storm van Leeuwen, J.W. (2008) 'Nuclear power – the energy balance: energy insecurity and greenhouse gases'. Available: http://www.storm-smith.nl (accessed 18 January 2008).

3 Vale, B. and Vale, R. (2000) *The New Autonomous House*. London: Thames and Hudson, p. 210.

4 Available at: http:// www.statistics.gov.uk

5 Ibid.

6 The Urban Task Force (1999) *Towards an Urban Renaissance: Final Report of the Urban Task Force*. London: E&FN Spon, p. 46.

7 DETR (1996) *General Information Report No. 53: Building a Sustainable Future*. London: DETR, and SAFE Alliance Foodmiles campaign 1998.

8 See http:// www.statistics.gov.uk (accessed 2 February 2008).

9 DCLG (2006) *Building a Greener Future: Towards Zero Carbon Development – Consultation*. Available: http://www.communities.gov.uk/documents/planningandbuilding/pdf/153125 (accessed 28 January 2008).

10 See the documentary *Who Killed the Electric Car?* 2006, Sony Pictures Home Entertainment.

11 Available: http://www.zedfactory.com (accessed 18 January 2008).

16 Bo01 and Flagghusen: ecological city districts in Malmö, Sweden

1 Available: http://www.malmo.se/download/18.4a2cec6a10d0ba37c0b800012615/kvalprog_bo01_dn_eng.pdf. (accessed 4 December 2007).

2 Available: http://www.envac.net/docs/projects/405_Bo01%20Malm%F6.pdf (accessed 5 December 2007).

3 Available: http://www.malmo.se/download/18.7101b483110ca54a562800010420/westernharbour06.pdf (accessed 5 December 2007).

4 Online http://www.ekostaden.com (accessed 5 December 2007).

5 Persson. B. (2005) *Sustainable City of Tomorrow Bo01: Experiences of a Swedish Housing Exposition*. Stockholm: Swedish Research Council Formas.

6   In Europe, a dwelling is deemed to satisfy the PassivHaus criteria if the total energy demand for space heating and cooling is less than 15 kWh/m²yr treated floor area and the total primary energy use for all appliances, domestic hot water and space heating and cooling is less than 120 kWh/m²yr.

17   Stonebridge: negotiating between traditional and modernist models of city housing

1   Europan is a biennial Europe-wide design competition for architects under 40, that seeks to address current issues in housing and urbanism on a range of real projects.

2   Panerai, P., Castex, J., Depaule, J-C. and Samuels, I. (2004) *Urban Forms: The Death and Life of the Urban Block*. Oxford: pp. 90–113.

3   The planning authority required compliance with the British Research Establishment's (BRE) Report 209: 'Site layout planning for daylight and sunlight'.

4   Ibid.

18   'Made in Stockwell' and Deptford Wharves

1   Greater London Authority (2004) 'Green light to clean power', in *The Mayor's Energy Strategy*. Available: http://www.london.gov.uk/mayor/strategies/energy/docs/energy_strategy04.pdf (accessed 27 January 2008).

2   Greater London Authority (2005) *2004 London Housing Capacity Study*. London: GLA, Annex 3: PTAL Map of London. Available: http://www.london.gov.uk/mayor/planning/capacity study/docs/housing_capacity study2004.pdf (accessed 27 January 2008).

3   Greater London Authority (2004) *The London Plan, Spatial Development Strategy for Greater London*. London: GLA. Available: http://www.london.gov.uk/mayor/strategies/sds/london plan/lon plan all.pdf (accessed 27 January 2008).

4   DEFRA (2007) 'Construction and demolition waste management: 1999 to 2005, England'. Online: http://www.defra.gov.uk/environment/statistics/waste/kf/wrkf09.htm (accessed 27 January 2008).

5   DCLG (2006) 'Code for sustainable homes: a step-change in sustainable home building practice'. Available: http://www.planningportal.gov.uk/uploads/code for sust homes.pdf (accessed 27 January 2008).

6   BRE (2005) Putting a Price on Sustainability. Watford: BRE.

7   DCLG (2006) 'Planning Policy Statement 25: Development and Flood Risk'. Available: http://www.communities.gov.uk/documents/planningandbuilding/pdf/planningpolicystatement25 (accessed 27 January 2008).

19   Millennium Water: Vancouver's Olympic Village, Canada

1   EcoDensity, see http://www.vancouver-ecodensity.ca/index.php (accessed 29 October 2007).

2   City of Vancouver (2007) *Southeast False Creek Official Development Plan*. Available: http://www.city.vancouver.bc.ca/commsvcs/bylaws/odp/SEFC.pdf (accessed 17 October 2007).

3   For more information, or to download the Green Building Strategy, see 'Vancouver Green Buildings', City of Vancouver. Online: http://vancouver.ca/commsvcs/southeast/greenbuildings/index.htm (accessed 26 October 2007).

4   CanMET National Inventory Report, 1990–2005: Greenhouse Gas Sources and Sinks in Canada. Table A9-1. Available: http://www.ec.gc.ca/pdb/ghg/inventory_report/2005_report/ta9_1_eng.cfm (accessed 1 February 2008).

5   US Green Building Council, see online: http://www.usgbc.org and Canada Green Building Council. Online: http://www.cagbc.org (accessed 29 October 2007).

6   LEED™ for Neighbourhood Development, see http://www.usgbc.org/DisplayPage.aspx?CMSPageID=148 (accessed 29 October 2007).

7   Smart Growth is an urban planning and transportation theory that concentrates growth in the centre of a city to avoid urban sprawl; and advocates compact, transit-oriented, walkable, bicycle-friendly land use, including mixed-use development with a range of housing choices. Online http://www.smartgrowth.ca and http://www.smartgrowth.org (accessed 29 October 2007).

8   New Urbanism is an American urban design movement that arose in the early 1980s. Its goal is to reform all aspects of real estate development and urban planning, from urban retrofits to suburban infill. New Urbanist neighbourhoods are designed to contain a diverse range of housing and jobs, and to be walkable. A growing movement, New Urbanism recognizes walkable, human-scaled neighbourhoods as the building blocks of sustainable communities and regions. Online http://www.newurbanism.org and http://www.cnu.org (accessed 29 October 2007).

9   The seven principles of Universal Design are (1) Equitable Use; (2) Flexibility in Use; (3) Simple, Intuitive Use; (4) Perceptible Information; (5) Tolerance for Error; (6) Low Physical Effort; and (7) Size and Space for Approach. Online: http://www.adaptenv.org and http://www.universaldesign.com (accessed 29 October 2007).

10   Darby, S. (2006) *The Effectiveness of Feedback on Energy Consumption: A Review for DEFRA of the Literature on Metering, Billing and Direct Displays*. Oxford: Environmental Change Institute, University of Oxford. Available: http://www.defra.gov.uk/environment/climatechange/uk/energy/research/pdf/energyconsump-feedback.pdf (accessed 18 October 2007).

Appendix A   Solar energy, temperatures and photovoltaics

1   Thomas, R. (2001) *Photovoltaics and Architecture*. London: Spon.

2   Thomas, R. (2005) *Environmental Design*, 3rd edn. Abingdon: Taylor & Francis.

3   Bunn, R. (1998) 'Ground coupling explained', *Building Services Journal*, December: 22–27.

4   See Thomas, *Photovoltaics*, op. cit.

5   Adapted from online http://www.solarcentury.co.uk/knowledge base/ articles/pv_comparison table (accessed 1 February 2008).

Appendix B   Wind and water

1   Rayment, R. (1976) *Wind Energy in the UK*. BRE CP 59/76. Garston: BRE.

2   Thomas, R. (2005) *Environmental Design*, 3rd edn. Abingdon: Taylor & Francis.

3   Timmers, G. (2001) 'Wind energy comes to town: small wind turbines in the urban environment', *Renewable Energy World*, May–June: 113–19.

4   Anon. (1985) 'Water-to-water heat pumps'. *Technical Information EC 4708/8.85*. London: The Electricity Council.

5   Cooper, E. (1990) 'Utilisation of groundwater in England and Wales', *Water and Sewerage*, pp. 51–54.

Appendix C   Air quality

1   Liddament, M.W. (1997) 'External pollution: the effect on indoor air quality', in Rooley, R. (ed.) *Indoor Air Quality and the Workplace*. Cambridge: MidCareer College.

2   Department for Environment and Rural Affairs (2007) *The Air Quality Strategy for England, Scotland, Wales and Northern Ireland*, Vol. 1. London: DEFRA. Available: http://www.defra.gov.uk/environment/ airquality/strategy/pdf/air-qualitystrategy-vol1.pdf (accessed 2 February 2008).

3   Ibid.

4   Ibid.

5   Ibid.

6   Laxen, D.P.H. et al. (1987) 'Nitrogen dioxide distribution in street canyons', *Atmos*. Environ. 21.

7   1989–1903. Cited in Boucher, K. (1990/91) 'The monitoring of air pollutants in Athens with particular reference to nitrogen dioxide', *Energy and Buildings*, 15–16: 637–45.

Appendix D   Acoustics

1   DCLG (2004) 'Planning Policy Guidance Note 24: Planning and Noise'. Available: http://www.communities.gov.uk/documents/planningand-building/pdf/156558. (accessed 2 February 2008).

Appendix E   Fuel cells, turbines, engines and their energy sources

1   Lehmann, A.K., Russell, A. and Hoogers, G. (2001) 'Fuel cell power from biogas', *Renewable Energy World*, November–December: 76–85.

2   Larminie, J. (2000) 'Fuel cells', *Ingenia*, 1(4): 43–47.3
Stephens, M. (2002) 'Diesel still rules the standby power world', *Electrical Review*, 22 January: 18–19.

4   Anon. (2002) 'Microturbine CHP set for London district heating', *eibi* (energy buildings and industry), January: 20.

5   Carbon Trust (2007) *Micro-CHP Accelerator: Interim Report*. London: Carbon Trust.

6   Brahic, C. (2007) 'Forget biofuels – burn oil and plant forests instead', *New Scientist*.

Appendix F   Landscapes

1   Dimoudi, A. and Nikolopoulou, M. (2000) 'Vegetation in the urban environment: microclimatic analysis and benefits', in *PRECis: Assessing the Potential for Renewable Energy in Cities*. Pikermi, Greece: Centre for Renewable Energy Sources.

2   Nowak, D.J. (1999) 'The effects of urban trees on air quality'.

3   Cited in Rayden, D. (2000) 'State of the art on environmental urban design and planning', in *PRECis: Assessing the Potential for Renewable Energy in Cities*. Project Coordination: The Martin Centre, University of Cambridge.

4   Anon. (1964) *The Farmer's Weather*. Ministry of Agriculture, Fisheries and Food, Bulletin No. 165. London: HMSO.

5   Littler, J. and Thomas, R. (1984) *Design with Energy: The Conservation and Use of Energy in Buildings*. Cambridge: Cambridge University Press.

6   Holzberlein, T.M. (1979) 'Don't let the trees make a monkey of you', in Proceedings of the Fourth National Passive Solar Conference. Newark, Delaware: ISES – American Section.

7   Hrivnak, J. (2004) 'Environmental analysis of landscape: the effects of trees in streets: street trees as noise and air pollution absorbers, a case study in Fulham, SW6 London', Cambridge Darwin College, Cambridge University.

8   Arnold, H.F. (1993) *Trees in Urban Design*. New York.

Appendix G   Materials

1   Thomas, R. (2005) *Environmental Design*, 3rd edn. Abingdon: Taylor & Francis.

GLOSSARY

Acid rain Pollution caused principally by oxides of sulphur (SOx) and nitrogen (NOx) emitted during fossil-fuel combustion and metal smelting. This leads to formation in the atmosphere of acids, which are returned to earth.

Aerobic In the presence of oxygen.

Anaerobic Without the presence of oxygen.

BRE Building Research Establishment. The certification organisation behind EcoHomes and BREEAM.

Brownfield land Brownfield land is normally understood to mean land that has been previously built on but is now derelict, underused or of low ecological value.

Carnot efficiency The Carnot limit is the maximum efficiency for a heat engine, e.g. an internal combustion engine, and is given by: (TH – TC)/TH where TH is the temperature of the heat source and TC is the temperature of the heat sink in degrees Kelvin.

CFC A chlorofluorocarbon. A source of depletion of the ozone layer and a contributor to global warming.

CSA Canadian Standards Association.

dB Decibel.

dBA A measure of sound pressure level, weighted in a way that approximates the frequency response of the human ear (the A-scale). Normally expressed as a single figure.

d.c. Direct current.

Dioxin A name given to a number of chemicals formed at high temperatures (including in bonfires), some of which are carcinogenic.

Electrolysis In the electrolysis of water, the process whereby an electric current is passed through water to produce hydrogen and oxygen.

Electromagnetic spectrum The electromagnetic spectrum covers the full range of radiation from X-rays to microwaves. Solar radiation falls within this and consists of UV (290–400nm), visible (400–760nm) and infrared (760–2200nm).

Energy There are three forms of energy: (1) primary, i.e. that contained in fossil fuels in the form of coal, oil or natural gas or in nuclear energy or hydroelectricity; (2) delivered, i.e. that in the fuel at its point of use after allowing for extraction (or generation) and transmission losses; and (3) useful, i.e. the portion of the delivered energy that is of benefit after allowing for the efficiency of the consuming appliance.

Environmental footprint The concept of a land and water area that is needed to support indefinitely the standard of living of a given human population.

ETFE Ethylene tetrafluoroethylene.

Foodmiles The distance food travels from the producer to the consumer.

FSC Forest Stewardship Council.

Gasification See pyrolysis.

Geo-exchange A system where energy is exchanged, sometimes reversibly, i.e. heat extracted from, or heat rejected to, the earth at shallow depths where the energy is actually stored solar energy captured at the earth's surface.

Geothermal This comes from two Greek words: 'geo' meaning Earth and 'thermal' meaning heat. It is commonly used to describe the important resource (especially in volcanically active places such as Iceland and New Zealand) where heat energy generated at the Earth's core is available relatively close (250m deep) to the Earth's crust and can therefore be harnessed.

GGBS Ground granulated blast furnace slag.

GJ Gigajoule (1GJ = 278kWh).

Greenhouse gas A gas that absorbs infrared radiation emitted by the Earth's surface and by clouds. The gas in turn emits infrared radiation from a level where the temperature is colder than the surface. The net effect is a local trapping of part of the absorbed energy and a tendency to warm the planetary surface. Water vapour (H_2O), carbon dioxide (CO_2), nitrous oxide (N_2O), methane (CH_4) and ozone (O_3) are the primary greenhouse gases in the Earth's atmosphere.

ha Hectare. It is 10,000m² and equivalent to 2.47 acres

Habitable room A room used for dwelling purposes, including a kitchen but not a bathroom, hall or utility room.

HCFC Hydrochlorofluorocarbon. As for CFCs but less harmful.

Hz Hertz (1Hz = 1 cycle per second).

kcal Kilocalorie.

kW Kilowatt.

kWe A kilowatt of electrical output.*

kWh Kilowatt hour.

kWp A kilowatt peak. Power output of a PV module under standard test conditions (STCs).

kWth A kilowatt of heat output.*

L_{A10} The level of noise exceeded 10 per cent of the time when measuring in dBA (decibels with an A-scale rating). See dBA.

Low-E Low-emissivity. Often used to describe glass having a low-E coating which is transparent to visible light, and opaque to infrared radiation, thus lowering the total heat flow through the window.

MWh A megawatt hour (1,000kWh).

Nm 1 nanometre.

NR NR (noise rating) curves are a way of using octave bands to describe a noise with a single number.

Odt Oven dry tonne. An amount of material that weighs one tonne at zero per cent moisture content.

Ozone depletion potential A measure of the damage caused to the ozone layer by a substance.

PCM Phase change material.

PEFC Programme for the Endorsement of Forest Certification Schemes.

PFA Pulverised fuel ash.

Pyrolysis Gasification and pyrolysis are sometimes used interchangeably. Pyrolysis, in our case, is the breakdown of a material (typically biomass) in the absence of oxygen above 250°C. The process produces a solid (typically a char), a liquid (bio-oil) and a mixture of low-energy-content gases. Gasification is a type of pyrolysis and involves the transformation, through partial combustion, of a material (again, typically biomass) into a combustible gas, volatiles and an ash.

RSL (Registered Social Landlord) An independent housing organisation registered with the Housing Corporation under the Housing Act 1996. They may be industrial and provident societies, registered charities or companies.

Section 106 Agreement A Section of Town and Country Planning Act 1990 allowing a local planning authority to enter into a legally binding agreement or planning obligation with a developer, often requiring them to minimise the impact on the local community and to carry out tasks or make financial contributions, which will provide community benefits.

Shell and core A level of specification that includes the basic structure, envelope and services of a building provided as the base development for fitting out by a later occupier.

Silicon Silicon comes in two types: (1) P-type, i.e. a positive P-layer of silicon; and (2) N-type, i.e. a negative N-layer of silicon.

Sound Reduction Index (SRI) The reduction of the sound-pressure level as sound travels from one space to another through an element such as a wall, floor or roof. It is mainly dependent on the mass per unit area of the separating element. The SRI is approximately $= 20\log_{10}m + 10dB$ where m is the mass in kg/m².

Supplementary Planning Guidance (SPG) Non-statutory local authority approved policy which could be a material consideration when determining a planning application in England and Wales. SPG has now been superseded by Supplementary Planning Documents (SPD), which have statutory status but are not part of a statutory development plan.

Tarmac Short for tarmacadam. The term is used to refer to generic tar- or asphalt-penetrated road surfaces sometimes also called asphalt or 'blacktop' in the United States.

Temperature The unit of thermodynamic temperature in the SI system is the kelvin (K). For this reason, derived units such as thermal conductivity are expressed as watts per metre kelvin (W/mK). However, the Celsius (°C) temperature scale is also in common use (the Celsius scale is also known as the centigrade scale). Absolute temperature in degrees kelvin is found by adding 273 to degrees Celsius. Thus, 30°C + 273 = 303K.

Unitary Development Plan (UDP) A local authority plan which identifies particular areas as suitable for housing, industry, retail or other uses, and sets out the policies which the authority proposes to apply in deciding whether or not development will be permitted.

U-value The rate of heat flow per unit area through an element per degree of temperature difference.

W Watt (1W = 0.86kcal/h).

W/m²K (watt per m² of area per degree K of temperature difference) Heat transfer coefficient.

Wp Watt peak.

Watershed An area of land that drains downslope to the lowest point.

---

*Note: kWe and kWth are generally used when discussing combined heat and power to avoid potential confusion.

ILLUSTRATION ACKNOWLEDGEMENTS

The authors and publishers would like to thank the following individuals and institutions for giving permission to reproduce illustrations. We have made every effort to contact copyright holders, but if any errors have been made we would be happy to correct them at a later printing.

A Models/John Ross Photography: 18.18; 18.20; 18.21

Alan Baxter & Associates: 3.3; 3.4; 3.12

Alexander, Anthony: 3.9; 3.10

Andersson, J. E.:16.5a; 16.7; 16.9; 16.10;

Arups: 15.15; 15.20; E.3

BBC Photo Library: 9.1

BDA ZEDfactory Ltd: Tables 15.2 & 15.1; 15.1; 15.2; 15.3; 15.4; 15.5; 15.6; 15.8; 15.9; 15.10; 15.11; 15.13; 15.14; 15.16; 15.17; 15.18; 15.21; 15.22; 15.23; ; 15.24, page 142

BEAR Architecten, The Netherlands, 'National Environmental Education Centre': 6.11a

Binet, Helene: 3.6

Bodenham, Dave: 7.1

Borcke, Christina von: 4.1; 4.2; 4.3; 4.6; 4.7

Boucher, Keith: C.1

Building Services Journal: B.1

Cha, Jae: 13.4a

City of Malmö Planning Department: 1.3; 16.1; 16.2; 16.3; 16.12; 16.13; page 160

City of Vancouver: 19.1-19.4

Coin Street archive: 13.22, 13.23

Cook, Peter/VIEW: 1.1; 5.1

Commission of the European Communities, 1992: 6.19, A.1

Construction Resources: 8.4

Christiania Bikes – www.christianiabikes.com: 3.11

Crown Copyright: 3.7

Department for Communities and Local Government: 2.5; 2.6

DEFRA: 9.7

EarthEnergy Ltd. – www.earthenergy.co.uk: A.3a

E & F. N. Spon: 6.15b

ECD Architects: 1.6; 11.1–11.14; page 96

Editions Parenthèses: 17.3

Egbert H. Taylor & Company Ltd – www.taylor-ch.co.uk: 9.5

Electricity Council: B.2

Elemental Solutions: 9.9

English Partnerships: Tables 3.2, 3.3

Environment Agency: 6.17

Fawcett, Alex, Hoare Lea: 7.2

Fossum, Tor: 16.4

FXV Ltd: 18.5; 18.10; page 180

Gandemer, J., Guyot, A.: 6.13

Gilbert, Dennis / VIEW: 5.2; 6.11c

Gomberoff Bell Lyon Architects Group Inc. / Merrick Architecture Borowski Lintott Sakumoto Fligg Ltd: 19.11

Greater London Authority: Table 3.1

Greater London Authority / Brunel University: 1.5

Grandorge, David: 17.4

Gunther, Karle / PSFU: 6.15

Hall, Janet, RIBA Library Photographs Collection: 6.18c

Hancock, Linda: 15.7; 15.12

Hawkins/Brown: 5.8b; 18.1; 18.2; 18.4; 18.6; 18.8; 18.9; 18.11; 18.12; 18.13; 18.14; 18.15; 18.16; 18.17; 18.19; 18.22–18.28; Tables 18.1-18.3

Hayes Davison/Hamiltons Architects: 6.14

Hrivnak, Jess: 4.4

ISES – American Section: F.4

Koehorst, Mark, Ecofys/Delft University: 6.16

Kosuth, Koseph/Sean Kelly Gallery, NY: 13.1c

Lawson, Ian: page 132

Litracon Bt 2003: 7.4

Llewelyn-Davies: 2.2; 2.3; 2.4; 4.5

London Planning Advisory Committee/Greater London Authority: 2.7; 2.8; 2.9; 2.10; 2.11

Los Angeles County Museum of Natural History: 6.4a, c

Max Fordham LLP: 1.2; 1.4a–f; 1.8; 1.9; 2.1; 3.1; 3.5; 3.8; 5.3; 5.4; 5.10; 5.11; 6.1; 6.5; 6.6; 6.7; 6.9; 6.11e; 7.3; 7.6; 8.1; 8.2; 8.6; 9.2; 9.3; 9.4; 9.10; 15.19; 16.6; 16.8; 17.18; A.6; C.2; D.1; D.2; E.1; E.2; F.1; F.3

Mangold, D., University of Stuttgart: 6.8

Mannion, Micheline: 13.16

Mardaljevic, J., IESD, De Montfort University, Leicester, UK: 1.10

Marion Boyars Publishers: 6.4b

McMurtry, Colin, 3dpix: 12.6

Merrick Architecture Borowski Lintott Sakumoto Fligg Ltd: 19.5–19.10; 19.14

Millennium Water, Millennium SEFC Properties Ltd.: 19.15, page 196

NASA: 6.10

Phipps, Simon: 18.7

Polypipe Sanitary Systems: 8.5

Rakowitz, Michael, White Columns: 13.2

Recollective Consulting: 19.12; 19.13

Richard Partington Architects: A.12

RIBA Library Photographs Collection: 6.18 a, b

Royal Commission on Environmental Pollution: 9.6

RPA: 12.1; 12.3; 12.4; 12.5; 12.7; 12.9; 12.12; 12.13

RPA/Llewelyn Davies: 12.2

Ruff, Steve: 13.4b

Sayer, Phil: 13.12; 13.19; 13.21

Short & Associates: 14.1; 14.2; 14.3; 14.8; 14.9; 14.10; 14.11;
    14.13; 14.14; 14.15

Short, Alan: 14.5; 14.6; 14.7; 14.12

Sillén, Michael: 16.5b

Simpson, John, SEA Design/Peter Kirby: 18.3

Siza, Alvaro: 17.15; 17.16

Soar, Timothy: 12.8, 12.10, 12.11, 12.14–12.18, page 106

Sportworks Northwest Inc.: 3.2

Sternberg, Morley von: 13.11; 13.14; 13.15

Sumner, Edmund: 13.17

Swedish Research Council Formas: 16.11a, b

Terence O'Rourke Ltd: 17.1

Tomkins, Haworth: 13.6; 13.8; 13.9; 13.10a, b; 13.18; 13.20

University of Wales: 14.4

Vector Foiltec Ltd: 7.5

Vile, Philip: 13.13; 13.24; 13.25; page 116

Water & Sewerage Journal: B.3

Waterlines Technical Brief: 9.8

Witherford Watson Mann Architects: 0.1; 17.2; 17.5–17.11;
    17.13, 17.14, 17.17; page 170

Zaha Hadid Architects: *Nuova Stazione Alta Velocita di Napoli-
    Afragola design*: Zaha Hadid & Patrik Schumacher: 6.12

INDEX